CO AZU 154

MAKING IT IN THE KITCHEN
SPANISH STYLE

Hannah Milstein Shapiro

MAKING IT
IN THE KITCHEN
SPANISH STYLE

1982

MADRID

© HANNAH MILSTEIN SHAPIRO
Manuscript Registered in Congress, U.S.A. Nº 21-254

Reservados los derechos de edición
para todos los países.

IMPRESO EN ESPAÑA
PRINTED IN SPAIN

ISBN: 84-283-1159-5

Depósito legal: M. 38.281.—1981

 Magallanes, 25 - Madrid-15   (3-2844)

Impreso en Artes Gráficas Benzal, S. A. - Virtudes, 7 - Madrid-3

*To my family
Harold, Carol, Stanley, Nancy,
and Jo Ann*

My thanks to all the cooks and interested friends who have helped and encouraged me, to my husband who ate everything, and to my children who coaxed me to complete this book.

TABLE OF CONTENTS

¡Ay Señora! 19
A Typical Menu from a restaurant in Spain 21
Even a plate of beans can be prepared beautifully 23
A Spanish day 26
The Bus ride and the Shoe 29
Flamenco 31
How to work up a recipe 33
A few notes about the food in the recipes 33
Definitions of terms used in the recipes 34
Abbreviated terms 36
Measures and equivalents 36
Cooking utensils mentioned in the recipes 37
Converting Fahrenheit and centrigrade 37
Converting weight 38
Oven temperatures 39
Easy food decorations 40

APPETIZERS 41

"If you don't show who you are in the beginning..." 41
Souflee canape 42
Bean "nuts" 43
Grilled shrimp (Gambas a la plancha) 43
Chopped green peppers and tomatoes 44
Eggplant dip or salad, style 1 (picado de berenjena) 45
Eggplant dip or salad, style 2 46
Marinated cauliflower a la Isabel 46

Pickled smelts (Boquerones en vinagre) 47
Tuna or meat-filled pastries (Empanadillas) 48
French-fried squid (Calamares fritos) 49
Spanish croquettes (Croquetas) 50
Mixed-fry croquettes 51
Shrimp in pajamas (Gambas en pijamas) 52
Garlic shrimp (Gambas al ajillo) 54
Moorish kabobs (Pinchos Morunos) 54
Marinated octopus (Pulpo) 56
Baby Eels (Angulas) 57

SOUPS **59**

Of soup and love, the first is the best 59
Bread-balls for soup 60
Custard garnish for clear soup 61
Beef boullion 61
Creamed vegetable soup (Crema de legumbres) 62
Fifteen-minute soup (Sopa al cuarto de hora) 63
Clam soup 65
Fish soup (Sopa de pescado) 66
Cold Spanish soup (Gazpacho) 67
Chicken soup (Sopa de ave) 68
Dried salt-cod soup 69
Shrimp soup with mayonnaise 70
Shrimp-shell soup 71
Onion soup (Sopa de cebolla) 72
Garlic soup (Sopa de ajo) 73
Consomme with sherry (Consomé al jerez) 74
Cold jellied consomme (Consomé frío) 74
Bean and vegetable soup, Majorcan style 75
Spinach soup with chick peas 76
Spinach and green pea soup 77
Carrot puree soup 78
Blended tomato, potato and onion soup 78
Potato soup puree (Sopa de patatas) 79
Two-bean soup (Potaje blanco) 80

Bean soup from Gallego (Caldo Gallego) 81
Tapioca soup 81

EGGS 83

"What kind of meals do they serve?" 83
How to hard-boil eggs 84
Coddleg eggs 84
Plain omelette 85
Spanish potato omelette (Tortilla española) 85
Cheese omelette souflee made in a frying pan 87
Ham omelette (Tortilla con jamón) 88
Shrimp omelette (Tortilla con gambas) 88
Spring omelette 89
Ham and potato omelette 89
Mushroom omelette 90
Omelette with cooked beans 90
Gruyere cheese omelette 91
Asparagus omelette 91
Spinach omelette 91
Baked eggs on spinach, style 1 91
Baked eggs on spinach, style 2 92
Puffed baked eggs 92
Chicken or ham and egg custard 93
Baked eggs with ham and grated cheese 94
Lentils with fried eggs 94
Hard-boiled egg croquettes 94
Eggplant scrambled eggs 95
Stuffed-egg croquette 96
Eggs a la Riojana 97
Eggs a la Flamenca 97
Souflee 98
Coddled eggs Villaroy 100
White Mountain eggs (Huevos Monte Blanco) 101

VEGETABLES 103

"Sign your flourish" 103

Pisto with zucchini squash or eggplant 104
Carrots and spinach in vinegar sauce 104
Carrots a la Santanderina 105
Stuffed peppers with tomatoes and anchovies 106
Green peppers with raisins 107
Creamed cauliflower with grated cheese 107
Creamed cauliflower with egg 107
Cooked cauliflower 108
Cooked cabbage 108
Stringbeans with tomato 109
Eggplant supreme 109
Vegetable casserole (Budin de legumbres) 110
Vegetable medley (Panaché de verduras) 111
Spinach pie 113
Spinach and onions seasoned with cinammon 114
Creamed spinach (Espinacas con Bechamel) 114
Spinach, style 1 (Espinacas) 115
Spinach, style 2 (Espinacas) 116
Baked spinach 116
Spinach souflee 117
Artichoke hearts 118
Fresh artichokes (Alcachofas) 119
Peas with onions and mint 120
Green peas with sausage, ham, and onions (Guisantes a la Ex-
    tremeña) 120
Mushrooms with bread crumbs and parsley 121
Plain sauteed mushrooms 121

RICE, POTATOES, MACARONI 123
Todo el monte no es orégano 123
Rice with tomato and peppers 124
Peppers stuffed with rice 124
Rice (arroz) 125
Rice with tomato sauce, sausage, and pepers (Arroz a la Rio-
    jana) 126

Rice with veal or pork (Arroz Murciano) 127
Boiled potatoes with parsley 128
Pan-roasted potatoes 128
Potato garnish 128
Potatoes with paprika and vinegar (Patatas de Jáen) 129
Custard potatoes 129
Potatoes in tomato sauce 130
Potatoes in a sauce 130
Fried potatoes in sauce (Patatas al ajillo) 130
Potato croquettes 131
Duchess potatoes (Patatas Duquesa) 132
Macaroni in bechamel sauce (Macarrones con bechamel) . . . 133
Macaroni with tomato sauce, plain or baked (Macarrones con
tomate) 133
Baked macaroni 133
Macaroni in sauce with baked eggs 134

BEANS **135**

Barriga llena, corazón contento 135
How to prepare dried beans 136
Lentils with tomato sauce 137
Kidney bean stew, Asturias style (Fabada Asturiana) 138
Lentil stew (Potaje de lentejas) 139
Lima bean stew 140
Chick pea stew 140

SALADS **143**

En boca cerrada no entran moscas 143
Shrimp and potato salad supreme 144
Avocado, orange, and tomato salad 145
Lettuce salad (Ensalada de lechuga) 146
Gypsy salad 146
String bean, tomato, and potato salad 146
Tomato and green pepper salad 147
Tomato salad (Ensalada de tomate) 148
Potato salad (Patatas en salpicón) 148

Chopped egg and onion salad 149
Potato and egg salad 150
Potato and anchovy salad 150
Beet and potato salad 150
Potato and artichoke heart salad 150
Cooked beets with hard-boiled egg 150
Cauliflower, tomato, and anchovy salad 150
Cauliflower salad 151
Shrimp in a lettuce blanket 151
Sardine or perch salad (Ensalada de sardinas) 151
Lima bean, stringbean, and carrot salad 152

FISH **153**

Isabel's kitchen 153
Tips on preparing fish 154
Decoration to place around fish serving platter 155
　Spinach-shrimp molds 155
　Whipped potato-clam mold 156
　Hard-boiled eggs filled with anchovies 156
Fish court boullion 156
Deep-fry batter 156
Fried fish 158
Fried smelts Andalucia style (Boquerones Andaluz) 159
Fried trout 159
Baked trout 159
Dried salt cod in its own sauce (Bacalao al pil-pil) 160
Dried salt cod with peppers and tomatoes (Bacalao a la Rioja-na) 161
Spicy dried salt-cod in tomato sauce (Bacalao a la Vizcaína) . 162
Clams and rice 163
Fish pisto 164
Fish pudding 164
Paella, style 1 168
Paella, style 2 170
Grilled fresh sardines or perch (Sardinas a la parilla) 172

Galician fish and seafood pie (Empanada Gallega de mariscos) 173
Fish Basque style (Merluza a la Vasca) 174
Fish filet sauce 175
Filet of sole in wine sauce (Lenguado con crema y vino) . . . 175
Filet of sole au gratin (Lenguado au gratin) 176
Fish filet with bechamel sauce (Filetes de pescado con besamel) 178
Baked fish and potato chips (Pescado asado con patatas) . . . 178
Stuffed fish (Pescado relleno) 179
Stuffed fish Bella Vista 180
Fish in aspic 181
Salmon pie or tarts 182
Stuffed squid 183
Squid in black sauce (Calamares en su tinta) 184
Squid in tomato sauce 185
Why there are no snail recipes in this book 185

MEATS 189
Bueno es el vino cuando el vino es bueno 189
Dumplings 190
Meat and potatoes in wine sauce from Extremadura (Frite Extremeño) 190
Stuffed meat roast (Aleta) 191
Meat in onion sauce 193
Diced meat and tomatoes (Picadillo de carne) 194
Short ribs of beef 195
Ground-meat pie 195
Meat balls (Albóndigas) 196
Meat loaf 197
Meat and vegetable stew from Extremadura (Cocido Extremeño) 198
Madrid-style stew (Cocido Madrileño) 199
Beef (or veal) stew with potatoes (Estofado de vaca con patatas) 202
Veal roast with vegetables 203

Breaded veal chops or cutlets (Filetes de ternera empanados). 204
Veal cordon bleu 205
Veal Villaroy (Ternera Villaroy) 206
Stuffed green peppers with veal and chicken (Pimientos relle-
nos) 207
Smoked pork chops with cabbage and potatoes 208
Pork pie from Galicia (Empanada Gallega de lomo) 209
Roast whole baby pig (Cochinillo asado) 210
Bar-b-qued lamb ribs 210
Lamb ribs or short ribs with rice 211
Lam and potato stew (Potaje de cerdo con patatas) 212
Roast leg of lamb (Pierna de cordero asado) 213
Stuffed leg of lamb (Pierna de cordero rellena) 213
Roast stuffed leg of lamb with tomato sauce 214
Stewed lamb shanks 215
Roast whole baby lamb 216
Galician stew with navy beans (Pote Gallego) 216
Stew from Gallego with chick peas (Cocido Gallego) 216
Breaded liver (Hígado empanado) 219
Lamb tongues 219
Beef tongue 220
Lamb or veal kidneys 222
Calves fect with chick peas 223
Preparation of fresh tripe 223
Tripe a la Madrid (Callos a la Madrileña) 224
Gypsy stew 226
Pig's ears a la Leon 228

CHICKEN, DUCK, RABBIT, AND PARTRIDGE 229

Haz bien y no mires a quien 229
Broiled chicken 230
Roast chicken 230
Roast chicken stuffed with apples 231
Roast chicken with applesauce stuffing 232
Chicken in rum (Pollo a la Catalana) 233
Royal chicken (Pollo real) 234

Chicken medley (Pollo pepitoria) 235

Fried chicken breasts supreme (Pollo Villaroy) 237

Chicken in garlic and wine sauce (Pollo al ajillo) 238

Stewed chicken with tomatoes, peppers, and potatoes 238

Chicken stewed in tomato sauce 239

Country-style chicken (Pollo a la Campensina) 239

Duck in orange sauce 240

Hunter's style rabbit (Conejo a la cazadora) 242

Partridge in chocolate sauce (Perdiz en chocolate) 243

SAUCES 245

La mejor salsa es el hambre y buenas ganas 245

Salad dressing 246

Blond sauce (Salsa rubia) 246

Basic Spanish tomato sauce, style 1 (Salsa de tomate básico) . 247

Fast tomato sauce, style 2 248

Tomato sauce al Cognac . . . . ·249

Pink sauce Majorca style (Salsa rosa Mayorquina) 249

Mayonnaise 250

Garlic and olive oil sauce (Alioli) 252

Bechamel sauce 253

Hollandaise sauce 255

Mornay sauce 256

Bernaise sauce 256

Tartar sauce 257

Vinagrette sauce (Salsa vinagreta) 257

Green sauce (Salsa verde) 258

Orange juice sauce for roast chicken, duck, or pork 259

Anchovy sauce 260

Sauce for boiled fish 260

Chestnut puree 261

DESSERTS 263

Hombre de buena pasta 263

A true story 264

Plump is beautiful 264
Caramel-covered almonds 266
Cream puff shells 266
Orange cream gelatin 267
Applesauce souflee 268
Fried little cream pies 269
Churros (Spanish doughnuts) 270
Ice-cream cake 272
Baked Alaska 273
Meringue cookies or what to do with leftover egg whites . . . 274
Sponge cake (Bizcochón) 275
Meringue 276
Meringue shells 276
Gypsy's arm (Brazo de gitano) 277
Spanish apple pie 278
Dough for pies, style 1 279
Very easy pie dough, style 2 279
Pastry cream filling 281
Very easy pear pie 282
Peach pudding pie 282
Spanish custard (Flan) 283
An economical coffee custard (Flan económico) 284
Fruit and bread custard 285
Fried custard (Leche frita) 286
Fruit cocktail pudding 287
Applesauce pudding 287
Rice with milk dessert 288
Rice souflee dessert 288
Cockie balls 289
Annisettes (Roscos) 290
Cookies 290
Polvorones cookies 291
Very delicious nut cookies 292
Jane Baxter's nut cake 292
Chocolate souflee 293
Fritters (Buñuelos) 295

Crescents 296
Omelette in flames (Tortilla quemada) 297
Oranges in Kirsch (Naranjas al Kirsch) 297
Prunes in Cognac 298
Fruit cup in orange shells 298
Baked apples with pastry cream filling 298
Pastry-wrapped baked apples 299
Baked apples with honey 299
Baked apples with Cognac 300
Baked apples in wine sauce (Manzanas al vino blanco) 300
Baked apple flambe 301
Bananas flambe 302
Fruit salad in banana shells 303
Ice-cream with banana 303
Ice-cream with peaches 304
Ice-cream cup with champagne 304
Crepes (Tortillas rellenas) 304

BEVERAGES 307
El Español fino con todo bebe vino 307
Wines 308
Wine punch (Sangría) 310
    Red wine sangría 311
    White wine sangría 311
Eggnog (Ponche de Navidad) 312
Hot milk and egg punch 312
Vodka fruit drink 313
Hot chocolate, Spanish style 314

A story with a moral 314
The difference between "horse" and "gentleman" 315
Useful Spanish words and sentences for market and restaurant . . . 317
Index 319

ANECDOTES

¡Ay Señora! 19
Even a plate of beans can be prepared beautifully 23

The bus ride and the shoe 29
"What kind of meals to they serve?" 83
"Sign your flourish" 103
Isabel's kitchen 153
Why there are no snail recipes in this book 185
A true story 264
Plump is beautiful 264
A story with a moral 314
The difference between "horse" and "gentleman" 315

CARTOONS BY NANCY SHAPIRO

"That's not a bug in the paella, it's a type of crab!" 167
Why there are no snail recipes in this book 187
"This painting will be worth a fortune back home" 316

PROVERBS

Para trabajar mañana, para comer, ganas 23
Entre col y col, lechuga 26
Las sopas y los amores, los primeros son los mejores 59
Todo el monte no es orégano 123
Barriga llena, corazón contento 135
En boca cerrada no entran moscas 143
Bueno es el vino cuando el vino es bueno 189
Haz bien y no mires a quien 229
La mejor salsa es el hambre y buenas ganas 245
Hombre de buena pasta 263
El Español fino con todo bebe vino 307

PHOTOGRAPHS

Pisto . . . . between 104-105
Shrimp and potato salad supreme . . . . between 144-145
Avocado, orange and tomato salad . . . . between 144-145
Paella . . . . between 168-169
Roast chicken . . . . between 230-231

¡AY SEÑORA!

It seems that no matter where we live, we always have times when we have to play the waiting game.

I had ordered a dresser from a floor sample in a well-known furniture store in Madrid. The salesman said that I would receive it in two weeks. I think we both knew very well that it would never arrive in two weeks, but we played the game anyway. I waited for my dresser, and called the store manager every now and then. I understood that my calls would in no way speed things up, but at least I kept in touch. This is the way the conversation went.

January

Me: What happened to the dresser? When I ordered it in November you said it would be ready in two weeks.

Him: Ay, señora, the dresser that came for you was not good, so we ordered another. It will be ready in two weeks.

February

Me: What happened to the dresser? In January you said it would be ready in two weeks.

Him: One of the drawers did not fit, so we had to make another. It will be ready in one week.

March

Me: What happened to the dresser? You said it would be ready in one week.

Him: It rained and the varnish man could not varnish it. It will be ready in a few days.

April

Me: What happened to the dresser? You said it would be ready in a few days.

Him: The varnish man had a funeral and could not come to varnish it. It will be ready in a day or two.

May

Me: You delivered the wrong dresser!

Sometimes we wait for something with great anticipation and when it arrives it fills our dreams; othertimes it just lets us down. Make sure that at least the meals you serve never have the latter effect.

A TYPICAL MENU FROM A RESTAURANT IN SPAIN

Entremeses

Entremeses variados
Jamón serrano

Appetizers

Varied cold cuts
Mountain-cured ham

Sopas

Sopa al cuarto de hora
Sopa de ajo con huevo
Caldo de ave
Gazpacho a la andaluza

Soups

Fifteen-minute sopa
Garlic soup with egg
Chicken soup
Gazpacho (cold vegetable soup)

Huevos

Huevos revueltos con champiñon
Tortilla española
Tortilla a la flamenca
Tortilla con gambas

Eggs

Scrambled eggs with mushrooms
Spanish tortilla (potato omelette)
Gypsy-style tortilla
Omelette with shrimp

Pescados

Gambas al ajillo
Merluza a la vasca
Lenguado a la parrilla
Truchas al horno
Truchas fritas

Fish

Shrimp in garlic sauce
Hake, Basque style
Grilled filet of sole
Baked trout
Fried trout

Asados y Parrillas

Pollo asado, medio
Pechuga Villaroy
Chuletas de ternera
Filete de ternera con patatas
Solomillo con patatas
Estofado de vaca con patatas
Pierna de cordero asado

From the Oven and Grill

A half roast chicken
Fried chicken Villaroy style
Veal chops
Veal steak with potatoes
Sirloin with potatoes
Beef stew with potatoes
Roast leg of lamb

Legumbres

Guisantes con jamón
Espárragos con mahonesa
Alcachofas salteadas con jamón
Judías verdes con tomate y jamón
Ensalada de lechuga y tomate
Patatas fritas

Postres

Flan
Helado de vainilla o chocolate
Melocotón en almibar
Compota de frutas
Queso
Piña al Kirsch
Fruta del tiempo
Naranja al Kirsch
Tarta de manzana
Manzana asada

Café, té
Vino
Agua natural en botella
Agua con gas en botella

Vegetables

Peas with ham
Asparragus with mayonnaise
Artichoke hearts with ham, sautéed
Stringbeans with tomato and ham
Lettuce and tomato salad
French-fried potatoes

Dessert

Custard
Vanilla or chocolate ice-cream
Peaches (canned) in syrup
Fruit cocktail
Cheese
Pineapple in Kirsch liquer
Fruit of the season
Sliced orange in Kirsch liquer
Apple pie
Baked apple

Coffee, tea
Wine
Natural bottled water
Carbonated bottled water

EVEN A PLATE OF BEANS CAN BE PREPARED BEAUTIFULLY

> Para trabajar, mañana; para comer, ganas.
> *Work can be put off till tomorrow, but not the desire for food.*

In Spain there is an expression which says, "hay que comer bien," one ought to eat well. This means that food should taste great, look beautiful, be served with style, and be eaten in good company. So several times a day are set aside for the enjoyment of this activity.

Although breakfast consists of only bread and coffee, there are still a lot of things to do to prepare it. First, the hard-crusted loaves of bread have to be brought in from the local baker every morning so that they are fresh and crisp. Then the coffee beans have to be ground, and finally the milk has to be boiled to give the coffee that special creamy taste. Sugar and a lot of boiled milk are put into the coffee in the morning. Some people even add a bit of butter to make it extra rich. The coffee and the bread spread with butter and mermelade are just enough food to last until 11 a. m.

Eleven o'clock is "coffee time," which is similar to the American coffee break, except that in Spain even the school children stop for refreshments. Only a cup of hot chocolate, or coffee with boiled milk (café con leche) and a sweet roll are needed to stop the hunger pangs until the mid-day break at 1:30 or 2:00.

At one time everything closed between 1:30 p.m. and 4:00 p.m. except the restaurants and bars. The salesmen sent their customers out of the stores and locked up for the afternoon break even if the customer was in the middle of buying something! Business offices closed, even some taxi drivers refused to take calls because "es la hora de comer." it was time to eat, to go home to dinner. Although it wasn't easy to get home at 2 o'clock, most Spaniards considered it worth their while.

Recently this custom has been changed, and now many places stay open all day: stores, museums, and national places of interest. The hours for eating are more varied than before. People eat their main meal at different times, some in the middle of the day, some whenever they get home from work, and others have theirs at 9 o'clock at night.

There are many small bars called "tabernas" where people can stop to have appetizers before dinner or supper. They might order a few pieces of fried squid (see page 49) or two croquettes (see page 50), very popular appetizers, and have them with a small glass of wine while standing at the counter. Everything ordered is served very quickly; the orders are always very small, just enough food to tide you over so that you can battle the crowds and traffic until you reach home for dinner, the main meal of the day.

To prepare this meal, which is a banquet, the housewife probably went shopping that morning in one of the crowded open-air "mercados." These are market places where a variety of stores, from vegetable stalls to meat "carnicerías," are under one roof. Customers get individual attention here, since nothing is pre-packaged. The butcher will take a chunk of meat off the hook to cut the slices of "filetes," little steaks, that you order just the way you want them. The fishman will let you look at each fish's eye to see wich one is the freshest, and then wrap your pick in a old newspaper. All the food that is bought is placed into a basket which was brought along from home for that purpose.

Once completed, the main meal will probably consist of about six courses served one at a time. Soup will be served first, followed by fish or a tortilla (see page 85) Then a vegetable dish which is delicious enough to be served by itself will be presented, followed by the meat and rice course which will be served together on one plate; salad will be served at the end of the meal. Throughout the meal there will be hard-crusted Spanish bread and wine, and sometimes bottled water, "agua de solares". For dessert there will be cheese and fruit, or maybe flan. Afterwards, rest, "siesta,". Later on, before going back to work or out to visit or shop, there will be strong black coffee, "café solo," in small, demitasse cups.

Supper is hours away and won't be served until 10 o'clock or later. Now comes Tea Time, a good hour to visit with friends over a cup of coffee or tea and some pastries, either at home or in an elegant coffee house, hotel lobby, or in any one of the street cafes.

Another social activity before supper for those who want it is the cocktail hour. Either in the "tabernas" or at home, "se puede abrir el apetito," an appetite for supper can be encouraged by having a drink and an "aperitivo" about 9 o'clock. By 10 o'clock everybody goes home to supper.

The last meal of the day, supper, is considered to be small, since only three courses are served! Just food that is considered light enough to eat at that late hour will be prepated. The menu might look like this: chicken soup, either tortilla, fish, or chicken served with rice or potatoes, fruit and cheese for dessert.

And so a day with many enjoyable moments has been spent eating well.

The saying that one should eat well doesn't mean that expensive food has to be bought. Many great meals can be prepared with inexpensive items, as you will see when you cook some of the recipes in this book. But in that saying lies the idea that in order to eat well, care and time need to be taken to prepare the food as best as possible, and enough time has to be set aside to enjoy eating it. Even a plate of beans can be prepared beautifully and served with style!

¡Que aproveche!

A SPANISH DAY

> Entre col y col, lechuga.
> *Between cabbage and cabbage, lettuce.*
> *(Between something ordinary, something good.)*

Good eating, a pleasure all can pursue in varying degrees, is scheduled throughout the day and into the night.

Below are sample menus and a schedule most Spaniards like to keep between work and play, whether they are rich or poor.

7:00 a.m. to 9:00 a.m.

Breakfast	*El desayuno*
Hard-crusted Spanish bread	Pan español
Butter	Mantequilla
Peach preserves	Mermelada de melocotón
Strong coffee with boiled milk and sugar	Café con leche y azúcar

10:00 a.m. to 11:30 a.m.

Mid-morning snack	*Café (Almuerzo)*
Sweet rolls	Bollos dulces
Strong coffee, either black or with boiled milk	Café con leche o café solo

1:00 p.m. to 2:00 p.m.

Appetizers	*Aperitivos*
Fried squid	Calamares fritos
Wine, beer, or soda	Vino, cerveza, o soda

2:00 p.m. to 4:00 p.m.

Dinner	*La comida*
Soup	Sopa
Fish or Spanish tortilla	Pescado o tortilla
Vegetable	Verdura
Meat or chicken	Carne o pollo
Rice or potatoes	Arroz o patatas
Salad	Ensalada
Hard-crusted bread	Pan
Fruit and cheese	Frutas y queso
Wine, mineral water, and plain soda	Vino, agua mineral y sifón
Strong black coffee served in a demi-tass cup sometime after the meal	Café solo

6:00 p.m. to 7:00 p.m.

Tea Time	*Merienda*
Pastry	Pasteles
Cake	Tortas
A sandwich	Un bocadillo
Tea or coffee	Té o café con leche

8:00 p.m. to 10:00 p.m.

Cocktails	*Coctel*
Appetizers	Aperitivos
Olives stuffed with anchovies	Aceitunas
Mixed drinks	Combinados

10:00 p.m. to 11:00 p.m.

Supper	*La cena*
Soup	Sopa
Chicken, fish, or Spanish tortilla	Pollo, pescado o tortilla española
Salad	Ensalada
Wine, mineral water, and plain soda	Vino, agua mineral y sifón
Hard-crusted bread	Pan
Flan	Flan
Coffee	Café

THE BUS RIDE AND THE SHOE

The buses in Madrid were always packed at 1:30 in the afternoon, and on this particular day I had to stand all the way in the back where I had gotten on. (We entered from the rear and left from the front.)

In order to get off at one's stop, a cooperative effort was required of the passengers, especially if the rider who wanted to get off was at the back end!

The person who needed to leave called out "Por aquí" (here), and the caller would immediately be pushed from person to person to the front of the bus, in time to descend at the correct street.

When the bus neared my stop, I silently practiced these important words, trying to immitate the proper accent. I didn't want everyone to know I was a foreigner.

As soon as I uttered them, I had instant success. People pushed me from one to the other, toward the door and out of the bus.

It would have been a perfect exit, except that I landed with only one shoe on and my other one missing!

What had happened was that during my approach to the front of the bus another señora had hooked her heel into my shoe. I was pushed forward with such enthusiasm that I couldn't stop, and my shoe remained under her heel while my foot went along with the rest of me.

The shout of "Por aquí" had changed to "My shoe, my shoe," but the momentum of the system could not be stopped. Besides, no one understood what I was saying!

As I stood in the street with one bare foot yelling "My shoe" at the bus, someone inside opened the window and handed out my other shoe; then the bus drove off.

"Gracias," I called out to the back of the bus. I put my shoe on and walked home.

FLAMENCO

Tengo en mi casa un jardín	In my house I have a garden
por si viene un contratiempo	in order to sell flowers for you
vender yo flores pá tí.	if bad times come.
A mí me duele, me duele	My mouth hurts me,
la boquita de decirte,	gypsy, from asking you
gitana, si tú me quieres.	if you love me.
Lo he dicho, y lo voy hacé	I'm going to make, as I have said,
un teléfono sin hilo	a wireless telephone
pá sabé de tu queré...	in order to know of your love...
Er queré quita er sentío;	Love destroys the senses;
lo digo por esperiensia,	I talk through experience
porque a mí m'ha suseío.	because it has happened to me.
A mí me daban, me daban	I had
tentaciones de locura	crazy temptations
cuando de tí me acordaba.	whenever I thought of you.
Ven acá, falsa y refalsa,	Come here, false woman,
falsa, te vuelvo a decí...	false, I say again,
El día que me vendiste,	the day that you sold me out,
¿cuánto te dieron por mí?	how much did they give?
Cuando pases por mi verá	When you pass me by
orvía que me has querío	forget that you have loved me
y no me mires siquiera.	and don't even glance my way.
En un cuartito los dos,	If we were in a room together
veneno que tú me dieras,	I would do anything for you,
veneno tomará yo.	even take poison.

Typical gypsy verses of a Lively "Bulería," flamenco song and dance.

D.E. Pohren, *The Art of Flamenco*, Jerez de la Frontera, Spain: Editorial Jerez Industrial, 1962, p. 105

Me gustas más que el buen vino
y más que un pavo trufao!
Más que me gusta el tabaco
·y que estar siempre tumbao!
Con decirte que me gustas
más que el acta a un diputao!
Y eso que eres un tonel
y tu cutis se ha arrugao!
y tu cutis se ha arrugao!...
Más no sé que gracia tienes
ni qué tienen tus traseras
que te miro y me parece
que me das adormideras...

I like you more than good wine
and roast turkey!
and more than tobacco
and just lazing around!
I tell you that I like you
more than a lawyer likes court!
and this, even though you're a
barrel
and your skin is all wrinkles!...
I don't really know what charm
you and your buttocks have,
that when I look at you it seems
you've given me opium...

This is a Milongas, an Andalucian folklore song.

D.E. Pohren, *The Art of Flamenco*, Jerez de la Frontera, Spain: Editorial Jerez Industrial, 1962, p. *125*

HOW TO WORK UP A RECIPE

After preparing a recipe two or three times in close succession, it becomes easy to do, and reading the recipe again probably won't be necessary. At that time it becomes one of your own easy foods to prepare.

1. Read the entire recipe before starting to cook.

2. Make a list of the items to buy after checking the pantry.

3. Make notes as to when to prepare the different parts of the recipe.

4. Underline in pencil, in the book, the important things to remember.

5. Prepare all the ingredients, place them on plates, and put them near the stove so that they'll be ready to use.

6. Stay in the vicinity of the kitchen when you're cooking and look into the pot often to see that the food doesn't overcook or burn. Pay attention to the cooking and don't rush.

A FEW NOTES ABOUT THE FOOD IN THE RECIPES

Clams, mussels, and oysters must be alive when you prepare to cook them or they can make you ill. When they are alive, their shells are closed tightly; sometimes they open and close again. When they are dead, their shells open before cooking and never shut again. Discard clams, mussels, and oysters with shells that stay open before they are cooked. Stop the cooking as soon as their shells open so that they do not get overcooked. If they don't stay open after being cooked, discard them, also.

To fry food well, the food to be fried should be cold, and wiped dry with an absorbant towel before being dipped into batter.

To find out if the oil is ready for frying, drop a cube of bread into it. The bread should brown in 60 seconds.

To clear the oil for storing, drop a few pieces of potato into it and fry. Remove the potato before storing the oil.

To grind and prepare saffron for a recipe, put a few pieces of saffron, about three or four, into a mortar bowl and grind it. Add a small amount of liquid, and then add it to the food.

Substitute French or Italian bread for Spanish bread.

Substitute sweet Italian sausage or pepperoni for chorizo.

The wine used for these recipes is always dry, which means that it is not sweet. It may be an inexpensive one, but it should not be one labeled "cooking wine". Wine used for cooking should be good-tasting, one which may also be used for drinking, or else it will spoil the food.

In Spain, olive oil is used for all cooking and table use; however, you may use any oil you like for these recipes and the result will still be excellent.

DEFINITIONS OF TERMS USED IN THE RECIPES

MARINATE
Let the food stay in the mixture for a certain amount of time.

SIMMER
Cook the food just below the boiling point or just at the boiling point, but not at a fast boil.

SAUTE
Cook in a small amount of fat.

BLANCH
Rinse quickly with boiling water.

SALT TO TASTE
Taste the liquid and then salt it so that it has the correct amount of salt.

BROWN ONIONS
Fry onions in fat until they become brown, but not burnt.

FOLD IN EGG WHITES
Gently mix egg whites that have been beaten to a peak into the rest of the batter by turning the whites under the other part.

OIL FOR DEEP FRYING
Enough oil should be in the pot so that it will cover the food to be fried.

CLOVE OF GARLIC
A clove of garlic is one of the small bulbs inside a round, large mother bulb.

CHOP FINELY
The item may also be cut up into very tiny pieces.

DICED
Cut into very small pieces.

CUBED
Cut into small squares.

FLAKE THE FISH
Part fish into small pieces.

SOFT BREAD CRUMBS
The soft part of the bread is torn into small pieces.

BREAD STUFFING OR BREAD FOR STUFFING
Packaged unseasoned bread stuffing normally used to stuff fowl.

ABBREVIATED TERMS

tsp.	= teaspoon
tbsp.	= tablespoon
lb.	= pound
oz.	= ounce
in.	= inch
pkg.	= package

MEASURES

pinch	= less than 1/8 tsp.
3 tsp.	= 1 tbsp.
16 tbsp.	= 1 cup
1 cup	= 1/2 pint
2 cups	=1 pint
2 pints (4 cups)	= 1 quart
16 ounces	= 1 lb.

EQUIVALENTS

1/8 tsp. minced dried garlic = 1 clove fresh garlic
1/4 tsp. dried parsley = 1 tbsp. fresh parsley
1/8 tsp. minced dried bay leaf = 1 whole dried bay leaf
2 tbsp. lemon juice = 1 ounce or one average lemon
1/3 cup butter = 5 and 1/3 tbsp. buttér
1/4 cup butter = 4 tbsp. butter
1 slice bread = 3/4 cups bread cubes
3 to 4 slices bread = 1 cup dry bread crumbs
1 medium green pepper = 1 cup chopped green pepper
8 tbsp. butter = 1/2 cup butter = 1 stick butter = 4 ounces butter

COOKING UTENSILS MENTIONED IN THE RECIPES

SLOTTED SPOON
A spoon with slits or holes in it to allow food to drain. Used to lift food out of liquid.

WHISK
A bunch of wire loops in a handle used for beating or whipping.

MORTAR AND PESTLE
A bowl and an instrument, usually made of wood, used to grind spices.

SKEWERS
A long pin made of metal which is inserted into meat.

COLANDER
A metal container with holes in the bottom used for draining foods.

DOUBLE BOILER
Two pots made so that the top one fits part-way into the bottom one. Water is usually heated in the bottom pot so that the food can be warmed in the top.

CONVERTING FAHRENHEIT AND CENTIGRADE

To convert oven temperatures from Centigrade to Fahrenheit, use the following formula:

Fahrenheit equals the quantity 9/5 times centigrade plus 32:

$F = 9/5$ x centigrade $+ 32$

For example, if the recipe calls for a 150 degree centigrade oven, do the following arithmetic:

$$F = 9/5 \text{ x } 150/1 = 270$$

$$\text{Add } 32: 270 + 32 = 302$$

Round it off, and the Fahrenheit oven temperature to use will be 300 degrees.

To convert oven-temperatures from Fahrenheit to Centigrade, use the following formula:

Centigrade equals the quantity 5/9 times Fahrenheit minus 32:

$$C = 5/9 \times (Fahrenheit - 32)$$

First do the subtraction, then multiply 5/9 by it.

CONVERTING WEIGHT

Multiply ounces times 28 to equal grams.·
Multiply pounds times .45 to equal kilograms.

Multiply number of inches times 2.5 to equal centimeters.

Multiply teaspoons times 5 to equal milliliters.
Multiply tablespoons times 15 to equal milliliters.
Multiply fluid ounces times 30 to equal milliliters.
Multiply cups times .24 to equal liters.
Multiply pints times .47 to equal liters.
Multiply quarts times .95 to equal liters.
Multiply gallons times 3.8 to equal liters.

U.S. SYSTEM OF MEASURES	METRIC SYSTEM
EQUIVALENTS	
1 ounce	28.3 grams
1 pound	454 grams
2.2 pounds	1 kilo (1,000 grams)
1 pint	0.47 liter
1 quart	0.95 liter
1 gallon	3 78 liters

TEMPERATURES

Fahrenheit
32 degrees = freezing
212 degrees = boiling

Centigrade (Celsius)
0 degrees = freezing
100 degrees = boiling

OVEN TEMPERATURES

Slow oven = 250 degrees to 300 degrees
Slow moderate oven = 325 degrees
Quick moderate oven = 375 degrees
Hot oven = 425 degrees to 450 degrees
Very hot oven = 475 degrees to 500 degrees

How to calculate number of pounds of roast to buy for a given number of people.

If you will serve 1/2 pound per person, and you will have 6 people for dinner, work the following arithmetic:

$$1/2 \times 6/1 = 6/2 = 3 \text{ pounds of roast}$$

How to calculate the amount of time to roast meat.

If you are going to roast the meat for 35 minutes per pound, and the roast weighs 3 pounds, work the following arithmetic:

Multiply 35 minutes per pound
x 3 pounds
_____
105 minutes roasting time

Divide by 60 minutes to find roasting time in hours:

1 hour 45 minutes
105
- 60
_____
45

EASY FOOD DECORATIONS

Slice hard-boiled egg and place the slices overlapping on top of the food.

Put quarters of hard-boiled eggs in soups and in cooked vegetable dishes.

Slice raw red or green pepper into circles and arrange them overlapping on top of food. The circles may also be sautéed first.

Pitted black olives can be used as a decoration, either whole or when sliced into circles.

Whole asparagus spears can be used to separate different foods on one plate, or to decorate the plate.

Artichoke hearts make a nice addition.

Cucumber slices are good to adorn cold dishes.

Crescents, from the Crescent recipe on page 296, make a beautiful and unusual decoration.

Appetizers

From the short story, *El Conde Lucanor* by Don Juan Manuel, written in the fourteenth century, comes this advice:

"Si al principio no muestras quien eres, nunce podrás después cuando quisieres."

"If you don't show who you are in the beginning, you'll never be able to later when you want to."

The appetizer is a good way to show who you are from the start. Very simple ones such as green olives stuffed with anchovies and shelled almonds are popular in Spain, and they are not too filling before a large meal. A very fine restaurant in Madrid, El Callejón de la Ternera, always serves sliced onions and tomatoes that have been sprinkled with olive oil. For something more elaborate, croquettes would be a winner, and they're also more filling. Pickled smelts, for example, make a very nice first plate, either at the cocktail table in the livingroom or at the table in the dinning room. Some appetizers may also be used as a main dish.

SOUFLEE CANAPE

Easy and delicious. Serve as soon as it's taken out of the oven.

This recipe makes 16 one-inch rounds or squares.

Use a sharp cheese like sharp cheddar or roquefort.

Prepare the first two steps in advance.

> 2 egg whites
> 3 tbsp. grated sharp cheese
> 3 tbsp. flour
> 3 tbsp. butter or oil
> 1 cup warm milk
> 4 slices white bread, crusts removed
> 1 tsp. sugar

1. Cut bread into small rounds or squares.

2. Heat butter or oil in a pan, blend in flour, then slowly blend in the warm milk. Stir constantly to make a thick sauce. Remove from heat and let cool. Add cheese and let get cold.

3. At serving time, beat the egg whites until they begin to foam. Add sugar and continue beating until they form stiff peaks.

4. Fold into the cooled sauce.

5. Top each piece of bread with a teaspoon of the sauce. Place into a 450 degree oven until they rise, about 5 minutes.

BEAN "NUTS"

These crunchy beans are served like nuts for an appetizer or snack.

They do NOT have to be soaked overnight; just cook them, dry them, and fry them! Store in a jar for several days.

> *large dried lima beans*
> *oil for deep frying*
> *salt*
> *cayenne pepper (optional)*
> *1/2 tsp. paprika per cup fried beans*

1. Put the beans into a pot of cold water and bring to a boil. Reduce heat and simmer for 15 minutes (not longer or the beans will be too soft).

2. Drain, place beans on a pan, and put them into a 350 degree pre-heated oven for two minutes to dry.

3. Fry in very hot boiling oil (oil should cover beans) until light brown. Drain on absorbant paper.

4. Place into bowl and toss with salt, paprika, and a small amount of cayenne.

GRILLED SHRIMP
(Gambas a la plancha)

In Spain you can find places which specialize in serving shrimp, although most taverns serve grilled shrimp.

It's easy to identify a shrimp place — just look at the floor. If it's covered with a mixture of shrimp shells, crumbled napkins, and sawdust, you've found the spot.

You'll stand at the bar and the shrimp will be served in their shells, so shrimp-eating etiquette calls for the following: peel off the shells with your hands, drop them on the floor next to your own feet, and keep the counter and your dish clean. (The bartender has enough to do without cleaning up your mess, too!)

When you serve Gambas a la plancha, provide a finger bowl for washing and a bowl for the discarded shrimp shells.

1. Wash shrimp and drain dry. Leave shells on.

2. Oil griddle very lightly, sprinkle coarse salt on it, and heat until it's quite hot.

3. Lower heat, place shrimp (with shells on) on the griddle. Grill for 5 minutes on one side, turn and grill for 3 minutes on other side. Watch them so that they won't burn. Remove from griddle and serve immediately. Each person removes shells from their own shrimp.

CHOPPED GREEN PEPPERS AND TOMATOES

Serve this recipe warm or cold, as an appetizer on toast or crackers, or as a relish.

Serves 6.

2 green peppers
1 chopped clove garlic or 1/8 tsp. dried garlic
3 small chopped onions
3 fresh tomatoes or one one-pound can tomatoes, chopped
oil
1 tsp. paprika
pinch cayenne pepper (optional)
pinch sugar

1. Put the peppers under the broiler until the skin blisters Remove, cool, and peel. Discard seeds. Chop coarsely.

2. Heat the oil and sauté the chopped onions and sliced garlic until slightly brown.

3. Add the peppers and tomatoes, cayenne, salt, paprika, and a pinch sugar. Cook covered on low heat until peppers and tomatoes are soft and very little liquid remains, about 30 minutes. When done, add oil if it is too dry.

EGGPLANT DIP OR SALAD, STYLE 1
(Picado de berenjena)

This eggplant mixture is good as a spread on crackers or as a salad on lettuce.

It may be made the day before serving.

> *1 medium-size eggplant*
> *2 hard-boiled eggs*
> *1 medium onion*
> *1/4 cup olive oil*
> *1/8 cup vinegar*
> *salt and pepper*

1. Place the whole, unpeeled eggplant on an ungreased pan and bake in a 350 degree oven until it is completely soft. (About one hour.)

2. Cool and peel. Salt slightly and let it set for 15 minutes. Drain off liquid.

3. Grate the onion or finely chop it.

4. Finely chop the eggplant and hard-boiled eggs.

5. Mix all the ingredients together and serve.

45

EGGPLANT DIP OR SALAD, STYLE 2

To serve as a salad, place on a leaf of lettuce; for an appetizer, serve with crackers.

> *1 eggplant*
> *1 clove mashed garlic or 1/8 tsp. garlic powder*
> *1/4 cup olive oil*
> *2 tbsp. lemon juice*

1. Bake the whole, unpeeled eggplant in an ungreased pan in a 350 degree oven until it is completely soft.

2. Let it cool and peel it. Salt slightly and let it set for 15 minutes. Drain well.

3. Mix lemon juice, oil, and mashed garlic or powder in a flat plate.

4. Cut up the drained eggplant, and chop or mash it. Place it in the plate with the lemon juice and other seasonings and blend. Taste, and add more seasoning if necessary.

MARINATED CAULIFLOWER A LA ISABEL

The cauliflower is served cold, and may be used as a salad, an appetizer, or as a vegetable side dish.

Prepare it at least 12 hours before serving. This recipe is for about 6 people when used as a salad or vegetable dish.

> *1 medium head fresh cauliflower (do NOT use frozen cauliflower for this recipe)*
> *1/4 cup vinegar*
> *1/2 cup oil, preferably olive oil*
> *salt to taste*
> *1 small onion, finely chopped*
> *1 small tomato, peeled and chopped (fresh or canned may be used)*
> *2 tbsp. fresh parsley (or 2 tsp. dried parsley)*

1. Cook whole cauliflower for 10 minutes in 2 cups water which has been salted to taste. Be careful not to overcook cauliflower. The vegetable should not be very soft.

2. Remove the cauliflower from the pot and let it cool. Separate the flowerettes from the whole cauliflower.

3. Mix vinegar, oil, onion, tomato, parsley, and salt to taste in a bowl. Place the cauliflower pieces into it and toss them gently to cover them with the sauce. Be careful not to mash the cauliflower.

4. Let the cauliflower marinate in the mixture, covered, for at least 12 hours. Serve it cold.

PICKLED SMELTS
(Boquerones en vinagre)

Prepare this recipe at least 9 hours before serving.

> *2 lbs. smelts or fresh sardines (do not use frozen or canned fish)*
> *In Spain, use boquerones.*

1. Wash off scales, remove heads, remove spines, and discard them.

2. Separate each fish into two pieces lengthwise.

3. Place them into a bowl in layers, and cover each layer with vinegar, sprinkle liberally with lemon juice, and let set for about 8 hours in the refrigerator.

4. Drain off the vinegar and discard, after 8 hours.

5. Mix the following in a bowl:

> *1 tbsp. fresh parsley, chopped*
> *1/4 cup vinegar*
> *1/2 cup olive oil*
> *2 or 3 cloves finely chopped garlic*
> *salt*

6. Place a layer of fish on a flat serving dish and using a tablespoon, pour some of the oil and vinegar mixture over all the fish on the plate. Add another layer of fish, and add more oil and vinegar mixture. Continue in this manner until all the fish have been placed on the dish and covered with the oil and vinegar mixture.

7. Place the dish in the refrigerator for at least one hour before serving.

Serve plain, or wrap each slice of fish around a gherkin or pitted olive and secure it with a toothpick.

TUNA — OR MEAT-FILLED PASTRIES
(Empanadillas)

These may be made hours before serving and then reheated in the oven.

> *Pie dough recipe, style 2, page 279, for a two-crust pie*
> *Fast tomate sauce, style 2, page 248*
> *mushrooms*
> *1 cup drained tunafish or cooked ground meat or chopped cooked chicken for the filling.*

1. Prepare a thick tomato sauce using mushrooms. It should not have much liquid.

2. Prepare the pie dough, roll it out and cut it into circles with the rim of a cup.

3. When the sauce is done, stir in the filling.

4. Place one teaspoonful of sauce onto half the circle of dough, fold over, and press the edges with the tines of a wet fork to seal.

5. Deep fry in hot oil until the pastry is brown.

FRENCH-FRIED SQUID
(Calamares fritos)

Served as an appetizer in almost every "taberna" (bar) in Spain, french-fried squid is also eaten in small hard-crusted rolls with pieces of it sticking out from all sides!

Squid is a firm, white, sweet-tasting meat, something like shrimp, but much less expensive.

> *1 egg*
> *1 small squid per person*
> *flour*
> *salt*
> *milk*
> *oil for deep frying*

1. How to clean squid:

Hold the body of the squid in one hand and take hold of all the tentacles with your other hand.

Pull the tentacles out of the squid's body along with the entrails. Cut the tentacles from the entrails, and throw away the entrails. Cut the tip from the squid's body, and throw it away. Peel the skin from the body and the tentacles. Cut off the suction cups from the tentacles, and throw them away. Wash the inside of the body, peel off any loose skin, and remove the bone.

2. Slice the body of the squid into one-quarter-inch circles.

3. Place into slightly salted milk for 10 minutes. (This tenderizes the meat.)

4. Drain the squid after 10 minutes, dip it into salted flour, and shake off excess flour. Dip into slightly beaten egg.

5. Fry it in hot oil until the squid is golden brown.

SPANISH CROQUETTES
(Croquetas)

Every woman in Spain knows how to prepare ''croquetas''. The ''croqueta'', one of the most popular appetizers, is served at home, at weddings, in bars, everywhere. The reason is that it is delicious, looks great, fills you up, and it's cheap.

At first it is complicated to prepare, but after you make it twice, you won't need to read the recipe, it will be so easy.

Prepare the croquettes in advance, and re-heat then in the oven before serving.

The first three steps must be prepared at least one hour before frying the croquettes so that the bechamel sauce will be cool enough to handle.

> *flour*
> *beaten egg*
> *fine bread crumbs*
> **bechamel sauce, page** *253*
> *filling:*
> > *Use either one of the following:*
> > *1. One small can tuna fish. Drain tuna fish and mash.*
> > *2. Chopped ham.*
> > *3. Chopped breast of chicken.*
> > *4. Two chopped hard-boiled eggs.*

1. Prepare filling desired and set aside.

2. Prepare bechamel sauce. Leave onions in the sauce.

3. Add filling to bechamel sauce, stir it in, and pour sauce onto a large platter so that it may be cool. Sauce MUST be cold before it can be shaped.

HOW TO SHAPE CROQUETTES

1. Set up a plate of flour, a plate of beaten egg, and a plate of fine bread crumbs, in that order, one next to the other.

2. Take a tablespoon of bechamel sauce, and place it onto the plate of flour, roll it into the shape of a miniature football, and cover it all over with flour.

3. Lift it out and shake off the excess flour. Dip it into the beaten egg.

4. Lift it out and let the egg drain off a little bit. Dip it into the bread crumbs, and cover it all over with crumbs.

5. Fry it in deep hot fat until brown, for about a minute. (Fry one croquette first to test fat.)

MIXED-FRY CROQUETTES

> *Bechamel sauce, page 253*
> *sliced mushrooms*
> *cubed ham*
> *canned artichoke hearts cut into wedges*
> *shrimp cut into pieces*
> *chicken livers cut into pieces*
> *oil for frying*
> *flour*
> *beaten egg*
> *fine bread crumbs*

1. Prepare the bechamel sauce. Divide it into four parts on separate plates.

2. Sauté the mushrooms and ham in oil or butter.

3. Fry the chicken livers.

4. Fry the shrimp.

5. Combine the mushrooms and ham with the bechamel in one plate, the artichoke hearts with the bechamel in another plate, the chicken livers with the third plate, and the shrimp with the last plate.

6. When cold, set up the following:

Put flour in one plate, in another put beaten egg, and in a third put fine bread crumbs.

Take a tablespoon of bechamel sauce, place it onto the plate of flour, roll it into the shape you want covering it with flour. (Form the bechamel from each plate into a different shape. For example, form the mushrooms and ham into a ball, the shrimp into an oval, the livers into a square, the artichokes into a triangle.)

Lift it out, shake off excess flour, and dip it into beaten egg. Lift it out and let the egg drain off a little. Dip it into the bread crumbs and cover it all over with crumbs.

Fry in deep hot oil until brown, about a minute.

place on absorbant paper to drain.

When serving, separate the different croquettes by placing sliced tomatoes between them.

SHRIMP IN PAJAMAS
(Gambas en pijamas)

The "pajama" that the shrimp wears is a delicious fried batter which adds taste and size to it.

Steps 1 to 5 must be made a half hour in advance. Also, the entire recipe may be made hours earlier and reheated in the oven before serving.

This recipe serves 6 people as an appetizer.

> *oil for deep frying*
> *1 lb. shrimp*
> *1 cup flour*
> *1/2 tsp. salt*
> *1/2 tsp. baking powder*
> *1 cup hot milk*
> *3 eggs*

1. Remove shrimp shells, but leave the tail on. Wash shrimp, sprinkle with lemon juice and salt, and set aside. (Shrimp shells may be used for Shrimp shell soup, page 71.)

2. Mix flour, salt, and baking powder in a bowl.

3. Separate the egg yolks from the whites. Don't let ANY egg yolk get into the egg whites or the whites won't whip up.

4. Beat egg yolks.

5. Add hot milk to the flour and stir it in. Add egg yolks. Do not stir very much, just enough to form a batter.

6. Set aside for a half hour.

7. Beat the egg whites until stiff and fold in quickly with as few strokes as possible. Do not stir it very much or the batter will lose its fluffiness.

8. Dip the entire shrimp into the batter, and deep-fry until brown. Lift the shrimp out with a slotted spoon and drain the oil from it.

Leftover batter may be dropped by the teaspoonful and fried the same way. Serve it with the shrimp.

GARLIC SHRIMP
(Gambas al ajillo)

Almost every tavern in Spain has Gambas al ajillo on their menu. They serve it sizzling hot in the same small, individual earthenware dishes in which it is cooked.

Not only are the shrimp delicious, but the sauce is, too. Everyone always soaks up what remains on the dish with a chunk of Spanish bread. It's especially good washed down with a "caña," a small glass of beer.

> *4 shrimp per person, or more, depending on the size of the shrimp*
> *1 clove garlic*
> *one-inch piece hot red pepper, or 1/4 tsp. crushed red hot pepper*
> *1 tbsp. oil*
> *salt*

1. Remove shrimp shells and wash shrimp. (Save the shells for Shrimp shell soup, page 71).

2. Blot shrimp dry with a paper towel.

3. In an earthenware pan, heat the oil, and add the garlic and hot pepper.

4. When the oil is sizzling hot, add the shrimp, salt to taste, and cook the shrimp for 5 minutes.

5. Turn shrimp over to cook on the other side for another minute, and serve piping hot immediately.

MOORISH KABOBS
(Pinchos Morunos)

Prepare this recipe the day before cooking it, so that the meat can marinate in the sauce for 24 hours.

Use skewers that are about seven inches long. Ones that have points which are narrower than the rest of the skewers are best. If the points are wide, the hole in the meat will get too large when it is pushed up on the skewer, and the meat will slip off when it is cooked.

Thread six pieces of meat on each skewer, and in between each piece of meat place a mushroom cap, a chunk of green pepper, a cherry tomato, and a 2-inch square chunk of bacon.

Another way of preparing kabobs instead of placing the vegetables on the skewers is to sauté the green pepper, cherry tomato, and mushroom cap in a pan with a small amount of oil, and skewer only the meat and the bacon chunk. Then serve the vegetables on the plate with the meat.

To serve the Kabobs as an appetizer, stick the skewers into a grapefruit, and place small plates nearby for each guest. To serve the Kabobs as a main dish, bring the skewered meat to the table on a serving dish, and push the meat off the skewers on to each person's plate. Place the empty skewers back on the serving dish, and remove them.

This recipe yields one skewer of meat per person for an appetizer, and two skewers per person as a main dish.

2 lbs. tender meat, either beef(steak), veal, lamb, or pork: cut it into 48 one-inch cubes.

Marinade Sauce

2 or 3 cloves finely chopped garlic
1 tbsp. finely chopped fresh parsley or 1/4 tsp. dried parsley
2 tbsp. dry white wine
2 tbsp. olive oil
1 sliced onion
1/2 tsp. salt
a pinch of black pepper
1/4 tsp. thyme
1/4 tsp. paprika if pork is used

1. Cut up the meat into one-inch cubes.

2. Mix together the marinade sauce.

3. Stir the meat into the sauce and place in the refrigerator for 24 hours.

4. Remove from sauce, thread the meat onto the skewers, alternating it with the vegetables and bacon, and either grill it over charcoal, broil it in the oven, or fry it in a small amount of oil.

5. Sprinkle with salt and serve.

MARINATED OCTOPUS
(Pulpo)

This recipe may be prepared the day before using. However, it must be prepared at least three hours before serving so that the octopus can marinate.

It serves 6 people.

> *1 small octopus*
> *3 tbsp. vinegar*
> *3 tbsp. olive oil*
> *salt*
> *1/2 bay leaf*
> *2 onions*
> *1 sprig fresh, chopped parsley*

1. Have the fishman remove the stomach and eye of the octopus.

2. Wash octopus very well and clean the suction cups with running water.

3. Place octopus on the table, and beat it with a mallet to soften the meat.

4. Cook it in water to cover, with salt to taste, bay leaf, and one onion until the meat is tender, about a half hour.

5. Remove the octopus from the water and let it cool. Peel the skin from the body and the legs. Cut off all the suction cups and throw them away.

6. Slice the meat of the legs into 1/4 inch thick slices. Slice the body into strips.

7. Place the cut up octopus into a bowl, and add the vinegar, oil, one sliced onion, and parsley. Stir it so that the meat gets coated with the sauce. Let it marinate in the refrigerator for at least three hours. Serve it cold.

To serve the octopus, remove it from the marinade, place it on a dish, and stick toothpicks into several pieces.

BABY EELS
(Angulas)

There are very few places in the world where baby eels can be found on the market, and Spain is one of these places.

Baby eels, called "angulas," are small, thin, and look like little pieces of spaghetti. They have a very delicate flavor which can easily be spoiled by cooking them poorly or with the wrong utensils.

Always cook them in an earthenware pan and use only a wooden spoon to stir them. After they are cooked, serve them immediately. This recipe serves two people.

1 large earthenware flat dish for frying the eels
1 wooden kitchen spoon
1/4 lb. baby eels
1 clove sliced garlic
olive oil, enough to cover the bottom of frying pan in which eels will be cooked
one-inch piece of hot red pepper

1. Heat oil over medium heat.

2. Add garlic and hot pepper.

3. When the garlic is browned, add the eels. Stir and toss them for 5 minutes.

4. Remove from heat, and add salt to taste. Serve immediately.

Soups

Las sopas y los amores,
los primeros son los mejores.

Of soup and love,
the first is the best.

BREAD-BALLS FOR SOUP

This is so fast and easy to prepare, and it makes a delicious addition to the soup.

Use a good bread.

Makes 26 balls.

2 slices bread, crusts removed
1 tbsp. chopped onion
1 egg
2 tbsp. oil

1. Soften the bread in water, then press out the excess liquid.

2. Fry the onion in two tablespoons oil, then blend in the bread. (It becomes a dough).

3. Remove the pan from the heat and blend in the beaten egg. Add salt to taste. Return the pan to low heat and work in the egg for a few minutes until the dough becomes thick. Put it on a plate and let it get cold.

4. When it's cold, make little balls the size of a chick pea and fry in very hot oil.

Place it in individual bowls at serving time, and pour the soup over it. Serve immediately, because if the balls stay in the soup long, they soften.

CUSTARD GARNISH FOR CLEAR SOUP

Small squares of custard decorate the soup.

> *1 cup boullion or milk*
> *2 egg yolks*
> *salt*

1. Beat the egg yolks with the cold boullion or milk, add a pinch salt, and pour in into a shallow pan. Put the pan into another pan of water and bake it in a 350 degree oven for 10 or 15 minutes until it gets firm.

When the custard is cold, remove it from the pan and cut it into small squares.

At serving time put several squares into each bowl and pour the consommé over them.

BEEF BOULLION

> *1/2 lb. beef for soup*
> *several marrow bones or plain bones*
> *1 large onion*
> *1 carrot*
> *1 celery stalk*
> *fresh or dried parsley*
> *1 leek (optional)*

1. Put the bones and the meat in the water. When it comes to a boil, remove the foam. Add the other ingredients, salt and pepper to taste, cover the pot and simmer for about three hours.

2. After this time, strain the liquid and let it get cold. When the fat is solid, remove it from the soup and discard.

The meat may be used in other recipes, for example, as a filling for croquettes.

CREAMED VEGETABLE SOUP
(Crema de legumbres)

This recipe was given to me by the soup cook of a famous Madrid restaurant, the Corral de la Morería, where you can see excellent Flamenco dancing while dining on superb food.

I was in the restaurant kitchen when he cooked this. Afterwards, when I sipped a bowl of it I knew that this was a recipe to include.

The egg yolk, sweet cream, and cornstarch given as optional in the list of ingredients make the soup richer, but they may be omitted. If you are going to add them to the soup, do so after the soup is done cooking, after step 5, just before serving. You may also cut the amount of butter from the 4 tablespoons listed to one tablespoon. (The instructions are given at the end of the recipe).

This recipe serves 6. It may be prepared in advance.

> *2 sliced potatoes*
> *1 leek or onion, finely chopped*
> *1/2 head cauliflower, broken into small pieces*
> *1 sliced carrot*
> *1/4 cup flour*
> *2 quarts water*
> *4 tbsp. butter (or 1 tbsp. butter)*
> *optional: 1 egg yolk, 2 tbsp. sweet cream*
> *cornstarch to thicken soup*

1. Melt the butter in the same pot in which the soup will be cooked. Add the leek, carrot, cauliflower, and potato. Mix it all in with the butter.

2. Add the flour and mix it in with the vegetables.

3. Stir in the water and cook the soup covered until all the vegetables are very well done. Stir the soup from time to time so that the flour doesn't stick to the bottom of the pot. Cook over low heat.

4. When the vegetables are very tender, put the entire soup through a sieve or blender.

5. Return the soup to the pot and place it over very low heat until it is very hot again. (Soup should be served very hot).

If the soup isn't thick enough, you may thicken it by mixing 1 tbsp. cornstarch with a 1/2 cup water and adding it to the soup. Continue heating and stirring it for a few minutes.

For a richer soup, add the following at serving time:

1. Beat one egg yolk with 2 tbsp. sweet cream.

2. Remove the soup from the heat, stir the mixture into the hot soup, and serve immediately. Do not let this cream-egg mixture cook with the soup.

If you are going to use the above mixture, you may cut the 4 tbsp. butter used in step 1, to 1 tbsp. butter.

FIFTEEN-MINUTE SOUP
(Sopa al quarto de hora)

It's supposed to take fifteen minutes to make this soup, that's how it got it's name. This is a hearty soup which may be used as a main dish when served with Spanish or French bread, salad, and dessert. This recipe serves six people.

1 tbsp. olive oil
1 tbsp. chopped onion
1 cup peas
1 large canned or fresh tomato, chopped, (peel and discard seeds before chopping)
1 slice ham, cut into small pieces
1 lb. small shrimp, shells removed
4 fish filets cut into small pieces, (any white meat fish may be used)
1/2 lb. small clams, well cleaned (about 30 clams)
2 tbsp. uncooked rice, rinsed and drained
1 tbsp. chopped parsley or 1/4 tsp. dried parsley

salt to taste
a pinch pepper
1/2 tsp. paprika
1 hard boiled egg, chopped
6 slices Spanish bread or French bread

1. Prepare the above ingredients and set them on a plate. Be sure to wash the clams well. Throw away opened clams. (See "Tips" page 154).

2. Steam the clams in 1 1/4 cups water with 1/2 bay leaf, one sprig fresh parsley, and a pinch of salt, for 10 minutes, or until the shells open. (Throw away the clams that did not open).

3. Remove clams from shells, dip each clam into the clam broth and rinse all the sand off the clam. Set clams on a dish and save the clam broth for later use.

4. In a soup pot, heat 1 tbsp. oil and sauté the chopped onion and the ham pieces. Keep pot covered.

5. Add chopped tomato and sauté another 5 minutes.

6. Add paprika and stir quickly. Remove from heat.

7. Immediately add 6 cups water and return to heat.

8. Add the fish, shrimp, peas, rice, and parsley. Add 1 tsp. salt and a pinch of pepper. Stir with a fork and cook until rice is done, about 15 minutes.

9. While soup is cooking, fry or toast in the oven 6 slices Spanish or French bread. Place the bread into the soup tureen or into individual soup bowls.

10. When the soup is done, add the clams, the carefully drained clam broth (make sure no sand gets in), and the chopped egg to the tureen or individual bowls. Pour the hot soup over the bread and serve immediately.

CLAM SOUP

Serves 6.

> 1 lb. clams
> 1/2 cup tomatoes
> 2 tbsp. chopped onions
> 2 cubes beef boullion
> 2 tsp. paprika
> 1/2 clove mashed garlic
> 1 sprig fresh parsley or 1/4 tsp. dried parsley
> 2 tbsp. oil
> 3 thin slices toasted Spanish or French bread

1. Wash the clams well and put them into two cups slightly salted boiling water. When the shells open, remove the pot from the heat and take the clams out. Remove the clams from their shells when cool, rinse them in the clam broth to clean them, then carefully strain the broth. Put the clams and the strained broth back in the cleaned pot and set aside.

2. Heat oil in a pan and fry the onion until tender. Toss the tomatoes with the paprika, then add a little water, (if you're using canned tomatoes use a little of the tomato juice), and continue simmering for about 30 minutes.

3. After this time, put the sauce into a blender or through a strainer and return it to the pot with the clams and broth. Blend in the mashed garlic and the parsley.

4. Soften the boullion cubes and stir them in.

5. Add six cups water, salt to taste, and bring to a boil. Reduce heat and simmer for five minutes.

6. Put the toasted bread in the soup tureen, pour the soup on top, and serve hot.

FISH SOUP
(Sopa de pescado)

A chef who cooked for a famous restaurant in Madrid gave me this recipe. There it's served as the soup course before the main meal; however, it's really hearty enough to use by itself as the main dish when served with Spanish or French bread, salad, and then dessert.

This recipe is for four people.

The first six steps may be prepared the day before.

Although the recipe calls for a certain amount per person, the quantity may be increased if desired.

8 shrimp, (2 per person).
8 clams, (2 per person)
8 mussels (2 per person)
2 white-meat fish filets (a half piece filet per person)
1 tomato, peeled and chopped
1 leek or onion
1 carrot
2 cloves garlic
1 cup oil
1/4 cup cognac
1 tbsp. flour
1 tsp. saffron (optional)
a small dash Pernod
1/2 tsp. fresh chopped parsley
1 cup cooked rice
1 chopped hard-boiled egg
2 tbsp. cooked peas

1. Wash clams and mussels well. Remove shrimp shells and clean shrimp.

2. Slice carrot and leek or onion, and chop garlic. Fry in oil.

3. Stir in shrimp and the clams with their shells. Stir in the mussels with their shells.

4. Add cognac. Continue cooking and stirring over high heat.

5. Stir in tomato. Add flour, a half teaspoon fresh chopped parsley, and four cups water. Stir to combine all the ingredients. Add salt to taste.

6. Add the saffron. Remove any foam which may have risen to the top.

7. At serving time, place rice, peas, and the chopped egg into the soup tureen, pour the soup over them and add the dash of Pernod.

GAZPACHO
(Cold Spanish soup)

Gazpacho is a cold soup served in Spain during warm weather. It's not only healthy, but also refreshing. The recipe presented here is the way Gazpacho is prepared in Madrid, and served there in the best restaurants and private homes.

Many people use a blender to purée the ingredients, which makes the preparation time very short. If you don't have a blender, use a sieve. This recipe serves about 6 people. It may be prepared the day before using. As a matter of fact, it's better if it's prepared in advance, and stored in the refrigerator for several hours. It should be served very cold.

> 6 soft, peeled medium-size tomatoes, fresh or canned (about 2 lbs. tomatoes)
> 2 cloves garlic
> 1 green pepper (NOT a hot pepper)
> 1 cucumber
> stale bread, either Spanish, French, or Italian, about 5 inches long. (After the bread has been soaked and the water squeezed out of it, you should have about 1 and 1/4 cupsful of soaked bread.)
> 1/4 cup plus 1 tbsp. white vinegar
> 1/2 cup olive oil
> 1 1/4 tsp. salt
> 1/4 tsp. paprika
> 1 tsp. ground cumin seed (preferably freshly ground)
> 5 cups ice cold water

BLENDER METHOD

Cut up all the vegetables, squeeze the water out of the bread, and put everything into the blender, including the spices and oil.

Divide the ingredients so that you can put as much as will fit into the blender at one time. Set blender button at purée.

REGULAR METHOD

1. Soak the bread in cold water for about 5 minutes or until it gets soft.

2. Mash garlic and place it into a large bowl.

3.Chop the tomatoes and add them to the bowl.

4. Add the chopped green pepper and the chopped cucumber to the bowl. (Remove any large seeds from the cucumber).

5. Squeeze the water out of the bread, mash any large pieces, and stir it into the bowl with the vegetables, mixing it in well.

6. Stir in the oil, vinegar, paprika, salt, and cumin.

7. Add one cup water and put the whole mixture through a sieve.

8. Stir in the rest of the water and blend it in well.

Serve chopped cucumber, chopped tomato, and chopped green pepper at the table for people to add to their soup.

CHICKEN SOUP
(Sopa de ave)

This dish needs no introduction because it plays the same role in any country: to strengthen the sick and please the appetite of the healthy.

Use enough chicken to make a rich soup. Cut off as much fat from the chicken as possible before cooking it.

This recipe may be prepared the day before. It serves 4 people.

> *At least 3 pieces of chicken plus any giblets. Any parts of the chicken are good to use except the liver.*
> *1 large whole carrot*
> *3 whole small onions*
> *1 stick celery*
> *1 small parsnip*
> *2 sprigs parsley*
> *1 tbsp. uncooked rice, rinsed and drained*
> *1 3/4 tsp. salt*
> *white pepper*
> *1 tsp. lemon juice*
> *6 cups cold water*

1. Place chicken and water in a soup pot and bring to a simmer. Skim off the foam that may rise to the top. Add salt and pepper to taste.

2. Place the vegetables and rice into the soup (not the lemon juice), and cook the soup covered on low heat until the chicken is tender, at least one hour. Remove pot from heat, skim the fat from the top of the soup, and discard.

3. Remove the vegetables and chicken from the pot. Slice the carrot, and if you like, cut up some of the chicken and return it to the soup with the carrot. Discard the other vegetables.

4. Before serving, heat soup again, stir in lemon juice, and serve very hot. Warm the soup bowls before putting the soup in them.

DRIED SALT-COD SOUP

Serves 4.

> *1/2 lb. dried salt cod*
> *6 small sliced leeks, or 3 medium-size onions, chopped*
> *1 lb. potatoes*
> *2 garlic cloves*
> *paprika*
> *4 tbsp. oil*

Soak the salt-cod in cold water for 24 to 26 hours. Change the water several times. Then drain it, rinse it well, and use.

1. Place the cod into a pot with two cups cold water. When the water comes to a boil, remove it from the heat, and take the cod out of the water. Save the water to use later.

2. Remove the bones, and mash up the cod. Save for use later.

3. Heat the oil in a large pan, slice the garlic, and fry. Remove the garlic, and fry the onions and leeks.

4. Peel and cut the potatoes into small pieces. Add to the pan with the onions.

5. Add the cod. Lower the heat, stir. Cook it for a few minutes.

6. Add the liquid in which the cod was cooked, plus two more cups water.

7. Taste for salt, add paprika, and simmer for about one hour.

SHRIMP SOUP WITH MAYONNAISE

Serves 6.

> 1/2 lb. shrimp
> 1 stalk celery
> 1 onion
> 1 carrot
> 1 cup mayonnaise
> 3 slices Spanish or French bread

1. Separate the shells from the shrimp and save. (They're going to be cooked later on!).

2. Clean the shrimp and simmer them on low heat in two cups water until they turn pink, no longer. Remove them, cut into small pieces and save.

3. Rinse the shrimp shells in a colander, drain and add to the pot with 5 cups more water, the celery, onion, and carrot. Bring to a boil, then simmer for 20 minutes.

4. After this time, strain the soup and discard the vegetables and shells. Return the soup to the pot and heat slowly.

5. At serving time, put the mayonnaise in a bowl, slowly blend in some cooled soup, then return it to the pot.

6. Put the slices of bread in a soup tureen, pour the hot soup on top, and add the shrimp. Serve hot.

SHRIMP-SHELL SOUP

This is an unbelievable soup. It is actually made from something we naturally discard: shrimp shells. There's a lot of flavor and nutrition in the shell of the shrimp, and the Spanish cook can make a most delicious soup out of it.

1 lb. shrimp SHELLS, the shrimp removed
1 small onion cut into quarters
1 stick celery and the celery top
1 tomato finely chopped
1 potato
1 small turnip cut into quarters
1 sprig parsley or 1 tsp. dried parsley
  salt and pepper
1/4 tsp. paprika
  1 egg
2 tbsp. sweet cream (optional)

1. In a soup pot, saute onion and celery in butter until they are transparent.

2. Stir in paprika and the listed vegetables. Add 1/2 cup water.

3. Wash shrimp shells.

4. Add shrimp shells and 3 1/2 cups water to vegetables and stir. Turn heat up. When soup begins to boil, lower heat and remove foam from top of soup, and discard it. Season soup with salt and pepper, and cook for 15 minutes, covered.

5. Remove from heat and strain soup. Discard vegetables and shells.

6. Beat whole egg. Add 5 tbsp. soup to egg. Return this mixture to soup, stir, and serve.

Alternate to step 6:

At serving time, re-heat soup BEFORE adding the following:

Beat 1 egg YOLK with 2 tbsp. sweet cream and add to soup. DO NOT LET THIS COOK. Serve immediately.

ONION SOUP
(Sopa de cebolla)

This recipe serves 6 people. Up to and including step 4 may be made the day before.

> 6 cups beef stock, either homemade or made with boullion cubes or beef extract. It's very important to have a good soup stock. If you use boullion cubes, add a little beef extract to it.
>
> 1 tsp. olive oil
> 6 medium onions, finely chopped
> salt
> 1 1/2 tsp. flour
> 12 slices Spanish, French, or Italian bread, thinly sliced
> grated cheese
> butter

1. Prepare soup stock.

2. Heat oil in a pot large enough to hold soup later on. Add onions and saute until they are transparent. Add salt to taste and remove

pot from heat. Stir in flour and then stir in boullion very SLOWLY so that the flour doesn't lump.

3. Bring to a boil again, remove foam if any, and simmer slowly for 15 minutes. Taste the soup and add salt if necessary.

4. Brown the sliced bread in the oven until it's crisp. Watch it so that it does not burn. Remove it when it's done and butter it lightly.

5. Place the bread into a large soup casserole that is oven-proof, or into small individual oven-proof bowls. Pour the simmering soup onto the bread, and sprinkle liberally with cheese. It should have quite a bit of cheese on it.

6. Place the casserole (or the individual bowls set on a tray) into the oven under the broiler and heat until the cheese browns a little. (Watch it that it doesn't burn − cheese burns easily.) Serve immediately.

GARLIC SOUP
(Sopa de ajo)

Garlic may be a strange ingredient to make into a soup, but the amazing thing about this dish is that it doesn't have a very strong garlic flavor. Still, you need to like garlic to like this recipe.

"Sopa de ajo" probably originated as a poor man's food; however, its delicious flavor has made it one of the choice soups in Spain, for rich or poor folk.

This is a cold weather soup, and it's usually served in an earthenware bowl, like onion soup.

This recipe serves 6 people.

8 cups water or boullion
1/2 cup olive oil
3 medium-size cloves garlic, sliced
12 thin slices Spanish, French, or Italian bread. Use bread that is one day old. Leave the crust on.

1 tsp. paprika
salt
1 egg, beaten

1. Boil the water or boullion and keep it hot and covered for later use.

2. Heat oil in pot large enough to hold soup later on.

3. Add the sliced garlic and brown.

4. Add the sliced bread and fry until they're crisp on both sides. Remove bread from pot and set aside. Leave garlic in pot.

5. Remove pot from heat, add paprika to pot and IMMEDIATE-LY add the hot water all at once so that the paprika does not burn. (Paprika burns easily.) Return pot to heat and add salt to taste.

6. Beat egg in large bowl and slowly stir in 5 ladles of soup to egg.

7. Add egg mixture and fried bread to the pot, and don't stir.

Serve very hot.

CONSOMME WITH SHERRY
(Consomé al jerez)

Stir in 1/4 teaspoon DRY white sherry or other dry white wine to each cup of consomme. Simmer for a few minutes and serve very hot.

You may substitute 1/4 teaspoon lemon juice for the wine. Add the lemon juice AFTER you have heated the consomme.

COLD JELLIED CONSOMME
(Consomé frío)

A very famous restaurant in Madrid serves this consomme in the summertime. It's very light and refreshing. The consistency is that of a jello.

Prepare this recipe the day before or at least 12 hours before serving. It serves 2 people.

1 envelope unflavored gelatin
2 cubes beef boullion
beef extract (optional)
2 tbsp. DRY white sherry, or other DRY white wine. (You may substitute 2 tbsp. lemon juice for the wine.)

1. Bring one and three-quarter cups cold water to a boil. Add boullion cubes and dissolve them completely. Then add the wine or lemon juice, remove from heat and set aside.

2. Sprinkle gelatin on 1/4 cup cold water to soften it. Add it to the pot of boullion, and simmer it on low heat stirring constantly until the gelatin is dissolved, about 5 minutes.

3. Pour it into a bowl and let it set (gel). It'll take about 5 or 6 hours.

4. When it is completely set, like jello, stir it with a fork until consomme is all jumbled up. Return it to the refrigerator until serving time.

BEAN AND VEGETABLE SOUP, MAJORCAN STYLE

I ate this on the island of Majorca in a "bodega." The place was a cool, white-washed wine cellar that had big wooden barrels of wine caskets stored against its walls. In the center of the room people were eating at round tables which were covered with clean red-checked tablecloths.

The man who owned the place waited on us, and he recommended this soup that his wife had just made. It was so good. I asked him for the recipe. Both he and his wife told me how to prepare it.

It may be prepared the day before serving. See "How to prepare dried beans," page 136.

Serves 6.

> *1 3/4 cups dried white northern beans*
> *ham bone or ham hock (optional)*
> *2 peeled and chopped tomatoes, fresh or canned*
> *2 finely chopped onions*
> *1 tsp. olive oil*
> *1/2 cup of either one of the following: swiss chard, turnip greens,*
> *spinach, or cabbage. Cook and chop before measuring.*

1. In the same pot in which you are going to cook the beans, heat the oil and saute the onions until they are transparent.

2. Add more oil if necessary, and saute the chard. Do NOT cook the chard (or any other green vegetable you may substitute) thoroughly; it should be almost raw. Stir in the tomatoes and simmer 5 minutes. Remove this mixture from the pot and set aside for use in step 4.

3. In the same pot, place soaked beans, ham bone, and enough cold water to cover them plus 4 extra cups water. Add salt to taste and cook for two and one-half hours. Add more water if it is necessary.

4. When the beans are almost tender, add all the vegetable mixture from step 2 and cook 10 minutes more, until the green vegetable is done.

Be careful not to overcook beans or they will become too soft.

SPINACH SOUP WITH CHICK PEAS

Serves four.

> *1 medium-size can chick peas*
> *1 pkg. frozen leaf spinach*
> *2 egg yolks*
> *1 slice ham (optional)*
> *1 tbsp. flour*
> *2 tbsp. butter or oil*

1. Cook the spinach in four cups slightly salted water.

2. When the spinach is done, melt the butter in a pan large enough to hold the soup later on, and blend in the flour. Add about one cup spinach liquid, stirring constantly until it becomes a smooth sauce. Add salt to taste, and set aside. ·

3. Remove the cooked spinach from the pot, drain, cut it up, and mix it into the sauce.

4. Add the water in which the spinach had been cooked. Taste and season.

5. Stir in the chick peas, and simmer for 10 minutes.

6. At serving time, heat the soup, sauté the ham, and add it.

7. Remove the soup from the heat, put the egg yolks in a bowl and stir in two tablespoons water. Add it to the soup. (Do not heat after adding egg yolks.)

SPINACH AND GREEN PEA SOUP

This dark green soup looks beautiful served in white bowls.

1 pkg. frozen spinach
2 cups green peas
1 onion, chopped
several pieces of ham
parsley
celery

1. Put one cup peas, spinach, onion, parsley, celery into enough water to make a soup. Add salt to taste, and cook for about a half hour, or until the vegetables are done.

2. In another pan, heat a small amount of butter and sauté the ham. Add the one cup peas to a small amount of water, and simmer until the peas are done. Remove from heat and save.

3. When the soup is done, put it in the blender or through a sieve. Return it to the pot and heat. Add the peas and ham.

4. At serving time, beat one egg yolk with 2 tablespoons water and add it to the soup. (Do not heat soup after the yolk has been added.)

If desired, sweet cream may be used instead of the egg yolk.

CARROT PUREE SOUP

Serves 6.

> *4 medium-size potatoes*
> *8 medium-size carrots*
> *parsley*
> *8 cups chicken or beef boullion*
> *butter*

1. Slice the carrots and sauté them in butter in the same pot in which you are going to make the soup. Add half the boullion and salt to taste.

2. Peel and cut three potatoes into small pieces. (Save one for the garnish later on.) Put them into the soup and simmer for about one hour, or until all the vegetables are very soft.

3. Cool and put the soup in the blender or through a sieve. Return it to the pot, add the rest of the boullion, and simmer it again.

4. Heat oil for frying, peel and cut the leftover raw potato into slices, and then cut the slices into small pieces and fry.

5. At serving time, put the fried potato into the soup bowls, and pour the puree of soup over them.

BLENDED TOMATO, POTATO, AND ONION SOUP

Serves four.

> *1 large onion, chopped*
> *4 tomatoes, chopped (may be canned)*
> *5 medium-size potatoes cut into pieces*

1 stalk celery
parsley
2 beef or chicken boullion cubes

1. Sauté the onion in butter or oil in the same pan in which you're going to make the soup. Add the tomatoes, then the potatoes.

2. Dissolve the boullion cubes in boiling water, and add them to the vegetables. Add salt, parsley, the celery stalk, and enough water to make the soup. (About 5 cups.) Cook for a half hour, until the potatoes are very soft.

3. When the soup is done, taste for salt. Put it in the blender or through a strainer.

4. At serving time, heat the soup, beat one or two egg yolks with two tablespoons water, and stir into the soup. (Do not let the eggs cook with the soup.) Serve immediately.

Instead of stirring water into the egg yolks, stir in two tablespoons cream or milk, if desired.

POTATO SOUP PUREE
(Sopa de patatas)

2 large potatoes
2 carrots
1 onion
1 leek
a few pieces of cauliflower
1 tbsp. flour
salt and pepper

1. Peel and slice the potatoes, carrots, onion, and leek. Fry them in oil.

2. When they are fried, stir in the flour. Cover with about four cups water, add salt and pepper to taste, and cook until the vegetables are very tender.

3. After this time, remove them from the soup and purée them. Return them to the pot, stirring them in. Serve hot.

TWO-BEAN SOUP
(Potaje blanco)

Serves six.

1/2 lb. white beans
1 cup chick peas, dried or canned
2 or 3 medium-size potatoes
1 cup rice
1 onion
a piece of salt pork or 2 tsp. butter or oil
4 cloves garlic
1/2 bay leaf
salt and pepper

Soak the chick peas the night before preparing this recipe if you are using dried chick peas.

1. Bring water to a boil in a deep pot. Add the onion, garlic, bay leaf, salt pork, and the soaked chick peas. (If you are using canned chick peas, add them about ten minutes after you add the potatoes in step 5.)

2. In another pot, put the white beans into cold water, and when the water comes to a boil, pour out the hot water and add more cold water. Bring it to a boil again. Lower the heat and continue cooking.

3. When both beans have been cooking for about 30 minutes, add the white beans and the water to the chick peas. See that there is enough water for soup.

4. Peel the potatoes, cut them into small pieces, and add them to the beans. Add salt and pepper to taste.

5. When the potatoes are almost done, add the washed rice, and cook for another 15 to 20 minutes. Remove the pot from the heat, and let it set for awhile before serving.

BEAN SOUP FROM GALLEGO
(Caldo Gallego)

This soup is best prepared the previous day. When the soup is cold, take off the fat before reheating.

> *1 cup white navy beans*
> *2 large potatoes, peeled and cut into quarters*
> *1 bunch fresh turnip greens or 1 pkg. frozen turnip greens (defrost)*
> *1/2 lb. lamb ribs or lamb necks (remove as much fat as possible)*

1. Place beans in a deep pot with enough cold water to make a soup, and slowly bring to a boil. Lower heat and continue cooking.

2. When they are almost done, add the potatoes, turnip greens, lamb, and salt to taste. Cook until the meat is done. Serve hot.

TAPIOCA SOUP

Serves six.

> *6 cups chicken boullion*
> *1/8 cup tapioca*
> *2 egg yolks*

1. Bring the boullion to a boil. Slowly sprinkle in the tapioca, stirring constantly. Cook for 10 minutes until it gets transparent.

2. At serving time, heat the soup, beat the egg yolks, stir in a little soup and add the yolks to the soup. (Do not heat soup after the egg yolks are added.) Serve with croutons.

Eggs

"What kind of meals do those Americans serve?" the man who delivered eggs to our building twice a week asked María, our maid. "I don't urderstand how you can buy so few eggs. Don't your people eat tortillas and flan every day?"

We were his worst customers, and I thought I was buying a lot of eggs! The Spanish house-wife used many more than I did by adding eggs to soups, vegetables, and sauces to enrich them; by using hard-boiled eggs to decorate plates of food; and by serving Spanish Torti-llas and Flan almost every day.

HOW TO HARD-BOIL EGGS

Use eggs that are at room temperature or set them in warm water for 5 minutes.

Bring cooking water to a boil. Reduce to simmer, and set the eggs in the water with a spoon.

Simmer for 15 minutes. Remove them from the hot water and put them immediately into cold water. The cold water prevents a dark ring from forming around the yolks.

CODDLED EGGS

> *boiling water*
> *1/4 tsp. salt*
> *4 eggs*

1. Put enough water in a frying pan so that it will cover the eggs. Bring it to a boil. Lower the heat to simmer. Add salt.

2. Break one egg into a cup, and from the edge of the pan, quickly slide it into the simmering water. Continue doing this with all the eggs, one at a time.

3. When the eggs are done, (5 minutes for Eggs Villaroy), remove them, one at a time, with a slotted spoon.

PLAIN OMELETTE

1. Heat a heavy skillet or 8-inch omelette pan and put in one tablespoon butter.

2. Beat the eggs with a fork, add salt and pepper. (Some people also add one tablespoon cold milk or water to two eggs.)

3. Pour the eggs into the pan and cook over low heat. As the eggs cook, lift the edges toward the center with a spatula, and tip the pan so that the uncooked egg flows underneath the cooked portion.

When the bottom of the omelette is lightly browned, loosen the edges of the omelette with a spatula, and fold it in half.

Remove it from the pan with a spatula, and serve it on a warm plate.

SPANISH POTATO OMELETTE
(Tortilla española)

A word needs to be said about tortillas, since there are 2 kinds, one from Mexico and the other from Spain. The Spanish and Mexican tortillas are completely different. The ingredients are not similar, they're prepared differently, and they do not look or taste alike.

The Spanish tortilla is very much like an omelette, and it is a versatile dish because it can serve many purposes. It can be the main hot dish of a meal, the first course before the main dish, or it can be cut up into small triangles and served cold as an appetizer.

Use an 8-inch cast-iron or heavy aluminum fry pan. This recipe serves two people as a main dish. It may also be made in advance and kept warm in the oven.

> *2 large potatoes peeled and sliced as thick as a nickel (2 cups thawed frozen packaged potatoes, shredded or sliced, may be used instead.)*

      1 medium onion, thinly sliced or chopped
      oil for deep frying
      salt
      2 eggs (use 3 eggs if 2 cups frozen packaged potatoes are used)

1. Slice onion, peel and cut potatoes.

2. Heat oil for deep frying (about 2 inches deep) and brown the potatoes.

3. Add onions to the potatoes, and fry onions until they are transparent.

4. Remove potatoes and onions from the pan with a slotted spoon so that the oil drips off, and place them in a bowl. (Leave the oil in the pan.)

5. Beat the eggs lightly in a large bowl. Add salt to taste.

6. Add potatoes and onions to beaten eggs.

7. Pour off some of the oil that is left in the fry pan, but leave enough so that the bottom of the pan is covered generously.

8. Heat the oil then pour the eggs into the pan. Give the pan a shake so that the egg doesn't stick. If that doesn't work, use a spatula to loosen the tortilla from the bottom of the pan.

9. When the bottom of the omelette is firm and the sides come away from the pan but the top is still loose, slide omelette, firm side down onto a plate. Now you're going to flip the omelette over onto the fry pan and cook the other side, by doing this: place the empty fry pan upside down onto the omelette and flip the plate, omelette, and pan over at the same time, thereby landing the omelette onto the pan.

10. Fry for a minute, until the egg sets. Do not fry too long. Remove the tortilla to a plate, and serve hot as a main dish or let it cool and cut it into triangles to serve as an appetizer.

CHEESE OMELETTE SOUFLEE MADE IN A FRYING PAN

Easy to prepare and great tasting, this is an unusual way to souflé.

Cooked vegetables may be added to make this a heartier dish. (Nice for lunches.)

The following are variations of this recipe:

1. Omit the tomato sauce, bechamel sauce, and cheese; prepare it plain.

2. Omit the tomato sauce; add cooked, drained and puréed vegetable to the bechamel sauce and cheese.

3. For dessert, omit tomato sauce, bechamel sauce, and cheese; add cooked, drained, sweetened fruit. When done, sprinkle with powdered sugar. Then heat a skewer until it's red hot and place it on the sugar to sear it.

THE SOUFLE:

> *eggs*
> *2 tbsp. tomato sauce for each egg*
> *2 tbsp. bechamel sauce for each egg*
> *1 tbsp. grated cheese for each egg*

1. Prepare a half cup bechamel sauce (if more is needed, refer to Bechamel Sauce recipe, page 253) by heating two tablespoons oil in a pan. Stir in two tablespoons flour. Blend in a half cup milk, stirring continuously until in thickens. Remove from heal and set aside.

2. Separate the egg yolks from the whites, and beat the yolks.

3. When the bechamel sauce has cooled, blend it and the tomato sauce into the egg yolks.

4. Beat the egg whites until they form stiff peaks, and fold into egg yolk mixture with as few strokes as possible.

5. Divide the mixture into individual portions. Heat butter in a small frying pan and fry each portion separately on medium heat. Fry on one side until bottom is brown, then PLACE UNDER BROILER until top puffs up and browns. Serve immediately.

HAM OMELETTE
(Tortilla con jamón)

small pieces of ham
2 eggs per person

1. Sauté ham in a small amount of butter or oil.

2. Beat the eggs in a large bowl. Add salt to taste.

3. Mix in the ham.

4. Add more butter or oil and pour in the eggs.

5. As the omelette cooks, lift the edges toward the center of the pan with the spatula and tilt the pan so that the uncooked egg flows underneath the cooked portion.

6. When the bottom is lightly browned, loosen the edges of the omelette with the spatula and either fold in half or flip the omelette over onto the other side. Let it cook for another minute and serve. The inside should be soft.

If desired, cover with a bechamel sauce, page 253, or tomato sauce, page 248, or Hollandaise sauce, page 255.

SHRIMP OMELETTE
(Tortilla con gambas)

Prepare it the same way as Ham Omelette, but use cut-up pieces of shrimp instead of ham.

SPRING OMELETTE

Serves two.

> *several pieces of ham*
> *1 sliced carrot*
> *1 quartered potato*
> *1 tbsp. cooked peas*
> *2 or 3 canned asparagus tips*
> *2 eggs*

1. Fry the ham in butter and remove it from the pan. Add the carrots and potatoes and fry for a few minutes. Add water or boullion and simmer until the vegetables are done. Remove them from the pan and drain.

2. Place them in a bowl with the peas, asparagus, and ham.

3. Beat the eggs, add salt, and pour them into the vegetables.

4. Heat oil or butter in a pan, and pour the eggs in. Cook for a few minutes, or until the bottom is brown and the sides come away from the pan, but the top is still loose. Slide the omelette, firm side down onto a plate. Now you're going to flip the omelette over onto the fry pan and cook the other side, by doing this: place the empty pan upside down onto the omelette and flip the plate, omelette, and pan over at the same time, thereby landing the omelette onto the pan.

5. Fry for a minute, until the egg sets. Do not fry too long.

Remove the omelette to a plate and serve.

HAM AND POTATO OMELETTE

This omelette is prepared like the Spanish Potato Omelette, page 85.

> *1 slice ham per person*
> *2 eggs per person*

1. Fry the ham which has been cut into small pieces, then remove it from the pan and brown the potatoes. (Add more oil if necessary.)

2. Beat the eggs, add the ham, potatoes, and salt to taste.

3. Add more butter or oil to the pan and pour the eggs into it. Give the pan a shake so that the eggs don't stick. If that doesn't work, use a spatula to loosen the omelette from the bottom of the pan.

4. When the bottom of the omelette is firm and the sides come away from the pan but the top is still loose, slide the omelette over onto the fry pan and cook the other side, by doing this: place the empty fry pan upside down onto the omelette and flip the plate, omelette, and pan over at the same time, thereby landing the omelette onto the pan.

5. Fry for a minute, until the egg sets. Do not fry too long.

Remove the omelette to a plate and serve hot.

MUSHROOM OMELETTE

Sauté the sliced mushrooms in oil or butter until they are tender. Remove them from the pan and drain. (Save the liquid for a soup recipe.)

Prepare an omelette the same way that Omelette *with cooked beans* is made, except use mushrooms instead of beans.

OMELETTE WITH COOKED BEANS

> *2 tbsp. soft cooked beans per person*
> *2 eggs per person*

Beat the eggs, add salt to taste, and pour into a well-greased pan. When the bottom of the omelette is brown and the edges come away from the sides but the top is still loose, add the beans and fold one half of the omelette over onto the other. Heat for another minute but don't let it get dry. (The inside should be moist when served.)

GRUYERE CHEESE OMELETTE

Beat the eggs, add one cup whipped cream, grated gruyere cheese, salt and pepper. Cook it like the recipe for Plain Omelette.

ASPARAGUS OMELETTE

several asparagus spears per person
2 eggs per person

Prepare this omelette the same way that Omelette *with cooked beans* is made, except use asparagus instead of beans.

SPINACH OMELETTE

1/2 cup cooked chopped spinach per person
2 eggs per person

1. Cook the spinach in a small amount of slightly salted water. Drain well and press out the excess liquid. Blend in a pat of butter.

2. Beat the eggs, add it to the spinach, and fry it in butter as you would an omelette.

BAKED EGGS ON SPINACH, STYLE 1

1 egg per person
1/2 cup chopped spinach per person
bechamel sauce page 253
grated cheese

1. Place eggs in a saucepan of cold water to cover. Bring water to a quick boil. Remove from heat. Cover and let stand about four minutes.

2. After this time, put the eggs into cold water. Crack the shells and carefully peel them off, a little at a time.

3. Prepare the bechamel sauce.

4. Cook the spinach in a small amount of slightly salted water. Drain it very well by pressing out the liquid. Mix it in with the bechamel sauce.

5. Butter a baking dish or custard cups. Place the spinach on the bottom of the dish. Put the eggs on top of the spinach. Sprinkle the eggs with grated cheese and bake in a 450 degree oven until the cheese melts, about five minutes.

BAKED EGGS ON SPINACH, STYLE 2

1 pkg. frozen chopped spinach
4 eggs
2 slices ham cut into triangles
  toasted bread cut into triangles
  bechamel sauce, page 253

1. Cook the spinach in a small amount of slightly salted water. Drain it very well by pressing out the excess liquid. Blend in a pat butter.

2. Butter individual baking dishes, place the spinach in, then top with a raw egg. Cover with bechamel.

3. Bake in a 450 degree oven for 5 minutes, or until the whites of the eggs are firm.

4. At serving time, place a few pieces of fried ham on each egg and a triangle of toast on the rim of the dish.

PUFFED BAKED EGGS

Exclamations of surprise and delight will greet you when you serve this light and fluffy egg dish. It's so easy to prepare that it makes up in five minutes. An added bonus is that it looks beautiful and is delicious.

It should be eaten as soon as it is done because it "falls" when it's out of the oven for a little while.

1 egg per person
1/2 tsp. grated cheese per egg
a pinch sugar per egg

1. Heat oven to 400 degrees. Separate the egg yolks from the whites.

2. Beat the egg yolks, add the grated cheese, salt and pepper.

3. Beat the egg whites in a separate bowl until they foam. Sprinkle in sugar and continue beating until they form stiff peaks. Fold into egg yolks with as few strokes as possible so that the whites don't lose their fluffiness.

4. Butter individual custard cups and pour in eggs. Bake for five minutes, until the top browns. (When a toothpick inserted near center comes out clean.)

CHICKEN OR HAM AND EGG CUSTARD

Serves 2.

chopped cooked chicken or ham
1 egg
1 cup milk
1 cup bread stuffing cubes

1. Soak bread cubes in a half cup milk.

2. Beat the eggs, add a pinch salt, and combine it with the other half cup milk, the chicken or ham, and the bread cubes.

3. Pour into a buttered, round ceramic or glass baking dish.

4. Place it into a pan of water and put into a 350 degree oven. Bake for about 40 or 50 minutes, or until a knife inserted near center comes out clean.

BAKED EGGS WITH HAM AND GRATED CHEESE

This is an easy, elegant dish, and a different way to serve eggs.

1 slice bread per person
ham cut into small pieces
1 egg per person
grated cheese
bechamel sauce, page 253
bread crumbs

1. Prepare the bechamel sauce.

2. Mix the ham and grated cheese into the bechamel sauce.

3. Butter individual baking dishes or custard cups, fit 1 slice toast into each one (cut toast to fit if necessary), and place a raw egg on top.

4. Cover with bechamel sauce, sprinkle with bread crumbs, and bake in a 450 degree oven for about 5 minutes, until the eggs set.

LENTILS WITH FRIED EGGS

Prepare the "Lentils with tomato sauce" recipe (omit the Swiss chard or escarole).

Place the lentils into soup bowls, and place a fried egg on top of each serving.

HARD-BOILED EGG CROQUETTES

bechamel sauce, page 253
eggs
flour
very fine bread crumbs
oil for deep frying

1. Prepare bechamel sauce.

2. Hard-boil the eggs.

3. Butter a large platter.

4. Completely cover the cooled eggs with cooled bechamel sauce, and place on the buttered platter.

5. Let set for about 2 hours.

6. Prepare a dish of flour, a dish of beaten egg, and a dish of unseasoned bread crumbs.

7. When bechamel is cold, dip bechamel-covered egg into flour, shake off excess flour, and mold bechamel to egg.

8. Dip into beaten egg, then into bread crumbs, and fry in deep oil.

EGGPLANT SCRAMBLED EGGS

1 medium-size eggplant
2 eggs
1 grated onion
garlic
3 tbsp. oil

1. Bake the eggplant in the oven until it is soft and thoroughly cooked. Remove it and let it cool.

2. When cool, peel it, discard the skin, put the pulp in a bowl, and drain all the liquid.

3. Grate the onion, and add it to the eggplant. Blend in a pinch garlic, salt and pepper, and about three tablespoons oil.

4. Beat two eggs and blend them in.

5. Heat butter or oil in a pan and scramble the eggplant and eggs.

STUFFED-EGG CROQUETTE

This is a different way of presenting stuffed eggs.

> *eggs*
> *ham*
> *onion*
> *parsley*
> *bechamel sauce, page 253*
> *bread crumbs*
> *flour*
> *oil*

1. Prepare bechamel sauce.

2. Boil eggs.

3. Fry finely chopped ham, finely chopped onion, and finely chopped parsley in butter until the onion is tender.

4. Cut the cooled eggs in half lengthwise and remove yolks.

5. Mash the yolks with the ham mixture, add salt and pepper to taste, and fill the whites, making a mound.

6. Dip each egg into the cooled bechamel sauce and completely cover the egg with it. Let it set for about 2 hours.

7. Prepare a dish of flour, a dish of beaten egg, and a dish of unseasoned bread crumbs.

8. When bechamel is cold, dip the bechamel-covered egg into the flour, shake off excess flour, and mold bechamel to the egg.

9. Dip this into beaten egg, then into bread crumbs, and fry in deep hot oil.

EGGS A LA RIOJANA

This is a famous egg dish made with tomatoes, green peppers, and sausage. It's usually baked in a flat earthenware dish.

Serves two.

> 2 eggs
> ham cut into small pieces
> three-inch piece chorizo, or pork sausage cut into slices or pieces
> 2 chopped tomatoes, either fresh or canned
> red or green pepper, roasted, peeled, and cut into strips (may be canned pimiento)
> garlic
> thyme

1. Roast the pepper in the oven until the skin wrinkles. Remove, put it on a plate, cover it, and peel it when cool. Cut it into strips.

2. Fry the sausage and ham. Remove from pan.

3. Remove some of the fat, and in the same pan, sauté the tomatoes for a few minutes with a small amount of water, salt to taste, a pinch garlic, and thyme.

4. Pour this sauce into individual buttered baking dishes, preferably flat ones, place the raw egg on the sauce, decorate with the sausage, ham, and pepper, and bake in a 450 degree oven until the egg whites become firm, about 5 minutes.

EGGS A LA FLAMENCA

This very famous egg dish is from the south of Spain.

> 1 egg per person
> 1/2 onion per person, cut into thin slices
> 1/2 slice ham per person, cut into small pieces or 1/4 cup cubed ham
> 1 slice ham cut into triangles, for decoration

1 tsp. cooked peas per person
1 tsp. cooked cut-up string beans per person
a few pieces french-fried potatoes, cut in half, per person
1 strip canned red pimiento per person
1 stalk cooked asparagus per person, cut into pieces
three-inch piece sliced chorizo, or one cooked breakfast pork sausage per person
parsley
1 cut up tomato, either fresh or canned, per person

1. Sauté the pieces of ham and onion in butter. When the onion becomes tender, add the tomato, and simmer for five minutes.

2. Add the peas, string beans, fried potatoes, asparagus, sausage, salt and pepper, and simmer for five minutes.

3. Pour some of the sauce into greased individual baking dishes, preferably flat, place the raw egg on the sauce, put some of the sauce on top of the egg, sprinkle with parsley, place a strip of the red pepper across the top, and bake in a 450 degree oven until the white is set, about 5 minutes.

Fry the ham triangles, and at serving time, place them around the dish.

SOUFLEE

The souflé, a baked dish which is light and fluffy, can be used as a main course or as a dessert.

People always think that making a souflé is very difficult, but it really isn't. The only thing that is difficult is timing it so that it's finished when you are ready to eat because a soufflé falls after a short time.

Some of the preparations can be done in advance. For example, the bechamel sauce and the filling may be prepared much earlier. Then you have only to beat and add the egg whites at the last minute.

If a soft-crust top is desired, place the soufflé dish into a shallow pan of water.

SOUFLEE FOR MAIN DISH OR SIDE DISH

4 eggs
bechamel sauce, page   253
filling

The filling may be either one of the following:

Finely chopped cooked shrimp, a pinch thyme, and a pinch pepper.
Finely chopped chicken, a pinch ground cumin and a pinch pepper.
Mashed cooked cauliflower, well seasoned.
Finely grated cheese, such as cheddar, but not a processed cheese. Add the cheese after the egg yolks are mixed into the bechamel.

1. Prepare the filling and set aside.

2. Make a thick bechamel sauce, and let it cool.

3. Beat egg yolks and blend into cooled sauce.

4. Add cooled drained filling to the sauce.

5. Heat oven to 350 degrees so that it will be hot when the soufflé is ready.

6. Beat the 4 eggs whites until they form stiff peaks. With a rubber spatula. fold them into the filling with as few strokes as possible. (Too much stirring ruins the fluffiness of the egg whites.)

7. Place the soufflé into an ungreased soufflé dish, or any deep ceramic or glass baking dish. (About 7-or 8-inch width.) Bake for about 30 to 50 minutes, or until a knife inserted into the center comes out clean.

CODDLED EGGS VILLAROY

This breaded deep-fried coddled egg dish is unique. Not only is this manner of serving an egg unusual, but under the crisp brown crust lies a layer of creamy sauce.

Eggs Villaroy is also a good appetizer because the finished product is dry enough to be finger food.

The recipe may be made the day before and warmed up before serving, or the first five steps may be made the day before and the rest of the recipe completed about a half hour before serving.

> *bechamel sauce, page* *253*
> *eggs*
> *flour*
> *very fine bread crumbs*
> *oil for deep frying*

1. Prepare bechamel sauce.

2. Coddle eggs for 5 minutes, drain, dry, and set aside. (See recipe, page 84.)

3. Butter large platter.

4. Completely cover cooled eggs on all sides with cooled Bechamel Sauce, and place on buttered platter.

5. Let set for about 2 hours.

6. Prepare a dish of flour, a dish of beaten egg, and a dish of unseasoned bread crumbs.

7. When bechamel is cold, dip bechamel-covered egg into flour, shake off excess flour, and mold bechamel to egg.

8. Dip into beaten egg, then into bread crumbs, and fry in deep oil.

WHITE MOUNTAIN EGGS
(Huevos Monte Blanco)
(Eggs Monte Blanco)

Each mound of whipped potatoes has a poached egg on top, covered with Mornay sauce, ham, and slivered orange peel. Very nice for brunch or lunch.

Up to and including step 4 may be made hours before serving. The Mornay sauce may be made the day before if desired, and the rest of the recipe may be made a half hour earlier and then placed under the broiler just before serving.

Duchess potato recipe, page 132. (Prepare enough to equal two
mounds of potatoes per person)
Mornay sauce recipe, page   256
2 eggs per person
1/4 slice ham per person
orange peel, slivered

1. Cut orange peel into thin slivers. Cook in water until tender. Rinse with cold water. Drain and set aside.

2. Cut ham into thin pieces.

3. Prepare Duchess potatoes.

4. Place mounds of Duchess potatoes in buttered baking dish. Make a hollow with a spoon in each mound for the egg. Leave enough potato to cover bottom of hollow.

5. Make a mixture of 1 egg and 1 tablespoon milk. Paint outside of mounds.

6. Prepare Mornay sauce.

7. Coddle eggs for 5 minutes. Drain, and place one egg into each mound.

8. Cover with Mornay sauce.

9. Sprinkle shredded ham over one egg, and orange slivers over the other. (Serve each person 2 egg mounds: one with ham and the other with orange.)

10. Place under broiler to brown.

Vegetables

How do you sign your name? Do you end it with a flourish? I don't, and one day in Spain I almost didn't receive a special delivery letter because of this.

When the mailman gave me the letter, he asked me to sign for it, which I did.

"Finish your signature," he said.

"That's my signature," I replied.

"But you didn't finish it. Put your flourish on it."

"I don't have a flourish."

"No flourish, no letter."

So I developed a flourish and received my mail. There are times when a change from our usual way of doing things is necessary.

Sometimes the change is more interesting. Vegetables with a flourish changes a food which we feel we must eat into something we want to eat.

PISTO WITH ZUCCHINI SQUASH OR EGGPLANT

1 tbsp. oil
1 clove sliced garlic
1 tbsp. fresh chopped parsley or 1/8 tsp. dried parsley
1 green pepper, seeds removed and chopped
1 red pepper, seeds removed and chopped
2 medium chopped onions
4 chopped, peeled tomatoes, fresh or canned
4 medium-size zucchini squash or 1 medium unpeeled eggplant
  or both, cut into small pieces
2 or 3 beaten eggs

1. Heat the oil in a pan and stir in the onions, garlic and parsley. Sauté on low heat until the onions are tender.

2. Add the peppers, tomatoes, squash, and eggplant. Salt to taste, cover and simmer until the vegetables are very tender. Add a small amount of water if necessary.

3. When the vegetables are done, remove the liquid from the pan and stir in the beaten eggs over low heat. (There should be no liquid in the pan when the eggs are added.) Cook until the eggs are firm.

CARROTS AND SPINACH IN VINEGAR SAUCE

1 lb. carrots sliced thin
2 lb. fresh spinach cut into small pieces or 1 pkg. frozen leaf
  spinach

1 clove sliced garlic
1/2 cup vinegar
1 tbsp. paprika
1 tsp. ground cumin
salt
cayenne pepper (optional)

1. Cook vegetables separately. Drain, cool, and set aside.

2. Heat oil and brown garlic. Add paprika, cumin, and vinegar.

3. Stir in the carrots and spinach. Add salt to taste.

4. Toss the vegetables in the pan over low heat until they are coated with the sauce.

This dish from Spanish Morocco can also be served as an appetizer.

CARROTS A LA SANTANDERINA

The smooth sauce for these carrots has a very different taste.

This recipe serves four.

1 lb. carrots
1 tbsp. ground almonds
1 onion, chopped or thinly sliced
1 tbsp. flour
1 clove mashed garlic
1/4 tsp. ground cumin seed
1/8 tsp. ground saffron (optional)
1 tsp. parsley
salt
oil
croutons (optional)

1. Slice the carrots into half-inch pieces and fry them in oil for a few minutes. Add the onion and fry until tender.

2. Blend in the flour.

3. Slowly add enough water to cover the carrots. Add salt to taste, and simmer slowly.

4. Mix the ground almonds, cumin seed, saffron, and garlic together. Add a few drops of oil, and a little liquid from the carrots. Add this to the pot and simmer until the carrots are done.

At serving time, sprinkle with parsley and add croutons.

STUFFED PEPPERS WITH TOMATOES AND ANCHOVIES

A tasty stuffing for peppers, this is good as an appetizer, first dish, or side dish.

> *1 green pepper*
> *4 tbsp. bread crumbs per pepper*
> *3 anchovies with capers per pepper*
> *1 tbsp. black pitted chopped olives per pepper*
> *2 canned tomatoes per pepper*
> *parsley*
> *olive oil*

1. Put the peppers under the broiler until the skin blisters. Remove and let cool. Peel and remove the seeds and top.

2. Chop the anchovies, tomatoes, olives, and parsley.

3. Brown the bread crumbs in about a half cup oil, and combine with the tomato mixture.

4. Fill each pepper, place in a greased baking dish, brush with oil, and bake covered in a 350 degree oven until the peppers are done.

Instead of baking the peppers, they may also be simmered on top of the stove in tomato sauce.

Serve with rice, and also serve tomato sauce.

GREEN PEPPERS WITH RAISINS

This is an unusual combination from Malaga.

peppers
raisins
onions
oil

1. Put the peppers under the broiler until the skin blisters. Remove and cool. Then peel and remove the seeds. Cut pepper into strips.

2. Fry chopped onions and raisins in a small amount of oil until the onion is tender. Stir in the peppers, then put them into a 350 degree oven for a few minutes.

CREAMED CAULIFLOWER WITH GRATED CHEESE

cauliflower, either whole or cut into flowerettes
bechamel sauce, page 253
grated cheese

1. Cook the cauliflower in a small amount of slightly salted water and drain.

2. Prepare the bechamel sauce: Pour it over the cauliflower which has been placed into a baking dish. Sprinkle grated cheese over it. Bake in a 400 degree oven until the cheese browns. (Watch it carefully so that it doesn't burn.)

CREAMED CAULIFLOWER WITH EGG

cauliflower, either whole or cut into flowerettes
1 egg
bechamel sauce, page 253
butter

1. Cook the cauliflower in a small amount of slightly salted water and drain. (Save the liquid for soup.)

2. Beat one egg and blend it into the bechamel sauce.

3. Place the cauliflower in a casserole, cover it with the sauce, place a pat of butter on top, and put it into a 400 degree oven until browned.

COOKED CAULIFLOWER

cauliflower
garlic
oil
chopped hard-boiled egg
chopped fresh parsley

1. Clean cauliflower and remove the leaves. Leave it whole or cut it into pieces.

2. Put it into a small amount of slightly salted water and cook until tender. (Do not overcook or it will become too soft.) Place it on a serving dish when done.

3. Sauté 2 cloves chopped garlic in 2 tablespoons oil or butter and pour it over the cauliflower.

4. Combine chopped hard-boiled egg with chopped parsley and sprinkle it over the cauliflower. Salt to taste.

COOKED CABBAGE

1. Slice or shred a small cabbage and cook it in a small amount of slightly salted water until tender. Drain and set aside.

2. Fry two sliced cloves garlic in oil until brown. Add the drained cabbage and toss. Salt to taste and serve hot.

STRINGBEANS WITH TOMATO

> *stringbeans*
> *garlic*
> *canned tomatoes*

1. Remove stems and threads from the stringbeans. Slice them the long way.

2. Brown sliced garlic in oil, add tomatoes, the stringbeans, and salt to taste. Simmer slowly until the stringbeans are done.

EGGPLANT SUPREME

Even people who don't usually like eggplant love this because the tomato sauce disguises the strong eggplant flavor.

> *1 eggplant*
> *about 2 cups Tomato sauce recipe 1, page 247*
> *4 sliced mushrooms*
> *10 pitted sliced olives*
> *1 tbsp. grated cheese*
> *1/2 lb. ground meat (optional)*
> *1 or 2 eggs*
> *salt and pepper*

1. Boil eggplant in salted water to cover until soft. Remove from pot, cut in half and let it cool.

2. Prepare Tomato sauce recipe.

3. When the eggplant is cool, scoop out the pulp carefully so that the skin does not tear. Save the skin.

4. Chop the pulp and place it in the pan with the tomato sauce. Add the mushrooms, pitted sliced olives, and grated cheese.

5. If you're using meat, brown the meat in another pan, then add to the sauce.

6. Spread the eggplant skins in a greased baking dish, fill with the tomato sauce mixture, and bake in a 400 degree oven until the filling sets, about 10 to 15 minutes.

7. Remove from the oven and cover the top of the casserole with one of the following, then bake in a 450 degree oven until light brown:

FLUFFY TOPPING RECIPE:

Bechamel sauce, page 253
Thinly sliced cheese

1. Separate 4 eggs.

2. Beat 3 yolks with 1 tbsp. flour, a pinch salt, 2 drops vanilla, and a pinch cinnamon.

3. Beat the 4 egg whites until they foam, add a pinch salt, and beat until they form stiff peaks.

4. Fold the whites into the yolks with as few strokes as possible. Spread it on top of the eggplant. Bake in a 450 degree oven until the top is a light brown. Serve immediately.

VEGETABLE CASSEROLE
(Budín de legumbres)

This is a delicious and unusual way to serve vegetables. It's very important that the vegetables used in the preparation of this recipe be cooked properly so that they taste good even before putting them in the casserole. Use the vegetable recipes in this book for their preparation. This recipe serves 6 people.

mashed potatoes, quantity for 2 people
chopped, cooked spinach, quantity for 2 people
sliced, cooked carrots, quantity for 2 people

bechamel sauce, page 253
3 eggs
  nutmeg
  garlic
1 tbsp. capers (optional)

1. Prepare cooked vegetables, drain them well, and keep them in separate bowls.

2. Stir a pinch nutmeg into the potatoes, and a pinch garlic into the spinach if you haven't already done so in their preparation.

3. Mix 1 raw egg yolk into each cooked vegetable.

4. Grease casserole dish, and cover the bottom of it with half the amount of potatoes.

5. Cover the potatoes with a layer of carrots.

6. Cover the carrots with a layer of bechamel sauce.

7. Cover the bechamel sauce with a layer of spinach.

8. Cover the spinach with a layer of potatoes.

9. Place the casserole in another pan which contains a small amount of water, and place these into the oven. Bake in a 375 degree oven for about 1 hour, or until a tooth pick, when inserted into the vegetables, comes out clean.

10. Cover the top of casserole with bechamel sauce, and sprinkle with capers.

VEGETABLE MEDLEY
(Panaché de verduras)

This recipe serves 4 large portions. In Spain, it is usually served before the main dish because the vegetables taste so good.

1 package (about 10 oz.) frozen, defrosted artichoke hearts or 1 can artichoke hearts

> *4 asparagus spears*
> *3 cups raw carrots, sliced*
> *1/2 lb. raw stringbeans*
> *4 peeled, whole medium-size potatoes*
> *2 fresh mint leaves or 1/8 tsp. dried mint leaves*
> *several pieces of raw chicken to flavor the cooking water or two chicken boullion cubes*
> *1 onion*
> *oil for frying, preferably olive oil*
> *1 sliced clove garlic*
> *1 pat butter*
> *oil and vinegar cruets to serve at the table*

1. Cook peas with mint leaves and a small amount of salt. Be careful not to overcook peas.

2. In a separate pot, cook carrots, stringbeans, potatoes, onion, and chicken pieces with enough water to cover, and salt to taste. Cook until the vegetables are tender, but not too soft and mushy.

3. Prepare a serving platter which will hold all the vegetables. Arrange the asparagus on it and place it in a warm oven. As each vegetable is prepared in the following steps, place it on the platter and keep it in the oven so that the vegetables will be warm when served.

When the vegetables are done, drain them and prepare them in the following manner:

4. Melt butter in a frying pan and toss the peas with the butter. Remove them to the serving platter in the oven.

5. Prepare the carrots the same as the peas.

6. Add more butter to the pan, and prepare the potatoes the same way.

7. Add 1/8 cup oil to the pan and brown the garlic. Add the stringbeans and toss them with the garlic and oil. Remove to the platter.

8. Add more oil and garlic if necessary, put the artichokes in the pan and toss them with the oil and garlic. Remove to the platter.

At the table, each person pours oil and vinegar over his own serving of vegetables.

SPINACH PIE

This recipe may be made up as a pie or as spinach turnovers.

For turnovers, cut the dough into circles, place a spoon of spinach on each piece, fold over, and press edges with a fork to seal, deep fry in hot oil.

> *pie dough recipe 2, page 279 or ready-made pie crust for one-crust pie*
> *1 small chopped onion*
> *4 tbsp. butter or oil*
> *2 tbsp. flour*
> *1 cup warm milk*
> *garlic powder*
> *salt*
> *2 one-pound packages chopped frozen spinach*
> *2 eggs*
> *ground nutmeg (optional)*

1. Heat the oil or butter in a pan and blend in the flour. Remove the pan from the heat and stir in the warmed milk little by little. Put it back on the heat and continue stirring until the sauce becomes thick. Add the garlic, salt, and a pinch of nutmeg. Put a pat of butter on top of sauce.

2. Cook the spinach, and drain well, pressing out any excess liquid.

3. Fry the onion and mix it and the white sauce into the drained spinach.

4. Blend in the eggs and taste for seasoning.

5. Prepare the pie dough, place in pie plate, prick all over with a fork, and coat bottom crust with egg white to prevent it from becoming soggy from the spinach.

6. Pour the spinach into unbaked pastry shell and bake at 425 degrees for about 20 minutes to a half hour, until crust browns lightly.

Decorate with sliced or quartered hard-boiled egg.

SPINACH AND ONIONS SEASONED WITH CINAMMON

Serves 4.

> *1 pkg. frozen leaf spinach*
> *1 small chopped onion*
> *2 cloves sliced garlic*
> *1 tbsp. paprika*
> *1 tsp. vinegar*
> *1/4 tsp. cinammon*
> *croutons (optional)*

1. Cook the spinach in a small amount of slightly salted water. When done, drain well, and press out all the liquid. Cut it up into small pieces.

2. Heat oil in a pan and fry the onion until tender, then add the garlic and brown. Stir in the paprika, spinach, and vinegar.

3. Toss the spinach with the sauce and simmer covered over low heat for a few minutes.

4. Stir in the cinnamon and salt to taste. Add more vinegar if necessary. Serve with croutons.

CREAMED SPINACH
(Espinacas con Bechamel)

A delicious way to serve spinach; even children love it.

Up to and including step 3 may be made the day before. However, it's best to combine the spinach and bechamel just before bringing it to the table. Heat the spinach first, then add it to the bechamel.

Fresh spinach should be washed in 5 changes of water to remove the sand.

2 packages frozen chopped spinach or 2 lbs. fresh spinach
bechamel sauce recipe, page 253

1. Cook spinach in a small amount of slightly salted water.

2. Prepare bechamel sauce.

3. Drain spinach well when it is done by pressing out the excess liquid.

4. Combine the bechamel sauce with the spinach, mix it in well, and serve.

SPINACH, STYLE 1
(Espinacas)

The spinach is pre-cooked and then sautéed in this recipe.

This is the most popular style of preparing leafy vegetables in Spain.

1 lb. fresh spinach or 1 package frozen spinach
1 clove garlic or 1/8 tsp. minced dried garlic (less garlic may be
used if you prefer)
salt
a pinch grated nutmeg (optional)
1 tsp. olive oil

1. Wash fresh spinach in 5 changes of water to remove the sand.

2. Cook spinach, covered, in 1/2 cup slightly salted water for 10 minutes. Drain.

3. Heat oil in pan, and add sliced garlic. Brown slightly.

4. Immediately add drained spinach and toss, thoroughly coating spinach with oil. Add salt and nutmeg and toss again. Serve hot.

SPINACH, STYLE 2
(Espinacas)

The spinach is cooked with all the ingredients at the same time in this recipe.

> *1 lb. fresh spinach or 1 package frozen spinach*
> *1 clove garlic or 1/8 tsp. minced dried garlic (less garlic may be used if you prefer)*
> *salt*
> *a pinch grated nutmeg (optional)*
> *1 tsp. olive oil*

1. Wash fresh spinach in 5 changes of water to remove the sand.

2. Heat oil in pan and add sliced garlic. Brown slightly.

3. Immediately add spinach plus 1 cup water, salt, and nutmeg. Toss all together in pan.

4. Cook spinach for 10 minutes.

BAKED SPINACH

Serves 2.

> *1 one-pound package chopped spinach*
> *2 eggs*
> *1 tsp. butter*
> *2 tbsp. milk*
> *a pinch ground nutmeg*
> *salt*
> *a pinch garlic*

1. Cook the spinach in a small amount of slightly salted water. Drain well by pressing out the excess liquid.

2. Stir in the butter.

3. Beat the eggs, add the milk, and blend into the spinach.

4. Butter individual custard cups and fill with the spinach. Place in a pan of water and bake in a 350 degree oven for about twenty minutes, or until a knife when inserted in the center comes out clean.

SPINACH SOUFLEE

Serves 6.

An unusual way to serve spinach, this dish must be served as soon as it is removed from the oven. However, everything may be prepared in advance except for adding the beaten egg whites. They must be blended in the last minute, before placing the baking dish into the oven.

It takes about 40 minutes to bake, so time the sitting down at the table accordingly. This can be the first dish.

Make sure to remove the souflée from the oven when everybody is at the table ready to eat it, because it falls flat at room temperature.

1 one-pound package frozen chopped spinach
3 tbsp. flour
3 tbsp. oil or butter
1 cup warm milk
3 egg yolks
4 egg whites
a pinch nutmeg
a pinch garlic
1/2 a small onion, chopped

1. Cook spinach in a small amount of slightly salted water. Drain very well.

2. Warm the milk.

3. Heat the butter or oil in a pan and sauté the onions until tender.

4. Blend the flour into the butter. Remove pan from heat.

5. Blend the milk into the flour very gradually, stirring it into a smooth sauce. Add salt, garlic, and nutmeg. Return to heat.

6. Stir constantly until a sauce is formed. (About 10 minutes.) Blend it into the drained spinach.

7. Separate the egg yolks and whites. Set the whites aside for later use.

8. Beat the yolks well and mix it into the cooled spinach. Taste for correct seasoning.

9. Heat the oven to 375 degrees.

10. Beat the egg whites until they form stiff peaks. Fold them into the spinach with as few strokes as possible.

11. Pour it into a 7 or 8-inch glass baking dish or souflée dish, place it in a pan of water, and put it into the center of the oven. Bake for about 40 minutes, or until a knife when inserted into the center of the spinach comes out clean.

Serve immediately.

ARTICHOKE HEARTS

This vegetable may be served with the main dish or as an appetizer. It may be made in advance and served cold, or served warm.

> *1 can artichoke hearts, or 1 package frozen artichoke hearts*
> *which have been thawed*
> *2 tbsp. olive oil*

1 tsp. vinegar
salt to taste
1 clove garlic, sliced

1. If you're going to use frozen hearts, cook them in slightly salted water. Do not overcook.

2. Drain off the liquid from either the canned hearts or the cooked frozen hearts.

3. Heat oil in frying pan and brown garlic.

4. Add the artichoke hearts and toss them with the oil and garlic in the pan.

5. Remove them from the pan, sprinkle them with vinegar and salt, toss gently and serve.

FRESH ARTICHOKES
(Alcachofas)

One artichoke or one half artichoke per person may be considered a serving portion.

whole, fresh artichokes
1/2 tsp. lemon juice per artichoke
1/2 clove garlic, mashed, per artichoke
1 1/2 tbsp. fresh, chopped parsley per artichoke
1/2 tsp. olive oil per artichoke
salt

1. Remove small outer leaves which are tough and bitter, about two rows of leaves. Cut stem off flush with artichoke so that artichoke can stand up. Cut off about 1/4 of the top of the artichoke, thus cutting off some of the sharp points.

2. Take hold of the stem area, turn the artichoke over, and press the cut off end of the artichoke down on the table. This will open the artichoke. Rinse and drain.

3. Place artichokes in the pot, standing up and pressing against each other, with about 2 cups water, salt, and 1 tsp. lemon juice.

4. Mix parsley, garlic, and a little salt, and place a small amount in the center of each artichoke.

5. Mix lemon juice and olive oil and pour around the outer leaves and into the center of each artichoke.

6. Cover and simmer for 1 hour or until the outer leaves are tender. (It's done when you can pull a leaf off the choke.) Add more water to the pot if necessary, but not onto the artichokes.

May be served hot with Hollandaise Sauce, page 255, or cold with Vinagrette Sauce, page 257.

PEAS WITH ONIONS AND MINT

> *1 sliced onion*
> *1 package frozen peas*
> *a few mint leaves*

1. Boil a cup water, add the mint leaves, cover and let set for 5 minutes. Strain.

2. Sauté onion in a small amount of butter or oil, add the peas, the strained water in which the mint leaves were steeped, salt to taste, and simmer over very low heat for a short time, until the peas become tender.

If desired, pieces of ham may be added.

GREEN PEAS WITH SAUSAGE, HAM, AND ONIONS
(Guisantes a la Extremeña)

> *1 pkg. frozen thawed green peas*
> *1 three-inch piece chorizo or 1 sweet Italian sausage*
> *1 slice ham cut into pieces or cubed ham*
> *1 large sliced onion*
> *1 large potato*
> *salt and pepper*

1. Cut the sausage into slices about a half-inch thick. Fry it, then add the ham and onion to the same pan.

2. When the onion is tender, add the peas, just enough water to cover all the ingredients, salt and pepper.

3. Peel the potato, cut it into small cubes, add it to the peas, and simmer on low heat until the potatoes are done.

If a thick sauce is desired, put a tablespoon flour in a saucer, blend in some liquid from the peas, and add it to the pan. Simmer a few minutes until the sauce thickens.

MUSHROOMS WITH BREAD CRUMBS AND PARSLEY

Wash and dry the mushrooms, separate the caps from the stems, and fry them in butter with chopped garlic, bread crumbs, and chopped parsley for a few minutes. (Do not let them get too well-done.)

Season with salt.

PLAIN SAUTEED MUSHROOMS

Heat butter in a pan and sauté the washed, dried, sliced mushrooms for about five minutes.

Rice, potatoes, macaroni

> Todo el monte no es orégano.
> *All that glitters is not gold.*

Because a dish of food looks good does'nt mean that it tastes good. These recipes look and taste good.

RICE WITH TOMATO AND PEPPERS

Serves 4.

> *1 cup rice*
> *2 sliced onions*
> *2 green peppers*
> *2 large sliced tomatoes*
> *parsley*

1. Put the peppers under the broiler until the skin blisters. Remove and let cool. Peel and remove the seeds. Cut into strips.

2. Heat a small amount of oil in a pan. Stir in the washed, drained rice, add 2 1/2 cups water, salt to taste, cover and cook.

3. In another pan fry the onion. When it becomes tender, add the peppers and the tomatoes. Simmer covered for about 10 minutes.

4. When the rice is halfway done, add the tomato mixture and a small amount of chopped parsley. Continue cooking until the rice is done. Let it set for a few minutes, then serve.

PEPPERS STUFFED WITH RICE

> *1 large pepper per person*
> *1 tomato per pepper*
> *1/2 small onion per pepper*
> *2 tbsp. raw rice per pepper*
> *garlic*
> *1/2 cup chicken or beef boullion*

1. Heat oil in pan and sauté the onion, then add the tomato. Simmer for a few minutes.

2. Mix in the washed raw rice and let it cook for about five minutes.

3. Cut top from pepper and remove seeds. Fill the pepper with the rice and the sauce. Do not stuff too full because the rice expands. Stuff a square of bread into the opening to serve as a cover.

4. Place on a greased baking dish, and coat the peppers with oil. Pour about a half cup of boullion on the bottom of the dish and bake in a 350 degree oven for about one hour, or until the rice is done.

RICE
(Arroz)

This is the way rice is prepared in Spain when it is to be served with other foods, for example, on the dish with meat.

For the quantity of rice given in this recipe, one cup, use a two-quart heavy pot with a cover, or an eight-inch heavy skillet with a cover. A heavy pot, one that is made of a thick material, is best to use because the heat spreads slowly and evenly and therefore the rice is least likely to burn. The best way to keep the rice from burning, though, is to stay in the kitchen!

This recipe serves four people, and it may be prepared about one hour in advance.

1 tsp. olive oil
1 clove sliced garlic
salt
1 cup rice (not minute rice)
a piece of uncooked chicken, chicken bone, or chicken giblet
1 sprig fresh parsley

optional: a pinch saffron to give the rice a slightly yellow color

1. Rinse rice, drain and set aside.

2. Heat oil in pot, add garlic, and brown.

3. Add rice to pot and stir with a fork to coat rice with oil.

4. Add 2 1/2 cups water and stir rice with a fork. Saffron may be added at this time. Stir the rice after adding the saffron. Add salt and stir. Taste the water to see if it is salty enough.

5. Add chicken pieces and parsley. Cover and simmer for about 25 minutes. The rice should be tender, but do not let it get too soft.

6. When the rice is done, remove the pot from the heat and let it set for five minutes before serving.

RICE WITH TOMATO SAUCE, SAUSAGE, AND PEPPERS
(Arroz a la Riojana)

> *tomato sauce, style 2, page 248*
> *1/2 green pepper cut into pieces*
> *1 cup ham pieces*
> *1 3-inch piece chorizo or 1 sweet Italian sausage cut into slices*
> *1 medium-size chopped onion*
> *1 cup rice*

1. Fry the sausage and ham in a pan large enough to hold the rice later on. Then remove them from the pan and sauté the onions until soft.

2. Remove some of the fat if necessary and stir in the rice. Toss it in the pan for a minute, then add two and a half cups water and salt to taste. Return the sausage, ham, and onions and cook until the rice is done, about 25 minutes.

3. Prepare the tomato sauce, and fry the green peppers. At serving time, put the green peppers on top of the rice, and make a space in the center of the rice for the sauce, or serve the sauce separately.

RICE WITH VEAL OR PORK
(Arroz Murciano)

Serves 4.

1 cup rice
1 lb. veal or lean pork
2 or 3 medium-size tomatoes (may be canned)
3 sweet red peppers or green peppers
2 cloves garlic
 pinch saffron (optional)
1 tbsp. chopped fresh parsley or 1/4 tsp. dried parsley

1. Cut the meat into small cubes, the peppers into strips, and the garlic into slices. Plunge the tomatoes into boiling water so that the skin may be peeled easily, then cut them into small pieces.

2. Fry the meat in oil, remove it from the pan, and set aside. Fry the garlic in the same pan, remove it, and fry the peppers and tomatoes.

3. After the peppers and tomatoes fry for a few minutes, add the meat and garlic, and the parsley. Grind the saffron, add a tablespoon water to it, and add it to the pan. Add about a cup water, cover and simmer for 20 minutes.

4. Bring 2 cups water to a boil.

5. When the sauce becomes somewhat thick, stir in the washed, drained rice, add the boiling water, salt to taste, and bring it to a boil again.

6. As soon as it boils, remove it from the top of the stove, cover it, and put it into a 350 degree oven for one hour, until the rice becomes tender.

BOILED POTATOES WITH PARSLEY

Cook potatoes until tender. Drain and peel them. Shake the potatoes in the pan over low heat to dry them out. Add chopped fresh parsley and butter, and sprinkle them with salt.

PAN-ROASTED POTATOES

1. Boil medium-size potatoes for about 10 minutes.

2. Drain and arrange them around the meat roast about one hour before the meat is done. Turn them from time to time and baste them with the meat gravy from the pan.

3. When they are done, if they are not browned enough, put them in another pan and place them under the broiler for a few minutes.

4. To serve, place them around the roast and sprinkle them with paprika and parsley.

POTATO GARNISH

Decorate a plate of food with these whipped potatoes and eat the decoration.

Everything may be prepared in advance, except the last step. If the mashed potatoes are prepared in advance, place a pat of butter on top when they are stored in the refrigerator. Then heat them in the oven before using.

Serves 4.

> *4 potatoes*
> *1/4 cup heavy cream*
> *1 tbsp. butter*
> *a pinch nutmeg*
> *1 egg yolk*
> *salt and pepper*
> *pastry tube*

1. Prepare whipped potatoes using the butter and cream to make a fluffy but stiff consistancy.

2. Whip in egg yolk, nutmeg, salt and pepper.

3. Put into a pastry tube, use ragged edge tip, and decorate the edge of serving platter.

POTATOES WITH PAPRIKA AND VINEGAR
(Patatas de Jaén)

> *potatoes*
> *1 clove garlic for each potato*
> *1/8 tsp. ground cumin seed per potato*
> *1/4 tsp. paprika per potato*
> *1/2 tsp. oil per potato*
> *1/4 tsp. vinegar per potato*
> *salt*

Cook the potatoes in water, then peel and cube them and pour on the following:

Mix together mashed garlic, cumin, and paprika. Add the oil, vinegar, and salt to taste. Pour over the hot potatoes and toss. If desired, add more oil.

CUSTARD POTATOES

> *1/2 clove mashed garlic or garlic powder*
> *butter*
> *4 medium-size potatoes*
> *2 eggs*
> *1 cup plus 2 tbsp. milk or 2 tbsp. cream*

1. Peel the potatoes and slice them very thin. Place them in a casserole dish and sprinkle them with salt and pepper.

2. Beat the eggs, add milk (and cream) and pour it over the potatoes. (It should cover them.)

3. Bake in a 350 degree oven for about 45 minutes, until the potatoes are tender.

At serving time, dot with pieces of butter.

POTATOES IN TOMATO SAUCE

> *1 potato per person*
> *1 small tomato for each potato, either canned or fresh*
> *1/2 chopped onion*
> *garlic*
> *thyme*

1. Slice the potatoes very thin and keep them in cold water until ready to use. Cut the tomatoes into pieces.

2. Heat the oil in a pan and fry the sliced garlic. Remove it from the pan and fry the onion until slightly browned.

3. Add the tomatoes and thyme, and simmer for a minute or two.

4. Add the drained potatoes and salt to taste and simmer until the potatoes are done.

POTATOES IN A SAUCE

> *1 potato per person*
> *1 clove garlic per potato*
> *1 tsp. flour per potato*
> *1 tbsp. butter*
> *1/8 cup water per potato*

1. Slice the garlic and fry in oil. Remove it and fry the potatoes. (Add more oil if necessary.)

2. Put the flour in a bowl, stir in the water, and add salt.

3. Melt butter in a pan, blend in the flour and water mixture. Add the potatoes and garlic. Simmer for awhile and serve hot.

FRIED POTATOES IN SAUCE
(Patatas al Ajillo)

When María Luisa's father went to Switzerland to work as a cook so that he could save up enough money to come back to Spain and open a restaurant, she came to live with us as a maid. Her father had taught her well, and she was a good cook. One of her favorite recipes was Patatas al Ajillo, and even if it wasn't on the family menu for the day, she would prepare it for her lunch anyway.

Her father called for her when he settled down in his new job, and the recipe went with María Luisa. I had to write and ask her to send it to me from Switzerland. Here it is, as her father told it to her:

> *potatoes, sliced for frying*
> *ground cumin*
> *garlic cloves*

1. Fry potatoes until slightly browned in a small amount of very hot oil. Remove them from the pan and set them aside.

2. Add mashed garlic and ground cumin to the pan, plus about a half cup water. (The amount of water depends on the amount of potatoes. Use enough water to make a small amount of sauce.) Cover the pan and simmer until the garlic is soft.

3. Add the potatoes to the sauce in the pan, toss and coat the potatoes with the sauce. Add salt to taste. Cover the pan and simmer until the potatoes are done. If necessary, add a little more water to the pan while the potatoes are cooking.

POTATO CROQUETTES

These croquettes are good as an appetizer or as an unusual way to serve potatoes with the meal. Up to and including step 2 may be made in advance, or the whole recipe may be made in advance and then re-heated in the oven before serving. It serves 8 people.

> *potatoes, enough for 8 servings*
> *3 eggs*
> *butter*
> *milk*
> *nutmeg*

1. Prepare whipped potatoes, using butter and milk to make a rich, fluffy, but stiff consistency.

2. Whip in 2 beaten eggs, a pinch nutmeg, salt and pepper.

3. Make croquettes by rolling a teaspoonful of potato mixture in flour, shake off excess flour, then roll it in the beaten egg, and then roll it in the bread crumbs.

4. Deep fry in hot fat.

If you're preparing this recipe the day before serving it, place the mashed potatoes in a bowl with a pat of butter on top of them and store in the refrigerator until ready to use.

DUCHESS POTATOES
(Patatas Duquesa)

This is a novel way to serve whipped potatoes. Up to and including step 2 may be prepared in advance, even the day before serving. In order to store the whipped potatoes in the refrigerator, place a pat of butter on top of them until you're ready to prepare the recipe.

potatoes, enough for 8 servings
2 eggs, and 1 egg yolk
butter
milk
nutmeg

1. Prepare whipped potatoes using butter and milk to make a rich, fluffy, but stiff consistancy.

2. Whip in 2 beaten eggs, a pinch nutmeg, salt and pepper to taste.

3. Make mounds of potatoes on a greased baking dish. Paint the mounds with a mixture of 1 egg yolk mixed with 1 tbsp. milk.

4. Place under the broiler and brown. Serve immediately.

MACARONI IN BECHAMEL SAUCE
(Macarones con besamel)

This is a very easy dish to prepare, and it looks and tastes great. Up to and including step 3 may be made the previous day

> *macaroni*
> *chopped ham (or other cooked meat)*
> *bechamel sauce, page* 253

1. Make bechamel sauce.

2. Cook macaroni and drain it when done.

3. Toss macaroni with butter, add chopped ham, and place it into a casserole dish.

4. Cover the macaroni with bechamel sauce one hour before serving and let it set.

At serving time, place it into a 350 degree oven for 5 minutes. Serve very hot.

MACARONI WITH TOMATO SAUCE, PLAIN OR BAKED
(Macarones con tomate)

> *tomato sauce recipe, page* 247
> *macaroni*

1. Prepare tomato sauce recipe.

2. Cook macaroni according to directions on the package. Drain.

When the macaroni is cooked and drained, add the sauce to the macaroni, toss and serve.

BAKED MACARONI

> *bechamel sauce recipe, page* 253
> *tomato sauce recipe, page* 247

macaroni
grated cheese

1. Prepare the bechamel and tomato sauces. Keep them separate.

2. Cook the macaroni according to directions on the package. Drain.

3. Place the macaroni in a casserole dish, pour bechamel sauce over it so that the sauce covers all the macaroni. Let it set. After it sets, pour the tomato sauce on top, sprinkle with grated cheese, and heat in the oven for a few minutes.

Be careful not to burn the cheese.

MACARONI IN SAUCE WITH BAKED EGGS

macaroni
bechamel sauce, page 253
1 egg per person
grated cheese

1. Prepare the bechamel sauce. Cook the macaroni.

2. Mix the macaroni with the bechamel sauce and the grated cheese.

3. Pour it into a buttered casserole baking dish, and make a dent on the macaroni for the eggs.

4. Place a raw egg in each dent, sprinkle with grated cheese. Put a pat of butter on each egg.

5. Put into a 400 degree oven until the eggs set, about 5 minutes.

Beans

> Barriga llena, corazón contento.
> *A full stomach makes a happy heart.*

Bean dishes are an economical and healthy way of filling the stomach while making the mouth and heart happy.

HOW TO PREPARE DRIED BEANS

Cover beans with water and cook slowly. Add water when necessary so that they don't get dry and lose their skin.

It's better to add salt when they are half-way done.

Chick peas: Soak them the night before cooking in warm water that has been slightly salted. Put them into boiling water to cook.

High-grade white beans and colored beans: If they are a very good class of bean, they don't need to be soaked overnight. Start them cooking in cold water, and when the water comes to a boil, change them to cold water again.

Lower grade of white beans and colored beans: Soak them in water overnight. Start them cooking in boiling water.

Lentils: They don't need to be soaked at all. Start them cooking in a small amount of cold water, just enough to cover them. When the water comes to a boil, add more cold water. Do this three times for a fine result.

HOW TO SOAK BEANS

Rinse beans in a colander. Discard stones and spoiled beans. Then place them in a deep bowl (not metal), and cover with very slightly salted cool water, plus several inches more. (Beans absorb water, so there should be plenty.) Soak them for 12 hours. (A few extra hours won't matter.) Drain, discard the water, and use as directed in recipe.

FAST METHOD FOR SOAKING BEANS

Although this is a fast way to prepare the beans for cooking, they won't be as tender as they would be if they were soaked for 12 hours.

Wash the beans, put them in a pot with enough water to cover them, plus a few extra inches, and bring to a boil. Remove from heat and let set for 2 hours before using them in a recipe.

LENTILS WITH TOMATO SAUCE

This is a hearty dish which everybody seems to like.

It may be prepared the day before serving.

Lentils do NOT have to be soaked before cooking.

Serves 6.

> 2 1/2 cups lentils
> 1 ham bone or other meat bones
> 1 large chopped onion
> 4 chopped tomatoes
> 1 tbsp. chopped fresh parsley, or 1/4 tsp. dried parsley
> 2 sliced cloves garlic
>   salt and pepper or crushed red pepper
> 2 tbsp. oil
>   a pinch thyme

1. Put the lentils in a pot with enough cold water just to cover them and bring to a boil. As soon as it boils, add more cold water, the bones, and salt to taste. Simmer slowly until the lentils are almost done, about 20 or 30 minutes. Add more water if needed during cooking so that the lentils are always covered with water.

2. In the meantime, fry the garlic in oil, then remove it and fry the onions until tender. Add the tomatoes, parsley, thyme, the fried garlic, salt and pepper to taste, and simmer for about 15 minutes. Set aside.

3. When the lentils are almost done, stir in the tomato and onion sauce, taste for salt, and simmer for about 15 minutes longer.

Also, cut-up swiss chard or escarole may be added the last 15 minutes. Cook it, drain it, and sauté it in oil for 5 minutes before adding it to the lentils.

Place a quarter of hard-boiled egg in each serving.

KIDNEY BEAN STEW, ASTURIAS STYLE
(Fabada Asturiana)

Soak the beans the night before, according to directions on page 136. This dish may be served as the first course, or as the main course. It's a very hearty meal and easy to prepare.

1 3/4 cups dried red kidney beans
2-inch piece chorizo or sweet Italian sausage
1 lb. stewing meat, either veal or beef
1 ham bone or ham hock
1 slice bacon
2 slices country ham
a pinch saffron
salt and pepper to taste

1. Place all the ingredients except the saffron and the bacon into a pot of enough cold water so as to cover everything, and add a little extra water. (This dish, when finished, doesn't have much liquid.) Simmer covered.

2. After one hour of cooking, add the bacon. Grind the saffron in a mortar and pestle, or crumble it between the fingers, dilute it with a bit of liquid from the pot, and add it to the pot.

3. Add more water if necessary so that there is always enough water just to cover the beans and meat. Let it simmer until tender. Do not overcook the beans; they should be firm.

LENTIL STEW
(Potaje de lentejas)

This is a hunger satisfying stew. The meat and bones may be omitted to make this a meatless dish.

> 1/4 cup olive oil
> 1 onion
> 1 clove garlic
> 1 bay leaf
> 1 or 2 peeled tomatoes, either fresh or canned
> 1 green pepper
> 1 inch chorizo sausage or 1 inch sweet Italian sausage
> 1 lb. stewing meat, either lamb, veal, or beef
> 2 or more soup bones
> salt and pepper
> 1 1/2 cups lentils, washed and drained (lentils do NOT need to be soaked before using)
> 4 medium-size potatoes
> a few grains of red crushed pepper (optional)

1. Cut tomatoes into 4 pieces, pepper into 4 strips, and onion into slices.

2. Heat oil in heavy stew pot and sauté onion, garlic, bay leaf, chorizo, and green pepper. Add tomatoes and simmer, covered, for about a minute.

3. Add meat, lentils, and soup bones, cover with cold water, and bring to a boil. Skim off the foam.

4. Add salt and pepper and crushed red pepper, lower heat and simmer for 1 hour, or until meat is tender.

5. Add peeled, halved potatoes the last half hour of cooking.

6. Correct seasoning and add more water if necessary. This dish should have a lot of liquid to it, almost like a soup.

LIMA BEAN STEW

This hearty dish, which serves 5 people, can also become a meatless dish by omitting the sausage and ham bone.

A good menu using the Lima Bean Stew as a main dish would be to serve a French Omelette and vegetable first, followed by the stew, salad, and for dessert, cheese and fruit, with a dry wine served during the meal.

> *1 3/4 cups lima beans*
> *1 large onion*
> *2 cloves garlic*
> *1 tbsp. olive oil*
> *1 tsp. paprika*
> *salt*
> *1 chorizo sausage or 1 sweet Italian sausage*
> *1 ham bone or ham hock*

1. Place drained beans in pot, add cold water to cover beans plus 4 extra cups cold water.

2. Add onion, garlic, ham bone, oil, and chorizo. Cook for about 1 hour, or until beans are tender. Do not overcook the beans or they will become too soft and will absorb all the liquid.

3. At the end of the cooking time, sprinkle in paprika and shake the pot. Do not stir with a spoon or the beans will become mushy.

CHICK PEA STEW

This hearty cold-weather dish serves four.

> *2 cups canned chick peas, rinsed and drained*
> *6 tbsp. raw rice*
> *6-inch piece chorizo or 2 Italian sausages*
> *2 potatoes cut into pieces*
> *1 tsp. paprika*
> *2 cloves sliced garlic*

1. Heat oil in the pan in which you are going to cook the stew. Rinse and drain the rice, put it in the pan with the oil, and stir.

2. Add four cups water to the pan, and salt to taste. Simmer on low heat.

3. After 15 minutes, add the potatoes and continue cooking on low heat until they and the rice are almost done, about another 10 minutes.

4. After this time, add the chick peas and sausages, and simmer for about 10 minutes longer.

5. In another pan, fry the garlic in one tablespoon oil or butter, remove the pan from the heat, stir in the paprika, and add it to the stew.

Salads

En boca cerrada no entran moscas.
Flies don't enter a shut mouth.

A mouth that gives compliments to cooks is a pleasing one, and these salad dishes will bring forth many praises.

SHRIMP AND POTATO SALAD SUPREME

>   5 medium-size boiled potatoes
>   1 onion cut in half
>   1 tbsp. fresh parsley or 1/4 tsp. dried parsley
>   2 cloves mashed garlic
> 1/4 cup vinegar
> 2/3 cup oil
>   2 tbsp. water
>   1 tbsp. capers
>   2 cucumbers, peeled and cut the long way (cut each into 8
>   pieces)
>   olives
>   1 lb. shelled shrimp
>   2 sliced tomatoes
>   1 sliced avocado
>   2 or 3 hard-boiled eggs
> 1/2 stalk celery
>   1 tsp. lemon juice
>   1 chopped onion

1. Cook the potatoes in salted water. Peel and cube when done.

2. Mix the vinegar, oil, water, and garlic. Set aside.

3. Put 2 cups water in a saucepan, add the lemon juice, celery, onion, salt and pepper, and bring to a boil. Simmer covered for 15 minutes.

4. After this time, add the shrimp and simmer for about 5 minutes, until the shrimp turn pink, no longer. Remove from heat.

5. Cut half the shrimp into small pieces. Save the remainder for later.

6. Place the potatoes, chopped onion, cut-up shrimp, capers and parsley in a bowl. Pour about one-third cup of the vinegar sauce over them, and toss.

7. Pour the rest of the sauce over the remaining shrimp, tomatoes, avocados, and cucumbers and let set for about 15 to 20 minutes.

8. Arrange the potatoes in the center of a flat plate in the form of a pyramid. Place the strips of cucumbers around the pyramid. Place a shrimp between each cucumber. Arrange the egg slices around the pyramid between the cucumbers, and the tomatoes and avocados on the plate around them. Sprinkle the top with capers.

AVOCADO, ORANGE, AND TOMATO SALAD

segments of one large onion
1 small onion sliced into thin rings
1 thinly sliced tomato
1 sliced avocado
several radishes
several green pimiento-stuffed olives
lettuce
1/2 cup oil
1/4 cup vinegar or lemon juice
salt

Put the orange segments, avocado and tomato slices, and onion rings on a plate, pour the oil and vinegar or lemon juice over them, and let set for a half hour.

Arrange on lettuce leaves with radishes and olives.

LETTUCE SALAD
(Ensalada de lechuga)

In Spain, the lettuce, a romaine type, is arranged on a large, flat plate, or on individual flat plates, and the leaves are usually served whole.

Sometimes the dressing is poured on the lettuce before it is served, and othertimes the lettuce is brought to the table without dressing, and each person pours his own oil and vinegar from the cruets on the table.

Arrange lettuce, sliced tomatoes, sliced onions, and olives on a large flat plate. Mix 2 parts olive oil to 1 part vinegar (see Salad Dressing, page 246), and pour it over the salad. Add the salt at the table.

GYPSY SALAD

> *cucumber*
> *green pepper*
> *onion*
> *tomato*
> *oil*
> *vinegar*
> *cinnamon*

Cut up all the vegetables into very small pieces. Pour on oil and vinegar plus a few drops of water. Add salt and cinammon, and toss.

STRING BEAN, TOMATO, AND POTATO SALAD

Up to and including step 5 may be made hours earlier and placed covered in the refrigerator.

> *4 small potatoes*
> *1/4 lb. raw string beans (frozen or canned string beans are not good to use in this recipe)*

4 tomatoes
1 dozen olives
4 anchovies
1 tbsp. capers
1 tbsp. fresh parsley, finely chopped

Dressing:
6 tbsp. olive oil
2 tbsp. vinegar
1 tbsp. lemon juice
   salt and pepper to taste

1. Cook potatoes and string beans separately in slightly salted water.

2. Peel potatoes while hot and let them cool. Cut the potatoes into cubes, and cut the string beans into small pieces.

3. Cut the tomatoes into quarters, each anchovy in half, and each olive in half.

4. In a flat serving dish, arrange tomatoes and potatoes radiating in a line from the center of the dish like spokes in a wheel.

5. Arrange the string beans in the vacant places.

6. Place the anchovies and the olives on top of the tomatoes and potatoes.

7. Sprinkle with capers.

8. Prepare the dressing and pour it over the salad at serving time. More oil and vinegar may be used if desired. Use a mixture of 2 parts oil to 1 part vinegar.

TOMATO AND GREEN PEPPER SALAD

green peppers
tomatoes
oil
vinegar
salt

1. Put the tomatoes under hot water so that the skin may be peeled. Then peel and slice.

2. Put the peppers under the broiler until the skin blisters. Remove, cool, and peel. Discard seeds. Cut into strips.

3. Blend oil, vinegar, and salt to make a dressing, arrange the tomatoes and peppers on a plate and pour on the dressing.

TOMATO SALAD
(Ensalada de tomate)

>2 tomatoes
>2 hard-boiled eggs
>1 green pepper
>1 onion
>1 sprig fresh parsley
>salt and pepper

1. Chop parsley and onion very finely.

2. Slice tomatoes, pepper and eggs. Arrange on a platter.

3. Sprinkle parsley and onion over the tomatoes, pepper and eggs.

4. Mix 4 tbsp. oil with 2 tbsp. vinegar and pour over the salad.

5. Set in the refrigerator for one half hour to chill.

6. Just before serving, sprinkle with salt and pepper.

POTATO SALAD
(Patatas en salpicón)

This salad may be made hours earlier and stored in the refrigerator. It serves 4 people.

>1/2 cup olive oil
>1/4 cup vinegar
>(mayonnaise may be substituted for oil and vinegar)

4 cooked, peeled potatoes
1 chopped green pepper
1 finely chopped onion
1 finely chopped sprig fresh parsley
1 cooked and chopped carrot
1 1/2 tbsp. cooked green peas
1 tbsp. cooked kidney beans (optional)
1 can sardines (optional)
1 tomato
1 lemon
lettuce
1 hard-boiled egg

1. Cook potatoes and carrot together. (The vegetables should be firm, so do not overcook.) Cook egg.

2. Cut cooked potatoes into small cubes, and prepare the rest of the vegetables.

3. Place the potatoes, green pepper, onion, parsley, carrot, peas, and kidney beans in a bowl. Mix the oil and vinegar and pour it over the vegetables. If this is not enough oil and vinegar, make another oil and vinegar mixture and add some more to the vegetables.

4. Place the potato salad on top of lettuce leaves, and decorate the plate with sardines, sliced tomato, quartered egg, and lemon slices.

CHOPPED EGG AND ONION SALAD

1 hard-boiled egg per person
1/2 onion per egg

1. Pour a small amount of oil on finely chopped onions, sprinkle with salt, and let it set for at least 15 minutes.

2. Hard-boil the eggs.

3. Mix the chopped hard-boiled eggs with the onions, add more oil if necessary, sprinkle with salt, and serve on lettuce leaves.

POTATO AND EGG SALAD

Arrange sliced boiled potatoes on top of lettuce. Place sliced hard-boiled eggs on the potatoes. Top with an oil and vinegar salad dressing or a vinagrette sauce, page 257. Serve cold.

POTATO AND ANCHOVY SALAD

Slice boiled potatoes and place on a plate. Mash anchovies and mix them with chopped green pepper. Place on each potato slice and serve with mayonnaise or vinagrette sauce, page 257.

BEET AND POTATO SALAD

Drain sliced canned beets and alternate them on the plate with sliced boiled potato. Mix an oil and vinegar dressing, and pour it over the vegetables.

POTATO AND ARTICHOKE HEART SALAD

Arrange a few slices of boiled potato on individual serving plates. Place a small amount of finely chopped onion on top of the potato. Rinse the canned artichoke hearts in hot water and slice them. Put the artichoke heart slices on top of the potatoes. Put a dab of mayonnaise on each one.

COOKED BEETS WITH HARD-BOILED EGG

Arrange sliced cooked beets (may be canned) on a plate and top with chopped hard-boiled eggs. Pour an oil and vinegar salad dressing on top and sprinkle with finely chopped parsley.

CAULIFLOWER, TOMATO, AND ANCHOVY SALAD

Separate the flowerettes of the cauliflower, and simmer them in slightly salted water for a few minutes. Do not let them get very soft.

When the cauliflower is done, arrange them in the center of the serving dish, place sliced tomatoes around the cauliflower, and rolled anchovies on top of the tomatoes.

Serve with mayonnaise or vinagrette sauce, page 257.

CAULIFLOWER SALAD

> *cauliflower cut into flowerettes or whole*
> *mayonnaise*
> *sliced tomato*
> *hard-boiled eggs*
> *olives*

1. Cook cauliflower in a small amount of slightly salted water until it is just about done. (It should not be very soft.) When done place it in the center of a serving plate and alternate sliced tomatoes and sliced hard-boiled eggs around it. Cover the cauliflower with mayonnaise and place olives on top.

SHRIMP IN A LETTUCE BLANKET

Chop cooked shrimp and mix with mayonnaise and mustard. Wrap them in soft lettuce leaves, and tuck in the ends.

SARDINE OR PERCH SALAD
(Ensalada de Sardinas)

This recipe serves 3 people.

It can be prepared several hours in advance.

> *1/4 cup olive oil*
> *1/4 cup wine vinegar (or a little less than a 1/4 cup)*
> *1 onion, chopped*
> *3/4 lb. raw sardines or perch (2 or 3 fish per person)*
> *· 1 green pepper, chopped*
> *coarse salt*

1. Heat enough olive oil in frying pan to cover bottom of pan. Sprinkle salt on pan and fry fish on both sides.

2. Remove from pan and place on a serving platter. (Bones may be left in or removed.)

3. Cover fish with chopped, raw onions, tomatoes, and green pepper.

4. Mix oil and vinegar and pour over fish. Place in refrigerator for about half an hour.

LIMA BEAN, STRINGBEAN, AND CARROT SALAD

> *raw lima beans (NOT dried)*
> *sliced carrots*
> *stringbeans cut lengthwise*
> *chopped green pepper*
> *1 clove mashed garlic*
> *1/2 cup oil (preferably olive oil)*
> *1/4 cup vinegar*
> *2 tbsp. fresh parsley*

1. Cook the stringbeans, carrots, and lima beans. Cool.

2. Mix the oil, vinegar, parsley, and garlic.

3. Put all the vegetables in a bowl, pour the sauce over them, and toss.

If you need more or less salad dressing, always use the proportions of half as much vinegar as oil.

Fish

Isabel did housework for us from time to time. She was a tall, strong person, somewhat heavy-set, with a manner that attracted many boyfriends. A free soul who didn't like to work as a sleep-in maid because it tied her down too much, she did day-work for a chosen few when she needed money. Isabel liked to make her own decisions, delighted in her freedom, and adored her three-year-old son.

Sometimes, when she wasn't working for us, she would show up unexpectedly in the afternoon to visit. At those times she'd take command of the kitchen, announce that she's going to cook dinner so that we'd have a well-cooked meal, and nobody ever contradicted her!

One day she came with a newspaper-wrapped bundle of seafood to prepare a paella. When Isabel started the preparations, I left the room because Isabel's kitchen became a disaster area when she cooked! She did everything in a big way, but most unusual was that everything she peeled was thrown onto the floor. I once asked her why she did that and she said it's because she wanted to separate the food from the garbage. As long as I wasn't in there, I didn't mind because she always washed down the whole kitchen —floors, walls, everything— after she finished cooking.

That day my mother was visiting us and wanted to watch Isabel prepare the paella. She didn't know her ways.

"It's best for us to leave the kitchen," I counseled. "She'll call us when she's done."

"I'll stay," my mother said. "I want to see how a paella is prepared."

A few minutes later my mother slid out of the kitchen with her finger in the air, bitten by a crab! She learned the hard way never to poke around in Isabel's kitchen.

TIPS ON PREPARING FISH

In order to fry fish well, it's important to have enough oil in the pan at just the right temperature.

If there isn't enough oil, the fish will burn and taste bitter. If the oil isn't hot enough, the fish will soften and come apart. If the oil is too hot, the fish will burn on the outside and be raw on the inside.

To test for the correct temperature, drop a cube of bread into the oil; it should brown in 60 seconds.

Serve fish immediately after frying.

To bake fish
Usually, the fish is put into the oven without liquid. It is normally coated with oil or butter and other seasonings according to the recipe.

Fish slices should be baked for about 10 minutes.

If the fish is being baked whole, make some slices in its back, and bake for about 15 to 20 minutes, according to the size of the fish.

To broil fish
Pre-heat the broiler. Place fish close to the heat. Dot with butter or coat with oil and seasoning.

To boil fish
Fish should be started in cold water and slowly brought to a boil so that the skin doesn't come off.

Boiled fish looks good served whole on top of lettuce on an oblong platter.

Decorate with parsley and serve with boiled potatoes and boiled carrots or beets.

Sauce for the fish should be served separately when the fish is presented with its skin on.

When the skin is peeled off or when the fish is cut into steaks, the sauce is served on the fish.

A long rectangular pot that has a perforated shelf to hold the fish is best for boiling. The fish is placed on the shelf, and the cold seasoned liquid is poured over the fish until it covers it. The pot is then covered while the fish is slowly cooked.

For white-meat fish such as sole, put one cup cold milk in the pot for every four cups cold water. Add salt and pepper, half a sliced, peeled lemon, and the fish. Slowly bring to a boil. When it boils, add a cup of cold water and remove pot from heat.

For fish such as salmon, hake, and trout, put 3/8 cup dry white wine in the pot for every four cups water. Add a carrot, a thinly sliced onion, half a bay leaf, a sprig parsley, a pinch ground pepper, and the fish. Slowly bring to a boil. If it's a small fish and weighs less than 2 pounds, remove pot from the heat. If the fish is larger, simmer slowly for about 15 minutes, no longer.

Decorations to place around fish serving platter.

SPINACH-SHRIMP MOLDS

1. Grease several small custard cups or tart shells. Blend chopped cooked, well-drained spinach with butter and salt to taste, and place into cups.

2. Place chopped cooked shrimp on top.

3. Blend one beaten egg with one tablespoon milk and pour it on top of the spinach. Place the custard cups onto a pan of water and bake in a 350 degree oven until the egg sets.

4. When cool, remove from molds and place around fish. Serve with a dish of mayonnaise or vinagrette sauce, page 257.

WHIPPED POTATO-CLAM MOLD

1. Grease several small custard cups or tart shells. Prepare whipped potatoes, and place into cups.

2. Place canned chopped clams on top.

3. Place whipped potato on top of clams.

4. Blend one beaten egg with one tablespoon milk or clam juice (if the clam juice is tasty), and pour it on top.

5. Bake in a 350 degree oven until the egg sets.

6. When cool, remove from molds and place around fish.

HARD-BOILED EGGS FILLED WITH ANCHOVIES

Cut hard-boiled eggs in half lengthwise. Remove yolk and mash with anchovies and chopped olives. Mix with mayonnaise. Fill egg whites in a mound and place around dish.

FISH COURT BOULLION

> *1 1/2 cups water*
> *large fish head and bones*
> *pinch thyme*
> *1/2 bay leaf (or 1/8 tsp. dried leaves)*
> *1 leek or onion*
> *1 carrot*
> *1 small piece celery*

1. Cook the above ingredients until carrot and fish are tender.

2. Strain liquid and use according to recipe.

DEEP-FRY BATTER

Vegetables, fish, or seafood, cut into bite-size pieces, may be dipped and fried. This batter puffs up when fried and is delicious. Even people who don't like vegetables will like them cooked this way.

Food should be cold and dry when dipped into the batter. Place on a paper towel to drain after frying.

BATTER: Makes one cup batter.

1/2 cup flour
3 tbsp. water
1 egg, separated
salt and pepper

1. Mix flour, salt and pepper in a bowl. Make an indentation in the center, place the egg yolk and water in it, and blend until a batter is formed.

2. Beat the egg white until it forms a stiff peak. Fold it into the batter with as few strokes as possible.

3. Dip dry food into batter and fry immediately on high heat until browned.

VEGETABLES TO DEEP-FRY:

> *onions = Slice. Dip into batter raw.*
> *carrots = Cut into small pieces. Cook first, cool, and dry.*
> *asparagus = Cut into 2-inch pieces. Cook or use canned, dry first.*
> *mushrooms = Separate cap and stem. Fry raw.*
> *cauliflower = Separate flowerets. Fry raw.*
> *broccoli = Cut the flowerets and stems into bite-size pieces. Peel the stems. Fry raw.*

FISH AND SEAFOOD TO DEEP-FRY:

> *shrimp = Remove shells, clean shrimp, and dip raw into batter.*
> *oysters = Dip raw oysters into flour before dipping into batter.*
> *fish = Cut into bite-size pieces. Dip into batter raw.*

FRIED FISH

Whole small fish or medium-size pieces of fish filets can be used.

Test the oil by dropping a bread cube into it. If it browns in 60 seconds, the oil is hot enough for frying.

See Deep-fry batter recipe, page 156, if a thicker coating is desired. Also, see Tips on preparing fish, page 154.

fish
flour
beaten egg
salt and pepper

STYLE 1

1. Wash and dry fish.

2. Salt, dip into flour, then into egg.

3. Fry in deep hot oil until brown on both sides. Drain on absorbant paper.

STYLE 2

1. Dip fish into cold milk and drain.

2. Dip into flour that has been seasoned with salt and pepper.

3. Fry in about a half inch oil. Drain on absorbant paper.

STYLE 3

1. Dip fish into milk and drain.

2. Dip into fine bread crumbs that has been seasoned with salt and pepper, then into lightly beaten egg.

3. Fry in a half-inch oil. Drain on absorbant paper.

FRIED SMELTS ANDALUCIA STYLE
(Boquerones Andaluz)

Smelts are not the fish called "boquerones." However, I don't think that these can be found in the United States, so smelts is a fairly good substitute for them.

This dish may be prepared hours before serving, and then re-heated in the oven.

> *smelts*
> *milk*
> *flour*
> *salt*
> *oil for deep frying*

1. When you bring the fish home from the market, sprinkle them with lemon juice and salt.

2. Before cooking, clean fish by removing head and stomach, wash fish and drain.

3. Place fish in bowl and cover with milk. Let soak for 10 minutes.

4. Remove from milk, drain, dip into salted-to-taste flour, and, holding 3 fish together by their tails, drop into hot oil for deep frying. Do not crowd too many fish into pot. Fry until brown.

FRIED TROUT

Sprinkle salt on the inside and outside of the washed trout, and let it set in the refrigerator for at least an hour. When it is ready to cook, dry it with a paper towel, dip it in slightly salted flour, and fry it in hot butter on one side until it gets brown, and then on the other side.

BAKED TROUT

Mix together mashed garlic, lemon juice, and oil. Coat trout with it, sprinkle outside and inside of trout with salt, and let it set in the refrigerator for at least an hour. After this time, place it on a greased baking dish, and bake in a 400 degree oven for a half hour or so, depending on size of trout. Be careful not to overcook it.

Cod fish is so popular in Spain that young children taunt each other with this song when they fight, saying in effect, "Nah, nah, you can't hurt me."

No me mates con tomates,
Mátame con bacalao.
No me remojes en el agua,
Que me gusta ser sala'o.

Dont's kill me with tomatoes,
Kill me with cod.
Don't wet me with water,
Because I like to be salty.

DRIED SALT COD IN ITS OWN SAUCE
(Bacalao al pil-pil)

A very famous dish that many people don't know how to prepare is Cod fish al pil-pil. The sauce is extracted in a most unusual way, by shaking the pan! It seems that moving the skin of the fish in the hot oil on the surface of the pan is what makes a thick juice emerge and produce this sauce which looks like mayonnaise.

Once you start shaking the pan, don't stop until you serve the fish.

This recipe takes endurance!

2 1/2 cups or 1 lb. dry salt cod
2 cups oil
4 cloves sliced garlic
pinch cayenne

Soak the cod in cold water for about 24 to 26 hours. Change the water several times.

1. Discard the water in which the cod was soaked. Wash the cod very well and cut it into serving pieces. Rinse again.

2. Put the cod in a pot of water and heat it slowly without letting it come to a boil. When it starts forming foam on the water, remove the cod and dry it.

3. Heat oil in a pan, add the garlic, and brown. Remove from the pan and save.

4. Put the cod into the same pan of hot oil with the SKIN SIDE ON THE PAN, remove pan from heat, and shake the pan from side to side without stopping so that it moves the fish. (This movement of the skin of the fish on the pan extracts the gelatin and makes the sauce.) Keep moving the pan for 10 to 15 minutes without stopping. When the sauce appears to look like a loose mayonnaise, the sauce is done.

5. When the sauce is done, and while still shaking the pan, add the browned garlic and cayenne, and put the pan on the heat again. Keep moving it from side to side until it gets hot enough. Serve immediately.

DRIED SALT-COD WITH PEPPERS AND TOMATOES
(Bacalao a la Riojana)

> *1 lb. dried salt-cod, cut into pieces*
> *3-inch piece chorizo or one sweet Italian sausage*
> *1 chopped onion*
> *1 medium-size can tomatoes, drained and chopped*
> *1 green pepper*

Cook this dish in a pot that can be brought to the table.

Soak the cod for 24 to 26 hours before preparing this recipe. Change the water from time to time. Rinse the cod well before using. Serves 4.

1. Put the green pepper under the broiler until the skin blisters. Remove, cool, and peel. Remove seeds. Slice into wide strips.

2. Fry the sausage until done and set aside. Pour off excess fat, sauté the onion until tender, and remove from pan.

3. Put the cod in the pan, SKIN SIDE DOWN, and shake the pan for 10 minutes without stopping until a mayonnaise-like sauce is formed. (Moving the fish on its skin extracts a gelatin and makes the sauce.)

4. When this is done, mix the tomatoes and onions together and pour over the cod. Cover and simmer for about a half hour.

5. After this time, place the strips of pepper on top as if they were spokes of a wheel, and the sausage in-between. Simmer covered for another half hour, and serve hot in the same pot.

SPICY DRIED SALT-COD IN TOMATO SAUCE
(Bacalao a la Vizcaina)

> 1 lb. dried salt-cod
> 1/2 tsp. crushed red pepper
> 2 cloves sliced garlic
> 2 strips bacon
> 2 chopped onions
> 1 medium-size can tomatoes, drained and chopped
> flour

Have all the ingredients ready before starting to cook because the pan of cod needs to be shaken constantly and everything should be ready to use.

Soak the cod for 24 to 26 hours. Change the water several times, then rinse well before using.

1. Bring one cup water to a boil, add the crushed peppers, and remove from heat. Set aside.

2. Place the cod in a pot of cold water and slowly heat until a foam appears. Do not let it boil. Remove the cod from the water and cool.

3. Dry the cod, cut into serving pieces, and DIP ONLY THE MEAT SIDE OF THE FISH IN FLOUR (not the skin), and set aside.

4. Fry the garlic in oil and remove to a plate. Fry the bacon, pour off excess fat, and sauté the onion until tender. Remove frompan.

5. Place the cod in the pan, skin side down, and shake the pan constantly for 10 minutes over low heat until a mayonnaise-like sauce appears. (Moving the fish on its skin extracts a gelatin and makes a sauce.)

6. After this time, add the tomatoes, garlic, onions, and bacon.

7. Add the strained water from the peppers. Simmer for an hour over low heat.

CLAMS AND RICE

Serves 4.

> *2 lbs. clams*
> *1 chopped onion*
> *3/4 cup rice*
> *1 clove chopped garlic*
> *1 clove mashed garlic*
> *1 tbsp. chopped fresh parsley or 1/4 tsp. dried parsley*
> *1/2 bay leaf*
> *a pinch saffron (optional)*
> *oil*

1. Wash the clams very well to remove as much sand as possible. Steam them in 4 1/2 cups slightly salted water with a sprig of fresh parsley and the bay leaf, until their shells open. Remove them from the liquid, and when cool, remove them from their shells. Rinse the clams in their broth to clean them some more, then pour the broth carefully into another pot to remove the sand.

2. Heat oil in a pot large enough to hold the soup later on and sauté the onion until tender. Add the chopped garlic and brown. Stir in the

rice. Add the strained clam broth and the chopped parsley. Add salt to taste if necessary.

3. Mix the mashed garlic clove with the ground saffron and add it to the soup. Simmer until rice is done.

4. When the rice is done, add the clams to the soup and simmer for five minutes. Serve hot.

FISH PISTO

> 4 finely chopped green peppers
> 4 finely chopped tomatoes, either fresh or canned
> 1 1/2 pounds fish filets, cut into small pieces
> oil, preferably olive oil
> 2 tbsp. fresh chopped parsley or 1/2 tsp. dried parsley
> 2 cloves finely chopped garlic
> salt and pepper
> 1 bay leaf

1. Mix together peppers, tomatoes, onions, parsley, and garlic. Add salt and pepper.

2. Grease a baking dish and place a layer of the vegetables in it, then a layer of the fish on top of the vegetables. Sprinkle with oil, salt and pepper. Place another layer of vegetables on top, and sprinkle with more oil. Place pieces of bay leaf around the dish, cover and place into a 350 degree oven and bake until the vegetables are tender.

FISH PUDDING

Señora Mallart's husband was in the State Department and they were being sent to the United States for duty. I helped Cuca polish up her English and one of her gifts to me was this recipe.

It may be served either hot or cold; however, the sauce should always be hot.

The pudding may be made the day before serving.

Serves 8.

> 2 lbs. haddock or similar fish
> 2 large onions
> 1 can tomato paste
> 1 cup soft bread crumbs or bread for stuffing
> 2 eggs
> 1 cup dry white wine
> 1 clove finely chopped garlic
>   salt and pepper
>   oil
> 1 bay leaf
> 1/4 tsp. ground nutmeg
>   pinch saffron (optional)
>   6 to 8 shrimp for decoration

PUDDING

1. Put 4 cups water in a pot, add the wine, a half onion, the bay leaf, salt and pepper, and the fish. Slowly bring to a boil, lower heat and simmer for 15 minutes, no longer.

2. Finely chop the remaining onions and fry them and the garlic in oil. Remove pan from heat.

3. Cool fish and flake.

4. Moisten the bread with 1/2 cup fish broth so that it's thoroughly wet, press out excess liquid, and add it to the onions and garlic in the pan. Remove from heat.

5. Blend in one teaspoon tomato paste, a pinch saffron, nutmeg, two eggs, salt and pepper, and the flaked fish.

6. Coat a tube pan (a round mold that has a hole in the center) with butter and pour in the fish mixture. Bake in a 350 degree oven for about 30 minutes.

Remove it from the mold when cold and place on a serving dish. At serving time, pour the hot sauce on top and let it drip down center of mold.

Decorate with unshelled shrimp.

SAUCE

> *the remainder of the tomato paste*
> *1 finely chopped onion*
> *1 finely chopped clove garlic*
> *1/2 bay leaf*
> *a small amount oil*
> *1 lb. mussels*
> *1/2 lb. cooked, peeled shrimp*

1. Fry onion and garlic in a small amount of oil.

2. Dilute the tomato paste in the fish broth and add it to the pan. Add the bay leaf, salt and pepper, and simmer for 30 minutes.

3. Wash the mussels well and steam them in a small amount of slightly salted water for about 5 minutes, or until their shells open. (Throw away any that did not open.)

4. Add the mussels and shrimp to the sauce and simmer for about three minutes. Use hot.

"That's not a bug in the paella; it's a type of crab!"

PAELLA, STYLE 1

Paella has become one of the most well-known recipes of Spain. It is basically a rice dish which lends itself to many variations, and each region of Spain prepares it differently. In the southern area, for example, you might find a paella made with rabbit meat.

The following paella recipe is Madrid style. It was given to me by Dativo Pérez who was a chef in the Corral de la Morería, a famous restaurant in Madrid. Now he is a teacher in a large chef's school in Castellana de la Playa.

The paella is always served at the table in the pan in which it is cooked, usually a special round paella pan. If the food is removed from the pan to another serving dish, it becomes a mess, and cannot be re-arranged again.

The rice in the paella is always served slightly firm, so be careful not to overcook it. Watch the pot while it's cooking to make sure that the rice around the rim of the pot is cooking also.

Use a 12-inch skillet which distributes heat well, and has a cover.

> *1 dozen raw clams or mussels, well washed*
> *olive oil*
> *1 1/2 frying chickens, cut into eighths*
> *1/2 lb. tender pork, cut into small cubes*
> *1 large onion, chopped*
> *1/4 tsp. paprika*
> *1/2 cup tomato, peeled and chopped (fresh or canned)*
> *salt*
> *2 cloves garlic*
> *2 cups uncooked rice (NOT minute rice)*
> *1/4 lb. raw shrimp, shells removed*
> *1/8 tsp. saffron, mashed and mixed with 1 tbsp. water*
> *1 tbsp. fresh parsley, chopped, or 1/4 tsp. dried parsley*
> *1 tbsp. lemon juice*
> *1 cooked lobster in the shell, cut into pieces*
> *6 artichoke hearts, cooked (either frozen or canned)*
> *2 red pimientos, (either fresh and sautéed, or canned) cut into strips*
> *6 canned asparagus spears*
> *1/4 cup cooked peas (optional)*

1. If you are using mussels, cook them separately in a small amount of slightly salted water until the shells open. Remove them from the water, leave them in their shells, and set them aside for later use.

2. Prepare all the ingredients, chopping them or cutting them according to the directions and set them on a plate ready for use. Set the last 5 ingredients on a separate plate because they will be used last.

3. In a pan other than the paella pan, heat 1/3 cup oil, and brown the chicken, pork, and onion.

4. Add the paprika and the tomato, and stir it all together. Simmer for 10 to 15 minutes on low heat. Remove from heat and set aside.

5. In another pot, bring 4 cups water to a boil for later use in step 11.

6. Meanwhile, rinse rice and let it drain in a colander.

7. Mix one mashed garlic clove, chopped parsley, lemon juice, and 1/2 tsp. salt and set it aside for later use.

8. In paella pan, heat 1/3 cup oil, add one chopped garlic clove, and brown slightly.

9. Add rice, stir, and fry for 5 minutes.

10. Add meat and tomato mixture from step 4. Add the whole mixture all at once.

11. Add saffron to the 4 cups boiled water from step 5, and add the water to the rice mixture. Stir it in with a fork so that the meat mixture is mixed in with the rice. Cook it on high heat until it starts to boil.

12. When it boils, lower heat and arrange the following on top of the rice mixture:

A. Place the asparagus on the paella as if they were spokes from the hub of a wheel.

B. Place the pimiento strips in-between the asparagus.

C. Place the lobster, shrimp, artichokes, and raw clams (or cooked mussels) in-between the asparagus and pimiento.

13. Sprinkle the parsley mixture from step 7 over the whole paella.

14. Raise the heat, cover the paella, and cook for 15 minutes until rice is done. Or, instead of finishing the paella on top of the stove, remove paella pan from heat, and place uncovered into a hot oven for 15 minutes.

15. Sprinkle peas over top of paella, remove from heat, and let paella set for 5 minutes before serving it in the same pot in which it was cooked.

PAELLA, STYLE II

This paella is a variation of the first one given, and is faster to prepare. You may use any seafood you like, and eliminate those you do not want.

Use a skillet which distributes heat well, one that is about twelve inches in diameter and has a cover. Serve the paella in the pan in which it is made.

This recipe serves 6 people.

1/2 Lb. raw clams
3 raw crabs, or one can crab meat
1/2 lb. raw shrimp, shells removed
1 lobster, cooked and cut into pieces
2 medium-sized raw squid, cut into small pieces
1/2 lb. mussels
1/2 cup oil, preferably olive oil
1 1/2 frying chickens cut into small pieces, or any chicken parts desired
1 large onion, finely chopped

1 clove garlic, mashed
1 tbsp. fresh parsley, chopped, or 1/4 tsp. dried parsley
3 cups uncooked rice, rinsed and drained (NOT minute rice)
2 pinches saffron, mashed or ground with a mortar and pestle
6 cups water
1 tsp. salt

decoration:
6 strips canned pimiento and 6 black olives

1. Wash all seafood well. Steam mussels in a small amount of slightly salted water to which a bay leaf has been added, until shells open. When mussel shells open, remove pan from heat and set aside.

2. Heat oil in a large, heavy skillet in which the paella will be cooked.

3. When oil is hot enough, brown chicken, onion, and garlic.

4. When chicken, onion, and garlic are browned, add squid, rice, and parsley. Brown for a minute.

5. Add saffron and salt to the 6 cups water, and add to skillet.

6. When liquid comes to a boil, lower heat and add the clams, crabs, shrimp, and lobster in a design, along with the chicken, so that it creates a portion for each person which can be seen easily when it's served at the table. In other words, place the ingredients on the rice instead of mixing them in.

7. Cook the paella covered for 15 to 20 minutes. Be careful not to cook it longer or the seafood will be tough and the rice will get too soft. Paella rice should be on the firm side.

8. When this is done cooking, remove it from the heat and let the skillet set, covered, for 5 minutes. (It's important for it to set for at least 5 minutes before you serve it.)

9. Arrange pimiento, olives, and mussels in a design on the paella, and bring the paella to the table in the skillet in which it was cooked.

GRILLED FRESH SARDINES OR PERCH
(Sardinas a la Parrilla)

In some parts of Portugal, and in Portugalete (also called Santurce), Spain, the piquant smell of charcoal and grilled sardines fills the street air during mealtime.

Some restaurants grill the sardines right outside their doors instead of in their kitchens, and then bring the fish in to the customers.

One orders grilled sardines by the half dozen. Add to that salad, bread, and wine, and your meal is complete, with black coffee, (café solo) at the end.

The sardines from Santurce are so good, that the people made up a song about them:

Sardinas frescas!
Mis sardinitas,
Que ricas son!
Son de Santurce
Las traigo yo.

Fresh sardines!
My little sardines,
How delicious they are!
They're from Santurce
I'm the one who's bringing them.

prepare 2 or 3 fish per person

1. Wash fish and remove head and insides if you care to. The head and insides are not removed in Portugal or Spain. When the heads become golden brown, they are crisp and crusty and delicious to eat.

2. Spread oil on the grill or griddle, and let it get hot.

3. Salt the fresh fish to taste.

4. Place them on the hot griddle, lower heat to medium and let them get well browned, first on one side and then on the other.

GALICIAN FISH AND SEAFOOD PIE
(Empanada Gallega de Mariscos)

Serves 4 to 6.

> *pie dough style 1 or style 2, page 279, or 2 cans refrigerator*
> *onion roll dough*
> 1/2 lb. mussels (optional)
> 1/2 lb. clams
> 1/2 lb. shrimp
> 1/2 lb. scallops
> 2 cod fish filets
> 4 medium onions
> 1/2 cup olive oil
> 1 1/2 cups canned tomatoes, drained
> lemon juice
> 2 bay leaves
> thyme
> 1 egg yolk

1. Make empanada dough and set aside.

2. Wash the mussels and clams and steam them with a bay leaf in a small amount of slightly salted water until the shells open. Remove the meat from the shells and rinse each piece in the liquid to remove any sand. Place on plate without the liquid and set aside.

3. Remove shrimp shells, de-bone fish and cut fish and scallops into pieces.

4. Sauté shrimp, fish, and scallops in oil until done. Do not overcook. Set aside.

5. In the same pan, sauté chopped onions in 1/2 cup oil. When they are transparent, add tomatoes, bay leaf, pinch hot pepper, salt to taste, and thyme. Cover and simmer 15 minutes.

6. Roll out dough and line pie plate with half the dough. If refrigerator roll dough is used, pinch edges of each piece together to form one whole piece.

7. Pour sauce from step 5 onto dough in pie plate, arrange fish and seafood over sauce, sprinkle liberally with lemon juice, and pour 1/2 cup oil over all ingredients.

8. Top pie plate with the rest of the dough, prick center of dough with a fork, and coat dough with the yolk of an egg. Bake for 15 minutes, until dough is done, in a 400 degree oven.

FISH BASQUE STYLE
(Merluza a la Vasca)

This dish is made of the hake fish, which is called "merluza" in Spanish. It is one of the best and most popular fish dishes in Spain. The final result looks beautiful and elegant, and it is simple to prepare. Thick slices of cod fish may be substituted for the hake.

This recipe serves six people.

Heat the oven to 400 degrees. Up to and including step 4 may be prepared ahead of time and refrigerated.

> *6 thick slices of hake fish steaks (or cod)*
> *flour*
> *oil*
> **green sauce, page** *258*
> *2 hard-boiled eggs, sliced into 6 slices*
> *6 asparagus spears*
> *18 small raw steamer clams, well washed, with the shells on*
> *18 small raw shrimp, shells removed*
> *1/2 cup cooked peas*
> *1/4 cup dry white wine*
> *1 tbsp. lemon juice*

1. Prepare the green sauce.

2. Salt fish to taste and dip into flour. Shake off excess flour.

3. Heat oil in pan and brown fish on both sides. Place on slightly greased baking pan.

4. On top of each slice of fish place 1 slice hard-boiled egg. Between each piece of fish place 1 asparagus spear. Divide clams and shrimp to equal 3 per person and place on and around fish

5. Pour green sauce on top of fish.

6. Sprinkle wine over fish.

7. Sprinkle lemon juice over fish.

8. Bake in oven for 10 minutes, or until fish is done, and serve immediately.

FISH FILET SAUTE

> *fish filets, one per person*
> *lemon juice*
> *butter*
> *bread crumbs*

1. Sauté fish in butter, then place on baking pan.

2. Sprinkle with lemon juice, salt, and bread crumbs.

3. Place under broiler to brown, about 5 minutes. Serve immediately.

FILET OF SOLE IN WINE SAUCE
(Lenguado con crema y vino)

This recipe serves 4 people.

Up to and including step 10 may be prepared about an hour before serving.

> 4 filets of sole
> 1 shallot or onion, chopped
> 1 tbsp. lemon juice

1 tbsp. dry white wine, preferably Chablis
1 1/2 cups fish boullion, page 156, or water
2 tbsp. flour
3 egg yolks
butter

1. Butter baking dish.

2. Tuck ends of filet under to meet in center and place on baking dish.

3. Sprinkle fish with salt, shallots, lemon juice, wine, and pieces of butter.

4. Bake in oven for 10 minutes, remove fish from pan and set aside.

5. Remove any fish bones from the pan, add flour and stir it into the fish drippings.

6. Add boullion, little by little, and stir it in to make a thick sauce. Do not add all the boullion if sauce is getting too thin.

Stir sauce while simmering it in pan for about 10 minutes.

7. Beat egg yolks with one teaspoon water.

8. Place in top of double boiler, but DO NOT let water in double boiler come to a boil. Beat yolks with whisk until they are thick, but not set. Remove from heat.

9. Pour fish sauce from pan through sieve and into yolks in double boiler, stir it in.

10. Place fish back on baking pan, and pour sauce over fish.

11. Brown lightly in oven under broiler.

FILET OF SOLE AU GRATIN
(Lenguado au Gratin)

This recipe serves 4 people. Up to and including step 8 may be completed about an hour before serving.

> 4 fish filets of sole, one per person
> 1 shallot or onion, chopped
> 1 tbsp. lemon juice
> 2 tbsp. flour
> butter
> 1/4 cup milk
> grated cheese

1. Butter baking dish.

2. Tuck ends of filet under to meet in center and place on baking dish.

3. Sprinkle fish with salt to taste, shallots, lemon juice, wine, and pieces of butter. Bake in 400 degree oven for 10 minutes.

4. Take fish off pan and set aside.

5. Remove fish bones, if any, from pan and stir in flour to the fish drippings on pan.

6. Slowly add milk to the flour and drippings. Pour this sauce into a saucepan, and simmer, stirring constantly, until sauce is thick.

7. Add 1 tbsp. grated cheese, stir it in and remove sauce from heat.

8. Return fish to pan, pour sauce over fish, and sprinkle more grated cheese on fish.

9. Brown in oven under broiler for about 5 minutes, until top is light brown.

Serve immediately.

FISH FILET WITH BECHAMEL SAUCE
(Filetes de Pescado con Besamel)

This recipe serves 6 people. Up to and including step 4 may be completed an hour or so before eating. The bechamel sauce may be prepared the day before.

> *6 slices fish filets*
> *bechamel sauce, page 253*
> *grated cheese*
> *lemon juice*
> *butter*
> *lemon wedges*

1. Prepare bechamel sauce.

2. Sauté fish in butter. Sprinkle with lemon juice, and salt to taste.

3. Place in casserole dish and cover with bechamel sauce.

4. Sprinkle with cheese.

5. Place under broiler and brown for 5 minutes. (Watch carefully that the cheese doesn't burn.)

Serve with lemon wedges.

BAKED FISH AND POTATO CHIPS
(Pescado asado con patatas)

> *1 fish for baking*
> *1 clove garlic*
> *1 tbsp. fresh parsley or 1/4 tsp. dried parsley*
> *2 slices lemon*
> *about 2 tbsp. lemon juice*
> *2 small cherry tomatoes for eyes of fish (if you serve the fish with head)*
> *1 small onion for mouth of fish (if you serve fish with head)*
> *oil*
> *1 potato per person*

1. Rinse fish, remove eyes (or have fishman remove eyes), and cut 4 slits on one side of fish to hold lemon slices. Leave fish whole.

2. Chop garlic and parsley, and mix them together.

3. Cut each lemon slice in half and trim off rind.

4. Paint fish with oil and lemon juice, and place on baking pan.

5. Into each slit in fish place some chopped garlic and parsley and half slice lemon.

6. Place the cherry tomatoes into the eyes of the fish, and the onion into the mouth of the fish.

7. Peel raw potatoes, slice very thin, and place them on the same pan as fish. Pour oil over potatoes, and sprinkle fish and potatoes with salt.

8. Place pan into hot oven, 400 degrees, and bake until fish is done, about one hour.

STUFFED FISH
(Pescado relleno)

1 whole fish or center cut of large fish, center cut should be at
  least 6 inches long
1/4 lb. shrimp, shelled and cut up
1/4 lb. of any white meat fish, de-boned and cut up
  2 hard-boiled eggs
  6 black olives, pits removed, and olives sliced
  1 tbsp. cognac
  pinch dried parsley or fresh parsley, cut up
1/2 onion, chopped
  1 tbsp. flour
  1 tbsp. butter
  1 tomato, chopped
  1 clove garlic, chopped

1. Lightly salt fish on the outside and inside, and set aside.

2. Sauté onion and garlic in butter. Add the small pieces of fish, shrimp, and salt to taste. Sauté for 5 minutes.

3. Add cognac and stir it in. Stir in tomato and parsley, then stir in flour. Add the hard-boiled eggs and olives. Simmer for 10 minutes, then remove from heat.

4. Fill the fish with the above mixture, close the opening by sewing it together. Coat the fish with butter or oil and place it on a shallow, greased baking pan with a bay leaf. Bake, covered, in a 400 degree oven for 20 to 30 minutes.

When fish is done, remove from oven and let it set on baking pan for about 5 or 10 minutes before serving so that it won't fall apart when you cut it.

STUFFED FISH BELLA VISTA

Bella vista means "beautiful sight," and the following recipe provides your baked fish with a coating which makes it a sight of beauty and in addition, enhances its flavor.

This recipe should be prepared the day before serving, and served cold.

Bake fish long before you prepare the coating so that fish may be cold enough to coat.

> *stuffed fish recipe, page 179*
> *3 envelopes unflavored gelatin*
> *1 cup mayonnaise*
> *2 cups water*
> *green food coloring*

decorations:

> *black olives or truffles*
> *pimientos*
> *leek greens or onion greens*

1. Sprinkle gelatin on 1/4 cup cold water, dissolving it.

2. Boil the remainder of the water and add it to the gelatin.

3. Measure 1/4 cup of the prepared gelatin and place it in a separate bowl. LET IT COOL.

4. Add 1/2 cup mayonnaise to the 1/4 cup gelatin from step 3 and blend well. Let it cool until it's thick enough for coating, but not set firmly. It should still be liquid.

5. Set COLD fish on a dish. (Not the serving dish.)

6. Remove protruding bones so that fish is smooth.

7. Coat fish with a tablespoon, using the mayonaise-gelatin mixture. Coat ONLY the top side of the fish. Let set until firm.

8. When the mayonnaise-gelatin mixture on the fish is firm, melt the remainder of the clear gelatin (from step 2), and coat the fish again with it to give the fish a gloss.

To decorate the platter on which fish will be served:

1. Add a few drops green food coloring to the remaining melted gelatin and pour it onto the platter on which fish will be served. Let harden.

2. When the gelatin is firm and hard, set decorated fish on it.

Blanch leek greens (or onion greens) and cut them and the black olives and pimientos into designs for the top of the fish.

FISH IN ASPIC

A fish mold and the sauce makes this a very pretty, tasty white dish. Either mayonnaise or bechamel sauce may be used.

> *1 lb. fish filets*
> *1/2 onion*
> *1/2 stalk celery*
> *a sprig parsley*
> *1 tbsp. unflavored gelatin*
> *3/4 cup mayonnaise or bechamel sauce*

1. Sauté the onion in a small amount of oil, then add two cups water, parsley, celery, and salt to taste. Simmer for about 10 minutes.

2. Add the fish, let simmer for a minute, then remove pot from heat and let the fish cool in the liquid.

3. If you're using bechamel sauce, prepare it by heating 4 tablespoons oil in a pan, then blend in 2 tablespoons flour. Stir in 1 cup warm milk little by little until it's blended. Continue stirring constantly until a sauce is formed. Add salt to taste.

4. Prepare the gelatin using 1/4 cup cold strained fish liquid instead of the water called for on the gelatin package. Soften the gelatin in the cold fish liquid in the top of a double boiler. Place over boiling water and stir until the gelatin is dissolved.

5. Cut the fish into small pieces.

6. Stir the cooled gelatin into the mayonnaise or the bechamel sauce, add the fish, and pour into a fish mold or individual serving dishes that have been rinsed in cold water. Place in the refrigerator to chill.

When the mold is half-way set, cut up pitted black olives and decorate the top.

SALMON PIE OR TARTS

This recipe serves 4 to 6 people. It may be prepared in advance.

> *1 can salmon*
> *1/2 onion, sliced*

1/2 lb. shrimp
   bechamel sauce, page 253
   whipped potatoes, enough to cover bottom of an 8-inch pie
   plate, plus decoration around plate
   grated cheese
   yolk of one egg
   1 tbsp. lemon juice

1. Prepare whipped potatoes.

2. Boil 2 cups water and add sliced onion, salt and pepper to taste, and 1/4 of a bay leaf. Simmer for 5 minutes.

3. Add washed shrimp with shells on, and simmer for 5 more minutes. Remove shrimp. (Liquid may be discarded or saved for shrimp shell soup, page 71.)

4. Peel shrimp, and mix shrimp with salmon. Add lemon juice and grated onion, mix and set aside.

5. Prepare bechamel sauce, and add yolk of one egg to sauce when finished.

6. Line pie plate with whipped potatoes.

7. Add shrimp and salmon mixture to bechamel sauce, and fill pie plate.

8. Decorate border with whipped potatoes using pastry tube.

9. Sprinkle with grated cheese and place into hot oven to brown.

STUFFED SQUID

This recipe serves 4 people. It may be prepared the day before.

4 baby squid, cleaned, peeled, and the bodies left whole.
   2 tbsp. oil
1/2 onion, finely chopped
   1 tbsp. fresh parsley, finely chopped

1/2 clove garlic, mashed
2-inch piece of celery, chopped
1/2 tsp. cognac
1/2 cup cooked rice or mashed potatoes
toothpicks
Spanish tomato sauce, page 247, or 1 can mushroom soup plus
1/4 cup dry white wine

1. Heat oil and sauté onion, parsley, celery, garlic, chopped legs of squid, and cognac until squid is tender.

2. Add cooked rice and mix it all together. Remove from heat.

3. Stuff raw squid with mixture, and secure each squid with a toothpick.

4. Prepare tomato sauce, add squid to sauce, and simmer for about a half hour.

SQUID IN BLACK SAUCE
(Calamares en su tinta)

1 lb. small squid. Leave ink sacs, which are behind eye-balls, intact
5 tbsp. olive oil
3 medium onions, chopped
1 clove garlic, chopped
2 tbsp. fresh parsley, chopped or 1/4 tsp. dried parsley
3 large tomatoes
1 tbsp. flour (toast flour in 375 degree oven until brown)
1 tsp. cooked rice per squid, or a total of 3/4 cup rice
1 tbsp. pine nuts, toasted in frying pan with a little oil
toothpicks for securing squid

1. Clean squid, remove ink sacs and save for later use.

2. Cut up tentacles and flappers for use in stuffing.

3. Mix cut up tentacles and flappers, cooked rice, pine nuts, salt and pepper, and stuff into each squid. Secure opening with a toothpick.

4. Heat oil in pan and sauté onions, garlic, and parsley.

5. Stir in tomatoes, salt to taste, cover and simmer for 7 minutes.

6. Add squid and simmer 15 minutes longer.

7. Strain squid ink through a sieve, mix with the browned flour, and after the squid have cooked for 15 minutes, add this to sauce in pan of squid. Add a small amount of water if sauce is too dry and cook for another 15 minutes over low heat.

Serve this dish with cooked rice.

SQUID IN TOMATO SAUCE

1. Make a thick Spanish tomato sauce, page 247 or 248

2. Clean squid, cut into pieces, and add to sauce.

3. Simmer for 30 minutes and serve with noodles, spaghetti, or rice.

WHY THERE ARE NO SNAIL RECIPES IN THIS BOOK

I had never prepared fresh snails before, but the fishmonger assured me there was nothing to it. "It's easy, señora," he said. "Just fill the sink with water, put them in, and wash."

When I arrived home, I put the snails into a sink filled with water, but before I could do anything else, the phone rang. Since no one was home, I had to leave the kitchen to answer it.

What I found when I returned was unbelievable! Snails were crawling all over the room. They had been dormant when I bought them, but the water had evidentally revived them and they had marched themselves out of the sink, over the counters, up the walls, and onto the floor. They were leaving.

I wanted to leave, too. I needed to run out into the apartment lobby and call, "Help! Someone come in here and get these things out of my kitchen!" But pride kept me in. The only American señora in the building must not make a fool of herself.

Stoically, I began picking up snails from the floor and putting them back into the sink. However, as fast as I put them in, they crept out. Some had reached heights on the wall beyond my stretch, and a few attained the ceiling.

By now I noticed distinct personalities. Some immediately marched back from where I had retrieved them; others took a completely different direction. Their energy and determination were endless. I bent down to study them at close range. Such tiny creatures, they moved on their bellies and carried their homes on their backs. Their exodus from the sink must have been a long journey for them. Because their antennas moved up and down, I wondered if they were communicanting with each other, and if they were, what would the message be. They seemed indomitable.

It was at that point I knew I would not eat them.

Nevertheless, I had to keep gathering them from their sojourns, for they were restless wanderers and their travels could lead them anywhere.

I prayed that somebody would come home soon to relieve me and make a decision about their destiny; I couldn't.

I don't know how long I had been so creatively occupied when finally the door opened and my 12-year-old son Stanley arrived from school.

"Thank goodness you're home," I cried. Deliverance was here. "What shall we do?"

"Put up a pot of water," he said.

"Isn't there any other way?" I implored.

"The water," he commanded.

And that's what we did with the snails; however, I didn't eat them.

That's why there are no snail recipes in this book.

Meats

Bueno es el vino cuando el vino es bueno.
When the wine is good it's really good.

And great is the meal that is well prepared!

DUMPLINGS

The dumpling may be cooked in the stew at any time, then removed and saved until serving time.

> *1 egg*
> *1/2 cup soft bread crumbs made from stale bread (not fine crumbs, but pieces. Spanish or Italian bread is best.)*
> *1 clove mashed garlic*
> *1/2 tsp. fresh parsley finely chopped or 1/4 tsp. dried parsley salt*

1. Combine all the ingredients. The dough should be moist. However, if it's too moist add more crumbs.

2. Divide the dough into 6 portions. Drop by the tablespoon into hot oil and fry until the dumpling is brown and done inside.

3. Place the dumpling on top of the stew, in the liquid, and cook COVERED for 15 minutes. When it's done, remove to a plate and set aside until the stew is ready to serve.

MEAT AND POTATOES IN WINE SAUCE
FROM EXTREMADURA
(Frite Extremeño)

When I told Dr. Dionisio Ollero, a friend of mine who teaches at the University of Madrid, that I was writing this cookbook, he said that I must include this very popular recipe from his Extremeño region.

It's very easy to prepare.

This recipe serves 4.

> *1 lb. lamb meat cut into pieces (beef, veal, or pork may also be*
> *prepared this way.)*
> *4 medium-size potatoes, peeled and cut into quarters*
> *1/4 cup dry white wine*
> *2 cloves sliced garlic*
> *1/4 bay leaf*
> *2 tsp. paprika*
> *2 tbsp. oil*
> *salt*

1. Fry the garlic in the oil, remove from pan when done and save.

2. Brown the meat.

3. Lower heat, add the wine, bay leaf, paprika, 1/2 cup water, the fried garlic, salt to taste, and simmer covered until the meat is almost done. (If needed, add another 1/4 cup wine and 1/2 cup water.)

4. When the meat is almost done, add the potatoes and cook until tender.

STUFFED MEAT ROAST
(Aleta)

The "aleta," a very unusual roast, is a solid piece of meat stuffed with ground meat. Select either a flank steak or a veal breast, and have the butcher cut a pocket in the meat so that you can stuff it. In Spain, one asks the butcher for an "aleta" and he cuts a pocket without being told.

This recipe serves 6 people and it may be prepared the day before serving.

3 lbs. flank steak or 3 lbs. veal breast, with pocket for stuffing
prepared by butcher
1 large cooked carrot
1 French omelette made from 1 egg, and cut into 1-inch squares
bay leaf
1/2 tsp. oil
1/3 cup dry white wine, or 1 tbsp. cognac

The following are the ingredients for the meat stuffing which is packed into the pocket of the meat roast:

3/4 cup ground meat, veal or beef
3/4 cup pieces of bread for stuffing
2 eggs
10 green olives, coarsely chopped
2 slices chopped chorizo or sweet Italian sausage
1/4 tsp. crushed basil
less than 1/8 tsp. sage
1 crushed clove garlic
salt and pepper
1 tbsp. flour
1/8 tsp. ground nutmeg

1. Cook carrot; make omelette. Cut omelette into one-inch squares and set aside.

2. Sauté the onion, chorizo, and garlic. Set aside.

3. Pound the flank steak to flatten it, but be careful not to tear it. If it tears, make another French omelette, and line torn area, on the inside of the pocket, with the whole omelette.

4. Sprinkle 1 tbsp. water over the bread, and mix it thoroughly with the other ingredients of the meat stuffing.

5. Once all the ingredients of the meat stuffing are thoroughly mixed together, pack it into the pocket of the meat. Place the cooked carrot in the center of the stuffing which is in the meat. (This will be a decoration when the meat is sliced.) Pack the stuffing loosely, because stuffing expands when it cooks.

6. Sew up the openings of the meat.

To pot roast the "aleta":

1. Heat oil in pot in which roast will be cooked, and brown the roast. Add 1/2 cup water, bay leaf, and an onion. Pour 1/3 cup wine over the roast, and sprinkle with salt to taste. Simmer for about 1 1/2 hours.

To oven roast the "aleta":

Place the roast in a pan, pour 1/3 cup wine over it, coat it with oil, salt to taste, place 1 bay leaf in the pan and one onion cut in half. Roast it uncovered for 1 1/2 hours in a 350 degree oven.

To make the gravy:

1. Remove the roast from the pan. Add 1 cup hot water to the pan. Scrape the pan with a spoon and stir up roast juices. Add another cup hot water. Strain the gravy.

2. Re-heat gravy and taste it for salt and pepper.

3. For a thicker gravy, stir 1/2 cup cool gravy into 1 tbsp. flour, and stir that into the rest of the gravy. Slowly heat.

Let the finished roast set for 15 minutes to several hours before slicing so that the stuffing won't fall apart.

Roast may also be completely sliced earlier in the day and re-heated in a slow oven.

MEAT IN ONION SAUCE

A simple and delicious recipe.

Serve on rice or noodles.

> *1 lb. tender beef or veal, cubed*
> *1 chopped onion*

> *1 cup dry white wine*
> *3/4 cup beef boullion*
> *oil for frying*
> *flour*

1. Season flour with salt and pepper, coat meat and fry in hot oil until tender. Remove from pan and keep warm.

2. Sauté onion in same pan, add wine and boullion. Simmer until the onion melts into the sauce. Pour over the meat and serve.

DICED MEAT AND TOMATOES
(Picadillo de carne)

Serves 4.

The meat in this recipe is cut into very small pieces.

Serve on rice or mashed potatoes.

> *1 lb. diced meat*
> *2 strips bacon cut into small pieces*
> *1 finely chopped onion*
> *2 tomatoes cut into very small pieces (may be canned)*
> *1 or 2 cloves finely chopped garlic*
> *1 tbsp. paprika*
> *pinch ground black pepper*
> *1 hard-boiled egg for decoration*

1. Fry the bacon, then remove most of the fat and brown the meat.

2. Blend in paprika and immediately stir in the onion, garlic, and tomatoes. Add salt and pepper to taste.

3. Add about one cup water and simmer covered over low heat until the meat is tender. (Add a little more water if necessary, but the result should not have very much liquid.) Uncover pot the last 15 minutes.

At serving time sprinkle with chopped hard-boiled egg.

SHORT RIBS OF BEEF

> *tomato sauce recipe, page 247*
> *short ribs of beef (remove fat)*
> *oil*

1. Brown ribs in oil. Remove from pot and set aside.

2. In the same pot, cook tomato sauce recipe.

3. Add ribs and cook until they are tender. Add more water during cooking if necessary.

Serve with noodles.

GROUND-MEAT PIE

Either an 8- or 9-inch pie plate or tart shells can be used.

This pie is easy to prepare and everybody seems to like it.

> *pie dough recipe style 2 for a one-crust pie , page 279*
> *1 lb. ground meat, either veal, beef, or pork*
> *1 finely chopped onion*
> *1 raw egg yolk*
> *3 tbsp. unseasoned bread crumbs*
> *3 canned tomatoes plus 1/4 cup tomato juice from tomato can*
> *garlic powder*
> *salt*
> *3-inch piece chorizo or 1 sweet Italian sausage, chopped*
> *canned pimiento or sliced mushrooms for decoration (optional)*

1. Prepare dough and line pie pan. Prick with fork all over, and coat bottom crust with a small amount of egg white.

2. Brown the meat, sausage, and onion.

3. Chop tomatoes and add to meat. Add the juice, salt, and garlic. Simmer for 10 minutes. Remove from heat.

4. Blend in bread crumbs, then egg yolk. Taste for seasoning.

5. Pour into unbaked pastry shell and bake in a 450 degree oven for about 7 to 10 minutes.

Remove and decorate.

MEAT BALLS
(Albondigas)

This recipe may be made the day before serving, except for step 9, which must be prepared at serving time. Serves 4.

>*1 lb. ground beef*
>*1/4 tsp. salt*
>*1/2 tsp. cinnamon*
>>*pinch nutmeg*
>>*1 clove garlic, mashed (or 1/8 tsp. minced dried garlic or garlic powder)*
>>*1 onion, finely chopped*
>*1/2 tbsp. lemon juice*
>>*2 eggs*
>>*1 tsp. chopped fresh parsley (or a little less than 1/8 tsp. dried parsley)*
>*4 1/2 tbsp. bread crumbs*
>>*4 tbsp. milk*
>*1/4 cup oil*
>>*flour*

1. Mix the meat in a bowl with salt, cinnamon, nutmeg, garlic, half the amount of onion, lemon juice, parsley, bread crumbs and milk. Add 1 whole egg, and the WHITE of another. (Set aside the yolk for later use.) Mix all the ingredients in well.

2. Shape into meatballs.

3. Heat the oil. Coat meatballs with flour, and fry them in hot oil until they are browned. Do not put too many meatballs in pan at one time, or they won't brown well.

4.When the meatballs are done, remove them from the pan and set them aside. Pour off as much fat as possible from pan, but save the meat liquid.

5. Add the other half of the onion to the pan and brown. (Be careful not to burn onion.)

6. Add 1 tbsp. flour and stir until slightly browned.

7. Add 2 cups water, salt to taste, the meatballs, and simmer slowly, the pan covered, for a half hour. (Add a small amount of water from time to time if necesary.)

8. *At serving time,* place the meatballs in a serving dish and leave the sauce in the pan.

9. *Remove pan from heat,* and slowly add the yolk of the egg to the sauce, stirring it in.

This must be done at serving time, since the sauce must not be heated after the egg yolk has been added or it will curdle.

Pour sauce over meatballs and serve at once.

MEAT LOAF

1 lb. ground beef
2 sweet Italian sausages, casings removed
2 1/2 slices bread made into crumbs
2 eggs
1/4 cup milk
1 finely chopped onion
1/4 tsp. dried garlic powder
1/2 tsp. ground black pepper or powdered ginger
1/2 tsp. crushed cilantro leaves
1/4 tsp. crushed thyme or oregano
1 tsp. dried parsley
salt
1/4 tsp. ground nutmeg

1. Mash sausage and blend all the ingredients. Taste for seasoning.

2. Place into a deep narrow baking dish (like a bread pan). Leave enough room in the pan for the fat to gather. Bake in a 350 degree oven for about 45 to 60 minutes.

When done, remove from oven and pour off fats. Let it set for about 20 minutes before slicing.

Serve as an appetizer on a small round of bread, in sandwiches, or as a main dish. To serve as the main dish, place the slices on a plate, cover with tomato sauce and decorate with a slice of hard-boiled egg and a circle of sautéed green pepper.

MEAT AND VEGETABLE STEW FROM EXTREMADURA
(Cocido Extremeño)

A whole meal out of one pot, and very easy to prepare, too.

This stew is very popular in Spain.

Serves 6 to 8.

> *1/2 lb. beef or veal stew*
> *2 chicken breasts or any other parts desired*
> *1 lb. lamb neck, fat removed*
> *6-inch piece chorizo or 2 sweet Italian sausages*
> *3-inch piece of Morcilla and Morcón sausage, if available*
> *1 ham hock*
> *1 medium-size can chick peas or 2 cups dried chick peas which have been soaked for 12 hours.*
> *4 medium-size potatoes*
> *2 tbsp. rice*
> *2 medium-size onions*
> *1/2 small cabbage*
> *1/2 package frozen turnip greens*
> *2 tomatoes, either fresh or canned*
> *1 whole clove*
> *2 or 3 mint leaves*

1. Put the stew meat, chicken, lamb neck, Morcón, ham hock, onions with the clove stuck into one, and tomatoes in a pot, cover with water plus an extra 5 inches, and bring to a boil.

2. After it has boiled for 5 minutes, lower heat to simmer, skim off foam, taste liquid, and salt to taste. If you're using dried chick peas which have been soaked, add them now. Also add the mint leaves and remove them after five minutes.

3. About a half hour before the stew is done, add the cabbage which has been cut into wedges, the turnip greens, sausage and Morcilla. Also add the peeled cubed potatoes and the canned chick peas.

4. When everything is tender, pour off the soup into another pot and cook the rice in it until done. (Keep the food in the large pot warm.)

Serve the hot soup and rice first. Then cut everything into serving portions and arrange the meat and chicken on one serving platter and the vegetables and sausage on another.

MADRID-STYLE STEW
(Cocido Madrileño)

Cocido means "stew" in Spanish, and this recipe is a Madrid-style elegant stew that you can serve to company with pride.

People in the various regions of Spain add different foods to their cook-pot, and so each cocido reflects the distinct flavor of the area from which it comes.

Even though the recipe is long, the preparation is easy, and just look at all the dishes that will come out of one pot: soup and noodles, meat, chick peas, vegetables, and dumplings.

There are two ways to serve this dish:

1. You can serve the soup and noodles first, then serve the cut up vegetables, meat, chick peas and dumplings on a separate platter, or

2. You can serve everything, cut up, in a soup toureen.

Whichever way you serve it, everybody loves this dish, especially children.

> *2 cups dried chick peas, or canned chick peas*
> *(Dried chick peas must he soaked at least 12 hours before using them in this recipe. See page 136 for directions. Canned chick peas may be drained and used immediately. Do NOT soak them.)*
>
> *1 whole onion*
> *the white part of one leek, chopped (may be omitted)*
> *1 large whole carrot, or several small ones*
> *1/2 bay leaf*
> *salt to taste*
> *1/4 lb. salt pork or slab bacon*
> *1 ham hock or ham bone*
> *chicken: either 2 fryer breasts, or any other parts desired*
> *very fine egg noodles for use with soup if the soup will be served separately*
> *1/2 lb. stew meat cut into small serving pieces, either beef or veal*
> *vegetable: use either one of the following: cabbage, string-beans, brussel sprouts, or swiss chard*
> *chorizo or Italian sausage, not hot*

1. If you're using canned chick peas, do not put them in the pot now. If you're using chick peas that you soaked for 12 hours, place the soaked peas in a large pot, fill the pot with enough warm water to cover the peas, plus about 5 inches extra water.

2. Add all the ingredients except the noodles. Make sure the water covers all the ingredients, and that there is enough liquid to make enough soup. Bring to a boil.

3. After it has boiled for 5 minutes, lower heat to simmer, skim off foam and discard. Taste liquid and add salt to taste.

4. After half an hour, or when the carrot, chorizo, and bacon are tender, remove them from the pot and set aside.

5. Fifteen minutes before stew is done, add vegetable. (Stew is done when the meat, chicken, and chick peas are tender.) The vegetable may be prepared in either one of the following two ways:

    a. It may be cut up if it's cabbage or swiss chard, or left whole if stringbeans or brussel sprouts; and cooked in the stew until tender, or

    b. It may be cooked separately. Sauté sliced garlic in a small amount of oil in a pot large enough to hold the vegetable.

    Toss the vegetable in the oil, add salt to taste, and add a small amount of water. Cover the pot and simmer the vegetable until tender. Be careful not to overcook it. When it's done, do not add it to the stew, but set it aside until serving time.

6. If you are using canned chick peas, now is the time to add them to the stew, when the stew is about done. (Drain the peas first.)

Dumpling for the stew

The dumpling may be cooked in the stew at any time, then removed as soon as it's done and set aside until serving time.

> *1 egg*
> *1/2 cup soft bread crumbs made from stale bread (not fine crumbs, but pieces of bread), Spanish or Italian bread is best*
> *1 clove garlic, mashed*
> *1/2 tsp. fresh parsley, finely chopped, or 1/4 tsp. dried parsley pinch salt*

1. Mix the above ingredients together to make a moist dought. If dough is too moist, add more crumbs.

2. Divide dough into 6 portions. Drop by the tablespoon into hot oil, and fry until dumpling is brown and done inside.

3. Place the dumpling onto liquid of stew, and cook COVERED for 15 minutes. When it's done, remove to a plate and set aside until the stew is done.

Soup and Noodles

The soup and noodles are prepared this way only when the soup will be served separately from the stew.

1. When the stew is done, strain off liquid into another pot. Remove all the ingredients from the stew pot, cut up everything (except the dumplings) into serving pieces, and arrange them all on the platter from which they will be served. Cover this platter and place it into a warm oven until serving time.

2. Now bring the liquid in the pot (the soup) to a boil.

3. Add egg noodles and boil for a very short time, until the noodles are tender.

Serve the hot soup with the noodles immediately. (Soup should be served very hot.)

Then serve the platter with the rest of the stew as the next course.

Also, you may eliminate preparing the "Soup and Noodles," and just serve everything straight from the stew pot. (Cut up the vegetables and meat into serving portions.)

BEEF (OR VEAL) STEW WITH POTATOES
(Estofado de vaca con patatas)

This recipe serves four people, and may be made the day before serving.

> 2 lbs. stew meat (beef, veal, or any meat for stewing)
> 2 onions, chopped
> 1 clove garlic, chopped
> 6 mushrooms
> chorizo, one-inch long (or sweet Italian sausage)
> 1 green pepper, cut into strips
> 2 carrots, cut into chunks
> 2 tomatoes, canned or fresh (if fresh tomatoes are used, peel
> them)

1 cup dry white wine
1 bay leaf
1/8 tsp. thyme
1 sprig parsley
4 potatoes, peeled and quartered
salt and pepper to taste
small piece salt pork
olive oil

1. Render the salt pork in a heavy kettle, and brown the meat in it. (Do not put many pieces of meat in to brown at the same time, or the meat will cook instead of brown.) When the meat is browned, remove it from the pot and set it aside.

2. Heat 1 tbsp. olive oil in the same pot and sauté the onion and garlic. Add tomatoes. Stir it all together. Add wine, bay leaf, thyme, parsley, chorizo, meat, and water just to cover all the ingredients. Salt and pepper to taste. Cover pot and simmer for about 2 hours, or until meat is tender.

3. When meat is tender, add potatoes and carrots. Taste liquid and add salt if necessary. Cook covered until potatoes are done. Be careful not to overcook potatoes.

4. While the stew is cooking, heat butter in a saucepan and sauté the green peppers and mushrooms. Add to stew just before potatoes are done.

VEAL ROAST WITH VEGETABLES

2 lb. veal roast, any cut
1 tsp. oil
4 medium onions
4 carrots
4 potatoes
1 turnip (optional)
1/4 lb. string beans
1 sprig fresh parsley or 1/4 tsp. dried parsley
salt and pepper to taste
1 tsp. dry white wine

1. Heat oil in stewing pot and brown meat on all sides.

2. Add onions and brown.

3. Add 1 1/2 cups water, salt, pepper, and wine. Cook until meat is ALMOST tender, about 1/2 hour.

4. Add whole (uncut) vegetables, and continue cooking until vegetables are tender. (Do not overcook potatoes or they will fall apart.) Add small amount of water if necessary, about another 1 1/2 cups. If the vegetables start getting done before the meat is tender, remove them from the pot.

When the meat is tender, remove it from the pot and let it set for about 5 minutes before slicing.

This recipe may also be prepared well in advance, the meat sliced cold, then slowly re-heated in the sauce before serving.

BREADED VEAL CHOPS OR CUTLETS
(Filetes de ternera empanadas)

> *1 chop or cutlet per person*
> *oil*
> *milk*
> *salt*
> *flour*
> *1 beaten egg*
> *bread crumbs*

1. Dip steaks into milk, and let them set for 10 minutes. Drain.

2. Salt each steak to taste.

3. Set up three plates containing flour, the beaten egg, and the bread crumbs.

4. Dip each chop into first, the flour, then the beaten egg, then the bread crumbs.

5. Heat oil in pan, and brown the breaded steaks.

Squeeze a few drops lemon juice over the chops before eating them, or prepare the following sauce:

Sauce

> *oil*
> *1 slice bacon*
> *1 slice ham*
> *1 tbsp. flour*
> *2 tbsp. dry white wine*

1. Remove the bread crumbs from the oil in the pan in which the chops were fried.

2. To the pan, add 1 slice bacon, cut into 4 pieces, and 1 slice cut up ham. When browned, remove and place on top of chops.

3. Add the flour to the pan and brown it. Add the wine and 2 or 3 tablespoons water, and salt to taste. Simmer for a moment, and serve hot over the breaded chops.

VEAL CORDON BLEU

This is originally a French recipe, but since it is served very frequently in Spain, it is included in this book. It serves 6.

> *12 small veal cutlets (make sure that they do not have any holes*
>   *or the sauce will leak through)*
> *6 slices mozzarella cheese or swiss cheese*
> *6 slices ham*
> *6 tsps. sliced mushrooms*
> *flour, slightly salted, for coating veal*
> *1 beaten egg, slightly salted*

1. Pound veal cutlets flat. Salt to taste.

2. Place 1 slice cheese, 1 tsp. mushrooms, and 1 slice ham on top of one veal cutlet. Cover with another veal cutlet, and fold edges under.

3. Dip into flour, and then into beaten egg.

4. Fry in hot oil on both sides until done. Serve immediately.

VEAL VILLAROY
(Ternera Villaroy)

This is a fairly easy recipe to prepare, and it can be prepared well in advance. The last step can be made several hours before serving, and then the dish may be warmed in the oven at serving time.

You get several textures in each cutlet: the outside is fried crisp, under that is a creamy substance (the bechamel), and then the meat.

This dish always makes a big hit at a party. The recipe serves 6.

> *6 veal cutlets*
> *bechamel sauce, page 253*
> *flour*
> *2 eggs, beaten*
> *bread crumbs*
> *oil*
> *butter for greasing platter*

1. Sauté cutlets in small amount of oil until done. Be careful not to overcook them. Set them aside to cool.

2. Prepare the bechamel sauce. (Remove the onion from the sauce.)

3. Butter a large platter.

4. Place one veal cutlet on a fork, dip it into the warm bechamel sauce, and coat the veal well on both sides. Set veal onto buttered platter. Continue doing this with all the cutlets. Let them set on the platter until the bechamel coating becomes cold and doesn't stick to the fingers when you touch it. It should take about 2 hours.

5. When the coated veal is cold, dip into flour one at a time, shake off the excess flour, and mold the coating (bechamel) to the veal to form a smooth shape.

6. Dip coated veal into beaten egg and then into bread crumbs.

7. Heat oil and brown veal on both sides. Do not crowd pan with many pieces at once or it won't brown well.

STUFFED GREEN PEPPERS WITH VEAL AND CHICKEN (Pimientos Rellenos)

Serves 6.

> 6 green peppers
> 1/4 lb. ground veal
> 1/2 boned chopped chicken breast
> 2 beaten eggs
> 1 tbsp. flour
> 2 tsp. chopped fresh parsley or a little less than 1/4 tsp. dried parsley
> 1 clove chopped garlic
> 1 cup chicken boullion
> 1 slice toasted bread, chopped
> salt
> 1 slice untoasted bread

1. Put the peppers under the broiler until the skin blisters. Remove, and let cool. Peel carefully and remove seeds.

2. Put the veal, chicken, parsley, onion, and garlic in a pan, add salt to taste, and fry until the meat is done and the onion is tender.

3. Place in a bowl and blend in the beaten eggs. Taste for seasoning.

4. Carefully fill each pepper and cover the opening with a piece of soft bread stuffed inside the hole.

5. Heat oil in a pan large enough to hold all the peppers later on and carefully fry each pepper, then remove to a plate.

6. After the peppers are fried, blend boullion into the flour, a little at a time, and add it to the pan. Add the toast and salt to taste.

7. Place the fried peppers in the pan and simmer slowly for about 15 minutes until the peppers are done.

SMOKED PORK CHOPS WITH CABBAGE AND POTATOES

This is a simple dish from the Coruña region of Spain.

1 or 2 potatoes per person
1 small cabbage or enough to serve a wedge per person
1 or 2 smoked pork chops per person
2-inch piece chorizo or 1/2 sweet Italian sausage per person
1/2 slice bacon per serving, cut into one-inch pieces
1 chopped onion per serving
1 fresh or canned chopped tomato per serving
1/2 clove garlic per tomato
1/4 tsp. paprika per tomato
salt

1. Cook the potatoes in salted water, peel, and set aside.

2. Cook the cabbage, pork chops, and sausage in a small amount of slightly salted water in another pot. When done, remove from heat and set aside.

3. Fry the bacon and pour off the excess fat. Add the onion, tomato, garlic, paprika and salt to taste. Cover and simmer on low heat for 15 to 20 minutes. If necessary, add a small amount of the liquid from the pork chops pot.

To serve, cut the meat and vegetables into serving pieces and place on a platter. Pour the tomato sauce on the cabbage and potatoes.

PORK PIE FROM GALICIA
(Empanada Gallega de Lomo)

· Start this recipe the day before serving because the meat has to stay in the marinade for 24 hours.

1 lb. tender de-boned pork cut into serving pieces
4 medium chopped onions
1 cup dry white wine
2 cloves mashed garlic
thyme
oregano
1 tbsp. paprika
1/2 cup oil
salt
1 egg yolk for coating dough
pie dough recipe 1, for 2-crust pie; or 2 cans refrigerator onion-roll dough

1. Combine the garlic, thyme, oregano, paprika, salt and wine. Add pork and toss. Place in the refrigerator for 24 hours.

2. After this time, prepare the pie dough for a 2-crust pie.

3. Brown the pork and the onions in oil. Add a half cup wine, and simmer slowly, covered, until the meat is thoroughly cooked. Add a small amount of water if necessary.

4. Line pie plate with dough. Prick all over with a fork. (If refrigerator-roll dough is used, pinch edges of each piece together to form one whole piece.

5. Fill crust with meat and sauce, sprinkle liberally with the rest of the wine, and pour a half cup oil over all the ingredients.

6. Top pie with the rest of the dough, prick center of dough with a fork, coat dough with the egg yolk, and bake for 15 minutes in a 400 degree oven until dough is done.

ROAST WHOLE BABY PIG
(Cochinillo asado)

>*oil or pork lard*
>*3 cloves mashed garlic*
>*2 onions finely chopped; 1 whole onion*
>*2 tbsp. fresh parsley or 1/2 tsp. dried parsley (add more if desired)*
>*3 whole crushed cloves*
>*1 cup dry white wine*

Roast for 18 minutes per pound.

1. Wash the pig well, dry it, and rub with a mixture of oregano and salt. Coat with oil or pork lard.

2. Mix together garlic, onions, parsley, cloves, oregano, and wine. Rub on pig, inside and out. Let set for at least three hours.

3. After this time, put the pig on a rack in a roasting pan, put an onion and a sprig parsley inside pig, cover lightly with foil for the first hour and roast in a 350 degree oven.

After one hour remove the cover, but cover each ear so that they won't burn. Continue roasting until brown and tender.

BAR-B-QUED LAMB RIBS

>*1/2 lb. lamb ribs per person*
>*lemon juice*
>*oil*
>*parsley*
>*mashed garlic*
>*oregano*
>*salt and pepper*
>*sliced onions*
>*tomato paste or ketchup*

Have the butcher split the ribs into single rib pieces.

1. Place the ribs in a bowl and cover with a mixture of lemon juice oil, parsley, mashed garlic, oregano, salt and pepper, and sliced onions. Cover, place in refrigerator, and let it set for several hours or overnight. (A prepared Italian salad dressing may be used instead of the above listed ingredients.)

2. Blend 1/2 cup oil, 1/4 cup lemon juice or vinegar, salt and pepper, 2 tsp. tomato paste or ketchup. Set aside for later use.

3. Place the ribs in a pan and roast uncovered in a 350 degree oven for one hour, or until crisp and done. During the last half hour, baste frequently with the tomato paste mixture.

LAMB RIBS OR SHORT RIBS WITH RICE

2 1/2 lbs. lamb ribs or beef short ribs (remove as much fat as possible)
1 cube beef boullion
1 cup rice
1 chopped onion
1 clove chopped garlic
1 cup dry white wine

1. Brown the onion in oil. Add the garlic and meat. Toss. Add the wine, one cup water, and salt to taste. Cover and simmer on low heat until the meat is tender and the liquid almost gone.

2. Stir in the rice.

3. Dissolve the boullion cube in one cup hot water. Add to the rice. Add enough water so that the rice is covered, plus a little extra. Cook covered until the rice and meat are done. Check frequently to see that there is enough water.

The pot may also be placed in a 350 degree oven instead of cooking it on top of the stove.

LAMB AND POTATO STEW
(Potaje de cordero con patatas)

There are two ways of serving this stew. It may be served in soup bowls with the soup, meat, and potatoes all together, or the soup may be served first, then the meat and potatoes may be served on a separate plate. Any way it is served, it is economical and delicious!

This recipe serves four people.

1/4 cup oil
1 sliced onion
1/2 sliced clove garlic
1 tbsp. fresh parsley
1 bay leaf
1 peeled tomato, either fresh or canned
1 inch piece of chorizo or pepperoni
8 whole peppercorns
1 lb. lamb stew meat, or breast of lamb, or neck slices (remove fat)
4 medium size potatoes
1/4 tsp. paprika

1. Heat oil, and sauté onion, garlic, bay leaf, and parsley.

2. Add tomato, chorizo, meat, paprika, and stir it all together.

3. Add cold water to cover the food in the pot, and bring it to a boil. Skim off foam.

4. Add peppercorns and salt to the soup, and cook for 1 hour.

5. Add the peeled potatoes, cut in half, and cook for 1/2 hour. Be careful not to overcook the potatoes or they will fall apart.

ROAST LEG OF LAMB
(Pierna de cordero asado)

Marinate the leg of lamb in the sauce for two hours before placing it in the oven. Cooking time is about 35 minutes per pound in a 325 degree oven. Figure on one-half to three-quarter pounds raw lamb per person when you buy the roast. Lamb must be served hot, and this roast is best served the same day that it is roasted.

> *leg of lamb*
> *about 1/4 cup dry white wine*
> *some oil*
> *salt to taste*
> *mashed garlic or garlic powder*
> *1 sliced onion*
> *1 bay leaf*
> *about a tablespoon chopped parsley*

1. Coat leg with a mixture of wine, oil, salt, garlic, and parsley. Let it set for about 2 hours. (A little more or less time doesn't matter.)

2. Place the leg in a roasting pan, put the onions on top of the leg, a bay leaf in the pan, and roast the lamb until tender.

Serve hot.

STUFFED LEG OF LAMB
(Pierna de cordero rellena)

> *2 lb. leg of lamb (have butcher remove the bone for stuffing leg*
> *3/4 cup ground veal or ground pork*
> *1 slice ham*
> *2 eggs*
> *4 almonds, blanched and peeled*
> *butter*
> *dry white wine*
> *bay leaf*
> *oil*

salt to taste
pepper
1/4 tsp. dried parsley or 1 tbsp. chopped fresh parsley
1 tbsp. flour

1. Boil one egg.

2. Chop the hard-boiled egg, ham, and nuts.

3. Add the ground meat, flour, parsley, one raw egg, salt, and pepper, and mix it all together well.

4. Stuff the leg loosely because stuffing expands when it cooks. Sew up the open end.

5. Pour wine over the leg, sprinkle it with salt and pepper, and place one bay leaf in the pan. Bake the leg of lamb in a 300 degree oven for about 2 hours.

Instead of roasting the leg of lamb, it may also be cooked in a heavy pot on the stove in the following manner:

1. After stuffing it and sewing it closed, brown the leg in butter, pour wine over it, and salt and pepper to taste. Pour 2 cups water into the pot, and simmer it covered for 2 hours.

ROAST STUFFED LEG OF LAMB WITH TOMATO SAUCE

1 5-lb. leg of lamb, bone removed
1 6-inch piece chorizo or 2 sweet Italian sausages
1 clove sliced garlic
1 cup dry white wine
3 medium onions cut into quarters
6 small whole potatoes
1/2 cup tomato sauce

1. Chop the sausage, stuff the lamb with it, and sew the opening.

2. Place the lamb in a roasting pan with the onions and potatoes.

3. Brown the garlic in 4 tbsp. oil.

4. Add the wine, and pour over the lamb and potatoes. Salt lamb to taste.

5. Place it into a 325 degree oven for about three hours.

6. Prepare the tomato sauce.

7. When the lamb is done, remove it from the pan. Blend the tomato sauce into the pan drippings (remove any fat first), and serve hot with the lamb.

STEWED LAMB SHANKS

This recipe serves 2 people (one lamb shank per person). It may be prepared the day before serving. Start the recipe at least 2 hours before cooking the meat, because the lamb shanks need to be marinated for 2 hours first.

> *2 lamb shanks*
> *dry white wine*
> *oil*
> *salt*
> *garlic powder or crushed garlic*
> *parsley*
> *1 sliced onion*
> *1 tsp. tomato paste*
> *1 bay leaf*

1. Paint the lamb shanks with a mixture of wine, oil, salt, garlic, and parsley. Let them set for 2 hours. (They may set for more.)

2. After 2 hours, heat 1 tbsp. oil in the pot in which the shanks will be cooked, and brown the shanks. Add the onion, and sauté it.

3. Add the tomato paste and dilute it with 2 cups water.

4. Add 1 tbsp. wine, 1/2 tsp. parsley, and the bayleaf. Simmer until the meat is tender.

ROAST WHOLE BABY LAMB

> *oregano*
> *oil or .pork lard*
> *3 cloves mashed garlic*
> *2 onions finely chopped; 1 whole onion*
> *2 tbsp. fresh parsley or 1/2 tsp. dried parsley (add more if desired)*
> *3 whole crushed cloves*
> *1 cup dry white wine*

Roast for 18 minutes per pound.

1. Wash the lamb well, dry it, and rub with a mixture of oregano and salt. Coat with oil or pork lard.

2. Mix together garlic, onions, parsley, cloves, oregano, and wine. Rub on lamb, inside and out. Let set for at least three hours.

3. After this time, put the lamb on a rack in a roasting pan, put an onion and a sprig parsley inside lamb, cover lightly with foil for the first hour and roast in a 350 degree oven.

After one hour remove the cover and continue roasting until brown and tender.

GALICIAN STEW WITH NAVY BEANS
(Poté Gallego)

Poté Galego is a very hearty dish from Northern Spain, and it is especially good in cold weather.There is something very unusual about this recipe: there are no onions or garlic in the ingredients, two very common items in most Spanish dishes.

Although this is a very easy recipe to prepare, it doesn't look that way when you serve it. Add a dry red wine, Spanish or French bread, a simple salad, fruit and cheese for dessert, and you have a hearty, elegant meal.

216

This recipe serves six, and may be prepared the day before serving.

Soak the beans 12 hours before preparing the recipe, if they are a poor quality bean.

1 3/4 cups navy beans
1 lb. stewing veal, cut into pieces
1/2 chicken, cut into pieces
3 smoked pork chops
1 ham hock or ham bone
salt to taste
1 bunch fresh turnip greens, or 1 package defrosted frozen turnip greens (defrost before adding to stew)
4 small potatoes, cut in half
3-inch piece of chorizo or 3-inch piece of sweet Italian sausage
1 thick slice bacon, jowl, or salt pork (in Spain use manteca rancia)
2 thick ham slices, preferably country ham

1. Place beans, meat, chicken, pork chops, and ham hock into a large pot, cover with water, salt sparingly, and bring to a boil.

2. When it comes to a boil, lower heat and skim off foam which rises to the top. Discard foam.

3. Continue cooking for about an hour until beans are almost done. Be careful not to overcook. They should be firm.

4. After an hour, add turnip greens, potatoes, chorizo, bacon, and ham. Taste liquid and add salt if needed.

5. Continue cooking for about another half hour, or until potatoes are done. Again, watch the stew to see that the beans and potatoes do not get overcooked. Serve hot in individual bowls.

STEW FROM GALLEGO WITH CHICK PEAS
(Cocido Gallego)

A very famous dish is this hearty meal served from one pot. Soup, vegetables, legumes, and meat are cooked together to make this a delicious, easy recipe to prepare.

Serves 6.

>   *1 lb. stewing veal, cut into bite-size pieces*
>   *3 smoked pork chops*
>   *1 ham hock*
>   *1 6-inch piece chorizo or 2 sweet Italian sausages*
>   *1 small cabbage, cut into wedges*
>   *1/2 chicken, cut into serving pieces*
>   *1 cup canned chick peas or dried chick peas which have been soaked for at least 12 hours*
>   *4 medium-size potatoes, peeled and cut in half*

1. Put the veal, chops, ham, sausage, and chicken in a pot, cover with water plus add an extra few inches, and bring to a boil. Lower heat and skim off foam.

2. Add the soaked dried chick peas and continue cooking over low heat until the meat and chick peas are almost tender. (If you are using canned chick peas, add them after the stew is cooked, then simmer for 5 minutes.)

3. When the meat is almost done, add the potatoes and cabbage. Continue cooking until tender.

How to serve

Serve the soup first. Cut up the ham hock and serve in the soup.

Place the cabbage and potatoes on one plate, the chick peas and sausage on another, and the veal, pork chops, and chicken on a third.

BREADED LIVER
(Higado empanado)

Serves 6.

> *1 lb. liver*
> *salt*
> *1/2 clove chopped garlic*
> *1 tbsp. fresh chopped parsley or 1/8 tsp. dried parsley*
> *bread crumbs*
> *oil*

1. Drop the liver into boiling water for a second, immediately remove it and dry.

2. Salt to taste, place it in a bowl with garlic and parsley, and let it set for a half hour.

3. Remove the liver from the bowl after this time, dip it into bread crumbs, and fry it in oil over medium heat until brown, first on one side, then on the other. Serve immediately. (Be careful not to overcook liver or it will become tough.)

Serve with onions which have been sautéed separately.

LAMB TONGUES

Serves 6.

This recipe includes an edible decoration for the serving plate.

> *6 lamb tongues*
> *carrots*
> *thyme*
> *onions*
> *parsley*
> *a bay leaf*
> *mushrooms*
> *tomatoes*

Decoration

3/4 lb. potatoes
3/4 cup peas
1 egg yolk
1 tbsp. plus 2 tsp. butter

1. Wash the tongues well and place into boiling water for about twenty minutes. Remove, cool, and peel the skin. (See recipe for Beff Tongue.)

2. Place into a pot, add sliced carrots, chopped onions, parsley, bay leaf, thyme, and tomatoes cut into pieces. Cover with water and simmer until the tongues are tender. When they are almost done, add the mushrooms.

Decoration for serving plate

1. Cook the peas and the peeled, cut up potatoes in a small amount of water until they are very tender. Drain, and dry the potatoes in the oven for a little while.

2. Purée the peas and potatoes in a blender or sieve. Blend in egg yolk and butter. At serving time, place in a pastry tube, and use the ragged edge to decorate.

To serve, place the tongues in the center of a serving plate and make a border with the purée.

BEEF TONGUE

The difficult part about preparing tongue is peeling the skin.

Make sure to cook the tongue for at least one hour, so that it's tender enough to peel.

After that time let it cool for about 5 minutes before you begin to peel it. The trick to peeling the tongue is to get the skin started at the tip of the tongue by cutting a slit into it, grabbing a piece of skin, and peeling. In some places where the skin is thin, you have to scrape it with a knife to start it peeling.

The most popular parts of the tongue are the center and front parts, but the back is also very tasty and it's great cut up into cooked vegetables.

Mashed potatoes and spinach are especially good served with hot cooked tongue, and mustard enhances the tongue's flavor. Sliced tongue is also very good served cold in sandwiches.

1-3 lb. raw beef tongue
1 bay leaf
1 sprig fresh parsley or 1 tbsp. dried parsley
1/2 cup dry wine
1 large sliced onion
1 large carrot
1 or 2 large pieces of celery, including the leaves
several whole peppercorns
salt

1. Wash tongue well and place it into boiling water in which a bay leaf has been added. The water should cover tongue. If the tongue is too large to fit into the pot as a whole piece, cut off the back part of the tongue, and fit it in with the other piece. Boil for one hour or so. Remove tongue from pot and let it cool. Peel skin.

2. After peeling it, place the whole tongue in a fresh pot of water in which you have added the bay leaf, parsley, wine, carrot, onion, peppercorns, and salt. (Taste the water to see if there is enough salt in it.) Cook over medium heat for 3 hours. Skim off foam from time to time.

3. When tongue is tender, remove it from the pot and let it get cool before cutting it into fairly thin slices.

4. Remove enough liquid from the pot to make a sauce. Mash or purée the carrot and onion in a sieve or blender, add prepared mustard, and add it to the tongue liquid. Taste it, and add salt and pepper if necessary. Add the sliced tongue, heat, and serve.

221

LAMB OR VEAL KIDNEYS

Serves 2.

Preparing the kidneys this way makes a delicious food out of something most people don't like. The usual offensive taste and smell is absent with this recipe.

Served with mashed potatoes prepared in advance.

> *8 lamb kidneys or 2 veal kidneys*
> *2 tbsp. butter*
> *1 tbsp. oil*
> *1 tbsp. flour*
> *1 cup dry white wine*
> *1 tbsp. fresh parsley or 1/4 tsp. dried parsley*
> *vinegar*
> *garlic powder*
> *salt*

1. Wash the kidneys, remove the veins and all the white tubes. Use a scissors if necessary. (These give the kidney a bad odor.) Cut the kidneys into small pieces, put them into a bowl and cover with vinegar, add salt to taste and a little garlic powder. Let it set for an hour.

2. After this time, remove the kidneys and drain. Place them in a hot pan and toss them until no more liquid emerges. (Pour off liquid as it comes out of the kidneys.)

3. When no more liquid comes out of the kidneys, remove them from the pan. Wash the pan, dry it, and return it to the heat.

4. Put the oil and butter in the pan and when it gets hot add the kidneys and fry quickly. Don't cook them long or they will get tough.

Remove the pan from the heat, stir in the flour and salt, and return pan to heat. Add the wine and parsley, and toss. Remove pan from heat and serve.

CALVES FEET WITH CHICK PEAS

This is a hearty thick soup which is especially good in cold weather.

Serve with Spanish or French bread.

Serves 4.

> 2 calves feet cleaned and sawed into pieces by butcher. (Do not let butcher chop bones because chopping causes tiny segments *of bone, which will get into the sauce)*
> 1 cup canned chick peas
> 2 medium onions
> 3 cloves garlic
> 2 sprigs fresh parsley or 1/2 tsp. dried parsley
> 1 small bay leaf
> salt
> 2 hard-boiled eggs
> 4 lemon wedges

1. Cook feet until tender (about 2 hours) with onion, garlic, parsley, bay leaf, and salt to taste in enough water to cover them plus some extra water.

2. Boil the eggs.

3. When tender, remove feet from the pot and let them cool. Cut meat from bones and chop or cut into small pieces. Discard bones.

4. Return the meat to pot, add chick peas, and simmer for a few more minutes.

5. At serving time, cut hard-boiled eggs into quarters, place 2 pieces into each soup bowl, then pour the soup on top. Serve hot with a lemon wedge on the side.

PREPARATION OF FRESH (NOT PRE-COOKED) TRIPE

1. Wash the tripe very well and soak it in cold water for 4 or 5 hours. Change the water from time to time.

2. After soaking it for 4 or 5 hours, scrub the tripe with a brush.

3. Place the tripe in vinegar for 1 hour.

4. After soaking the tripe in vinegar for 1 hour, wash it again, scrub it well, and change the water many times until the tripe is very clean. Make sure to clean out the grooves.

5. Cut the tripe into small squares, cover it with cold water, bring it to a boil, cook for 5 minutes, and drain off the water.

6. Cover the tripe with fresh water, bring it to a boil, add 1 tsp. salt to each quart of water, and cook it for 2 hours. Drain off the water.

7. Wash the tripe again in hot water. Make sure the grooves are well cleaned. Soak it in a bowl of hot water, and change the water several times.

8. Coat the tripe with lemon juice, sprinkle it with salt and dry white wine. Let it set for one hour.

The tripe is now ready to be cooked according to your recipe.

TRIPE A LA MADRID
(Callos a la Madrileña)

This is one of the most popular winter dishes in Spain. As Isabel used to say, "You get warmed-up just preparing it!"

There are food stalls in the open-air markets, the "mercados," which sell only the tripe and calves feet. The butcher knows exactly how to cut these meats without told when you say it's for "callos".

This recipe may be prepared the day before serving. It takes about 2 hours to prepare the ingredients, and about 2 hours to cook. (One hour of that time is used to marinate the tripe in wine and lemon juice.)

The kind of tripe to buy is one which is already cleaned and pre-cooked. If you are using fresh tripe, not pre-cooked, then follow the instructions for Preparation of Fresh Tripe, page 223 before starting this recipe.

> *1 lb. pre-cooked tripe, cut into small squares*
> *1 calf's foot, sawed in half by butcher (also ask him to remove the meat from the bone for you.)*
> *1 3-inch piece chorizo or sweet Italian sausage or pepperoni*
> *1 slice ham*
> *2 onions*
> *2 cloves*
> *1/2 tsp. parsley*
> *1 bay leaf*
> *salt*
> *pinch black pepper*
> *pinch hot pepper*
> *lemon juice*
> *1 cup wine*
> *1/2 tsp. paprika*

1. Wash the pre-cooked tripe very well in hot water. Make sure to clean out the grooves. Then soak the tripe in a bowl of hot water, and change the water several times.

2. After the tripe is well washed, cut it into small pieces, sprinkle it with salt and dry white wine. Let it set for one hour.

3. Wash the calf's foot, and place the foot, tripe, parsley, bay leaf, black pepper, salt, 1 cup wine, 1 clove garlic, and 1 onion into a pot. Cover the ingredients with cold water, plus about 3 inches extra

water. When the water comes to a boil, skim off the foam and throw it away.

4. Chop one onion and one garlic very finely. Cut the ham into pieces, and the chorizo into slices.

5. Heat 1 tbsp. oil in a fry pan, and fry the onion and garlic. Add the ham and chorizo. Stir in paprika and immediately remove the pan from the heat.

6. Add all the fried ingredients to the pot of tripe.

7. Continue cooking the food for 2 hours, over low heat, until the tripe and calf's foot are very tender.

Serve in soup bowls with Spanish (or French) bread.

GYSPY STEW

> 1 1/2 lbs. tripe
> 1 calf's foot
> 1 cup dried chick peas or 2 cups canned chick peas
> 1/2 cup cubed ham
> 2 pieces chorizo or sweet Italian sausage
> 2 green peppers cut into small pieces
> 2 tomatoes cut into small pieces
> 1/2 large finely chopped onion
> 5 cloves garlic
> 1 1/2 tsp. paprika
> 2 sliced carrots
> 1 ham bone
> 1 tbsp. fresh parsley or 1/4 tsp. dried parsley
> 3 mint leaves
> lemon juice
> 1 tsp. ground nutmeg
> a pinch saffron
> oil

If you are using fresh tripe, please see Preparation of Fresh Tripe, page 223.   If possible, buy tripe which is already cleaned and pre-cooked.

Soak the dried chick peas at least 12 hours in slightly salted warm water before cooking.

1. Wash the pre-cooked tripe very well in hot water. Make sure to clean out the grooves. Then soak it in a bowl of hot water, and change the water several times.

2. After the tripe is well washed, cut it into small pieces, coat it with lemon juice, sprinkle it with salt, and let it set for one hour.

3. After the tripe is soaked, put it and the washed calf's foot in a pot of water and bring it to a boil. Discard the water.

4. Put the soaked chick peas (if you're using canned chick peas, add them in step 5), onion, three chopped garlic cloves, paprika, carrots, parsley, mint leaves, and the ham bone in a pot with the tripe and calf's foot, and add fresh cold water to cover all the ingredients. Salt to taste and bring it to a boil. Lower heat and simmer.

5. When the chick peas, tripe, and calf's foot are tender (about 2 hours cooking time), add the sausage and cook for another 15 minutes. Add the canned chick peas now, if you're using them.)

6. Fry the green peppers in a small amount of oil. Add the tomatoes and the ham. Simmer until they are cooked. Add it to the pot of tripe.

7. Mash the rest of the garlic and add it to the stew. Add the nutmeg and salt to taste.

At serving time, cut the sausage into small pieces.

Serve hot in a deep bowl, accompanied by Spanish or French bread.

PIG'S EARS A LA LEON

2 ears
3 chopped onions
1 tbsp. flour
lemon
2 tbsp. boullion or water

1. Clean the ears well and cook in salted water. Cut up into small pieces.

2. Brown the onions in oil, then remove from pan.

3. Dry the ears and fry. Blend in flour. Blend in boullion or water. Add salt to taste. Continue stirring for a few minutes to make a sauce.

At serving time, sprinkle with lemon juice.

Chicken, Duck, Rabbit, and Partridge

Haz bien y no mires a quien.
*Do good deeds; it doesn't matter
who the recipient is.*

These good recipes will please and surprise you. Royal Chicken, for example, has an extraordinary sauce which contains chocolate, although the sauce does not have a chocolate flavor.

Roast Chicken stuffed with apples is unusual, Chicken Catalán gets its flavor from rum, and the Chicken Medley has a sauce so good that you won't want to leave any over. However, if you want a fast dish to prepare, Broiled Chicken is the one.

BROILED CHICKEN

broiler chicken
olive oil
lemon juice
dry white wine
crushed garlic or garlic powder
thyme
chopped parsley
ground cumin
salt and pepper

1. Split chicken in half or cut it into pieces.

2. Prepare a mixture of olive oil, a good amount of lemon juice, salt and pepper, a small amount of dry white wine, garlic, thyme, parsley, and ground cumin.

3. Coat chicken all over with this mixture, and let it marinate for at least 15 minutes, or longer. (A longer period of time will sharpen the taste.)

4. After it marinates, place it under the broiler, not too close to the heat, and watch it so that it doesn't burn. Turn the chicken so that it broils on both sides. Total broiling time is about 30 minutes.

ROAST CHICKEN

The chicken may be rubbed with seasoning the day before roasting.

1 whole roasting chicken or fryer
oil or butter for coating chicken
lemon juice
garlic
salt and pepper
1 onion
parsley
1/4 celery stalk

1. Blend lemon juice, oil, mashed garlic, salt and pepper. Brush on chicken, inside and out. Sprinkle with salt. Place celery, onion, and parsley inside.

2. Heat oven to 350 degrees, place chicken in roasting pan and roast uncovered for about 18 minutes per pound, until chicken is done. Baste from time to time.

ROAST CHICKEN STUFFED WITH APPLES

Soak prunes in the cognac the night before preparing recipe. This recipe is for a fryer-chicken which will serve 4 people. If you use a larger chicken, increase the stuffing accordingly. You don't have to measure the proportions exactly when you increase the stuffing. A few more or less prunes or chestnuts won't ruin anything.

1 whole chicken, fryer or roasting chicken
1 sour baking apple
1 cup unseasoned bread stuffing
4 to 6 prunes
enough cognac to cover the prunes
4 to 6 chestnuts
1 tbsp. butter (1/8 of a stick of butter)

1. Soak dried prunes in cognac overnight. Remove pits after soaking them.

2. Cook chestnuts according to step 1 in Chestnut Purée recipe, page 261. Remove shells and chop chestnut meat. Do not purée them.

3. Peel the apple, remove the core, and slice apple into quarters.

4. Coat chicken with melted butter inside and out. Sprinkle outside of chicken with salt to taste.

5. Mix unseasoned bread stuffing, prunes, chestnuts, apples, and pieces of butter together. Salt very lightly. Stuff chicken with the mixture.

6. Roast covered in a 425 degree oven for the first half hour. Then lower temperature to 350 degrees and continue roasting until done. (About another half hour.)

ROAST CHICKEN WITH APPLESAUCE STUFFING

The applesauce makes the stuffing somewhat sweet.

Serves 4.

> *1 chicken*
> *1 cup applesauce*
> *1 cup soft bread crumbs or unseasoned packaged bread stuffing*
> *1/2 cup dry white wine*
> *2 tsp. flour*
> *about 8 cooked chestnuts or 1 tbsp. raw peanuts or cashew nuts*
> *1 egg*
> *butter*
> *round toothpicks for closing chicken or thread for sewing*

1. To peel the chestnuts easily, cut a slit in each one and fry for a few minutes in hot oil, shaking the pan constantly. Then bake for about 10 minutes in a 350 degree oven. Peel both the hard shell and the inner brown one when cool. Leave them whole.

2. If you're using raw peanuts or cashews, fry them with the chicken liver. Chop the liver when cool.

3. Cook the giblets until tender; chop.

4. Combine the applesauce with the liver, giblets, nuts, bread, flour, egg, pieces of butter, and salt to taste.

5. Coat the cleaned chickens with butter inside and out. Stuff, and close openings.

6. Salt outside of chicken and roast covered in a 425 degree oven for the first half hour. Then lower temperature to 350 degrees and continue roasting uncovered until done, about another 40 minutes. When done, let chicken set for 10 minutes before carving.

CHICKEN IN RUM
(Pollo a la Catalana)

This recipe serves 4 people. Prepare step 1 at least one hour before cooking the chicken. The entire recipe may be completed a day in advance of serving, and re-heated before bringing it to the table.

> *1 chicken cut up into eighths*
> *2 tbsp. rum or enough rum to paint chicken*
> *salt and pepper*
> *butter*
> *1 onion, sliced*
> *2 green peppers cut into rings*
> *1 medium can tomatoes (a one-pound can)*
> *2 carrots cut into two-inch lengths*
> *1/2 cup water*
> *1/4 cup dry white wine*
> *1 hard-boiled egg, sliced*

1. Mix the rum, salt, and pepper, rub it on the chicken, and place the chicken in the refrigerator for about an hour or more. (It may marinate for many hours, but not for less than one hour.)

2. Melt the butter and brown the onions in the same pot in which you will cook the chicken.

3. Remove the onions to a plate and sauté the peppers carefully so that they do not break apart. Remove the peppers to a plate when they are done, for later use.

4. Add more butter to the same pot and brown the chicken.

5. Add the sautéed onions, tomatoes, carrots, water, and wine to the chicken in the pot. After 15 minutes, taste sauce and add salt to taste.

6. Cover the pot and simmer until chicken is tender.

Arrange the food on a serving plate and decorate with the green pepper and sliced hard-boiled egg. Serve the sauce in a gravy boat.

This dish is usually accompanied by rice.

ROYAL CHICKEN
(Pollo Real)

The reason this recipe is called Royal Chicken is because it's a dish fit for a king. The Blonde Sauce, which contains a very unusual ingredient, imparts an especially good flavor. Before serving, the cooked chicken is covered with the very tasty bechamel sauce to further enhance it.

The main part of the preparation is making the sauces, which may be done the day before serving. Also, the entire dish may be prepared the day before, except for the last step (6) when the chicken is covered with the bechamel sauce.

This recipe serves four people.

> *1 chicken, cut into serving pieces (or you may use any chicken parts you prefer)*
> *butter for browning chicken*
> **blond sauce, page** *246*
> *bechamel sauce, page 253*

Decoration for the chicken:

> *1 green pepper, cut into circles*
> *1 hard-boiled egg, sliced*

1. Melt butter and brown chicken. Remove chicken and set aside.

2. Sauté green pepper in the same pot. Be careful not to break up the circles of green pepper. Remove from pot for later use.

3. Prepare the blond sauce.

4. Place the chicken in the pot with the blond sauce, and simmer until the chicken is tender.

5. Prepare the bechamel sauce in a separate pot.

6. When the chicken is done, remove it to a serving platter. Cover the chicken with bechamel sauce, top with circles of green pepper and hard-boiled egg. Serve the blond sauce in which the chicken cooked in a gravy boat.

CHICKEN MEDLEY
(Pollo pepitoria)

This recipe serves 4 people. It may be prepared the day before serving.

> *1 chicken, cut into serving pieces*
> *flour*
> *2 hard-boiled eggs*
> *1 slice white bread, crusts removed*
> *oil*
> *1 clove garlic, sliced, or you may substitute 1/8 tsp. dried garlic*
> *1 tbsp. fresh parsley, or you may substitute 1/4 tsp. dried parsley*
> *1 whole bay leaf*
> *6 whole blanched and peeled almonds or 1 tbsp. chopped almonds*
> *1 whole onion, sliced or 1 tbsp. dried minced onions*

1/4 cup dry white wine
1/8 tsp. saffron, ground and mixed with 1 tsp. water

1. Hard boil the eggs. Slice one egg, and separate the yolk from the white of the other egg, and set them aside for later use.

2. Toast the bread lightly, and let it cool.

3. Heat the oil in the pot in which the chicken will be cooked.

4. Dip the chicken into lightly salted flour and brown in oil. Remove the chicken from the pot and set it aside.

5. Add a little more oil to the pot and brown the garlic, parsley, bay leaf, whole almonds, (if you're using chopped almonds, do not brown them), and onion. Remove these from the pot after they are browned and place them in a chopping bowl. Throw away the bay leaf.

6. Add the toasted bread and the one hard-boiled egg YOLK to the chopping bowl and finely chop all the ingredients. After they are chopped, return them to the same pot.

7. Add wine, one cup water, and the saffron to the ingredients in the pot. Stir them and add salt to taste.

8. Return the chicken to the pot, coat it with sauce, cover the pot, and simmer it until done. Baste the chicken with the sauce from time to time.

To serve the chicken, place it on a serving platter and arrange the sliced hard-boiled egg along the center top of chicken.

Separately chop the hard-boiled egg white very finely, and chop the parsley very finely, mix them together, and sprinkle them over the top of the chicken and egg.

Serve the sauce separately in a gravy boat. If you like a finer sauce, put the sauce through a sieve.

FRIED CHICKEN BREASTS SUPREME
(Pollo Villaroy)

Chicken Villaroy almost looks like ordinary fried chicken in a golden brown crust. However, when you bite into it you'll find a creamy white sauce hidden under the crust. That's what makes this dish so special.

This recipe serves 6 people. Up to and including step 5 may be made the day before. Step 8 may be completed about 3 hours before serving, and the food can be kept warm in the oven.

> *6 chicken breasts*
> **bechamel sauce, page 253**
> *flour for breading chicken*
> *enough oil to deep-fat fry*
> *butter for greasing platter*

1. Coat chicken with oil, salt chicken to taste, and roast it in a 350 degree oven until chicken is done, about 20 minutes. Do not roast chicken too long or it will get too dry.

2. When chicken is done, let it cool, and carefully remove the bones. Be careful not to break up chicken breast.

3. Prepare bechamel sauce, and remove onion from sauce.

4. Butter large platter on which you will place chicken to cool. (Not serving platter.)

5. Place chicken breast on a fork, dip it into bechamel sauce, and coat chicken well on both sides with the bechamel sauce. Place chicken on the buttered platter and let it set about two hours, until bechamel coating is cold and until it doesn't stick to the fingers.

6. When coated chicken is cold, dip it into flour, shake off excess flour, and mold coating to chicken.

7. Dip chicken into beaten egg, and then into bread crumbs, in that order.

8. Heat oil for deep frying, and brown chicken on both sides. Do NOT fry too many pieces of chicken at once; the pan should not be crowded or the chicken will not fry properly.

Test-fry one piece of chicken first to see that the oil is the proper temperature.

CHICKEN IN A GARLIC AND WINE SAUCE
(Pollo al Ajillo)

> *1 frying chicken cut into serving pieces*
> *oil for frying*
> *4 cloves sliced garlic*
> *flour*
> *2 tbsp. fresh chopped parsley or 1 tsp. dried parsley*
> *1 cup dry white wine*

1. Brown garlic in oil and set aside.

2. Add more oil if necessary and brown chicken. Place in baking dish.

3. Stir wine into frying pan and scrape up flour stuck to pan. Add parsley and simmer for a minute.

4. Remove from heat, add salt and pour over chicken.

5. Bake in 357 degree oven until chicken is tender.

STEWED CHICKEN WITH TOMATOES, PEPPERS, AND POTATOES

Serves 4.

> *1 chicken cut into quarters*
> *2 sliced onions*
> *3 fresh tomatoes or 1 medium-size can tomatoes, cut into quarters*

2 small green peppers cut into quarters the long way
2 cups dry white wine
4 potatoes cut into quarters
2 cloves sliced garlic
1/2 bay leaf
2 mint leaves

1. Brown the chicken in butter, remove from pan and set aside.

2. Brown the onion and garlic. Stir in tomatoes, peppers, and bay leaf. Simmer a few minutes. Add the wine, one cup water, and salt. Simmer for about 10 minutes. Add mint leaves. Simmer 5 minutes. Remove leaves.

3. Stir in the chicken and potatoes, cover pan and continue simmering until chicken is done.

CHICKEN STEWED IN TOMATO SAUCE

tomato sauce recipe, either recipe 1 or 2, pages 247, 248
1 chicken cut up into serving pieces
butter or oil
1/4 cup dry white wine

1. Prepare the tomato sauce.

2. Heat the butter or oil in a pan and brown the chicken.

3. Place browned chicken into the tomato sauce and simmer until done.

COUNTRY-STYLE CHICKEN
(Pollo a la campesina)

Serves 4.

1 chicken cut into serving portions
1/2 cup raw or frozen green peas

> *1 medium-size can tomatoes, chopped*
> *2 finely chopped onions*
> *1 green pepper*
> *1 cup dry white wine*
> *flour*
> *salt and pepper*

1. Put the peppers under the broiler until the skin blisters on all sides. Remove and let cool. Peel and remove the seeds. Slice into thin strips.

2. Combine the flour with the salt and pepper, put it in a paper bag. Put the chicken in and shake to coat with flour.

3. Heat oil in a pan, shake off excess flour and brown chicken. Place in a pot.

4. When the chicken is browned, brown the onions. Add the tomatoes and simmer for about 15 minutes. Pour over chicken, add wine, and one cup water. Taste for salt and continue simmering until chicken is done.

5. Add the green peas and green peppers and simmer five minutes longer.

DUCK IN ORANGE SAUCE

If you've always thought that duck was too greasy to eat, preparing it this way will change your mind. The first two steps really remove the fat.

This recipe is for 4 people.

> *1 4-lb. duck*
> *butter and oil to brown duck and render its fat*
> *1 onion cut in half*

1 carrot
1 cup orange juice
2 tbsp. lemon juice
1 cup dry white wine
2 tbsp. Cointreau or cognac
2 tbsp. orange marmalade, or apricot or currant jam

Decoration

segments of one orange
peel of one orange (white part removed) sliced into thin strips

1. Heat a small amount of butter and oil in a pan large enough to hold duck. Dry duck and brown for 10 minutes. Turn from side to side. (This will remove a lot of fat from under the skin.) Pour off fat from time to time.

2. After it is well-browned, remove it from the pan. Sprinkle it with salt inside and out, place an onion and carrot in its cavity, put it on a rack and roast uncovered in a 400 degree oven for another 10 minutes. Do not baste. This will remove more fat.

3. After 10 minutes take it out of the oven and remove the fat from the pan.

4. Lower oven heat to 350 degrees and continue roasting uncovered for 30 minutes.

5. Mix the orange juice with the lemon juice and set aside.

6. Put the orange strips into a pot, cover with water and boil for five minutes. Rinse with cold water, drain and save the strips. (Discard the water).

7. After the duck has been roasting for thirty minutes, add the wine to the orange juice and lemon juice, remove duck from oven, pour off fat, and pour orange sauce on duck. Continue roasting another thirty minutes.

8. After this time remove duck from pan, pour off as much fat as possible without losing gravy, and roast for another thirty minutes. (Throw away carrot and onion.)

9. When the duck is done, remove it from the pan.

10. Place the Cointreau in another pan with two tablespoons marmalade. Bring to a boil and immediately stir in the duck gravy. Lower heat.

11. Place duck on a serving plate, decorate it with the orange peels and segments, and pour on a small amount of the sauce. Bring the rest of the sauce to the table in a gravy boat. Serve duck and gravy hot.

HUNTER'S STYLE RABBIT
(Conejo a la Cazadora)

Serves 6 to 8.

Serve with rice.

> 2 medium-size rabbits cut into small pieces
> 1 small can mushroom pieces
> 1/4 cup cubed ham (optional)
> 2 sliced onions
> 1 clove chopped garlic
> 2 tbsp. cognac
> 1/4 cup dry white wine
> 1 tbsp. chopped fresh parsley or 1/4 tsp. dry parsley
> 1/2 bay leaf
> 1 medium-size can tomatoes, chopped

1. Brown garlic in oil, then remove to a plate. Fry the onion and ham until the onion is tender. Remove.

2. Add more oil if necessary and brown the rabbits, a few pieces a a time. Place the browned pieces into a pot.

3. Blend wine and cognac and pour over the rabbits.

4. Pour the chopped tomatoes on top, add bay leaf, salt and pepper, and cook on low heat until tender.

5. Add the mushrooms and simmer another 15 minutes.

PARTRIDGE IN CHOCOLATE SAUCE
(Perdiz en Chocolate)

This recipe was handwritten by an old cook, a woman who lived in Pamplona.

Here is the translated version, and below is the original.

"Heat half oil and half butter in a clay pot and fry the partridge until it's well browned. Then add onion, garlic, and parsley, which you stir in. When it begins to brown, add vinegar and boiling water.

"Cook it on low heat so that it doesn't burn."

"When it's cooked, add chocolate and bread crumbs."

"Finally, cook it for a few minutes."

"Mitad aceite y mitad manteca se ponen a calentar en una cazuela de barro y se echa allí la perdiz hasta que quede bien doradica. Entonces se le añade cebolla, ajo y perejil, lo cual se rehoga y cuando tome color, se le añaden vinagre y agua hirviendo.

"Cocerá a fuego lento para que no se queme."

"Cuando está cocida se le añade chocolate y pan rallado."

"Como final se hierve todo durante unos minutos." (1)

---

(1) *La Cocina Regional* de Isabel De Trévis, p. 53, Navarra, Vasca y Santanderina, Editorial Molino, 1959, Urgel, 245, Barcelona.

If you make this recipe, try using about 1/4 teaspoon to 1/2 teaspoon grated unsweetened baking chocolate.

La Cocina Regional de Isabel De Trévis, p. 53, Navarra, Vasca y Santanderina, Editorial Molino, 1959, Urgel, 245, Barcelona.

Sauces

La mejor salsa es el hambre y buenas ganas.
Hunger and desire are the best sauce.

SALAD DRESSING

Most of the time, in Spain, oil and vinegar cruets are place on the table and each person pours a little on his salad.

Whenever oil and vinegar, are used for salads, the ratio is always one part vinegar to two parts olive oil.

This dressing may be stored in the refrigerator and used when needed. There is enough dressing here to use on one head lettuce.

> 1/2 cup olive oil
> 1/4 cup vinegar
> 1 clove mashed garlic (optional)
> 2 tbsp. chopped fresh parsley

Place all the ingredients into a jar and shake them up. Use as needed.

BLOND SAUCE
(Salsa Rubia)

This is a very different kind of chicken sauce because of its very unusual ingredient, chocolate. The surprise is that the sauce, when completed, doesn't taste at all like chocolate. It seems that when the chocolate is mixed with the other ingredients it imparts a subtle special flavor that is delicious with chicken, and it becomes very difficult to identify. No one will guess what this sauce is composed of, and it's a good idea not to tell until the food is eaten!

This recipe will make enough sauce to cover one chicken.

       1 onion, chopped
       1 clove garlic, sliced or 1/8 tsp. dried minced garlic
       2 tbsp. oil
       1/2 tsp. dried parsley or 1 tbsp. fresh chopped parsley
       1 bay leaf
       1/8 tsp. ground nutmeg
       1/8 tsp. thyme
    1 1/2 tsp. flour
         salt
       1/8 cup dry white wine or cognac
       1 cup chicken boullion
       1 slice ham, chopped
         a pinch saffron, ground up
       1/2 tsp. grated UNsweetened baking chocolate

1. Sauté onion and garlic in oil until onion is transparent.

2. Add parsley, bay leaf, nutmeg, thyme, and stir.

3. Remove the above mixture from pan and chop finely (or place it in a blender) to make a smoother sauce.

4. Return to pan, add flour, and stir. Add wine, boullion, ham, saffron, and stir.

5. Add salt to taste. (Very little.)

6. Add chocolate.

7. Simmer for 5 minutes, and use. (Taste and correct for salt.)

BASIC SPANISH TOMATO SAUCE, STYLE 1
(Salsa de tomate básico)

This sauce may be prepared the day before, and stored in the refrigerator. This is the tomato sauce that is used in many dishes in Spain.

1 tbsp. olive oil
1 large, finely chopped onion
1 clove mashed garlic or 1 tsp. minced, dried garlic
1 tbsp. dry white wine (optional)
1 can (1 lb. size) tomatoes
1 can (about 5 or 6 oz. size) tomato paste
2 soup bones
1 one-inch piece chorizo or sweet Italian sausage
salt
a pinch thyme
1 bay leaf
2 sprigs chopped parsley
a small amount pepper or crushed red pepper

1. Heat oil in saucepan and sauté onion until transparent.

2. Add garlic, parsley, thyme, pepper, chorizo, and simmer for a minute or so.

3. Add tomatoes, tomato paste, soup bones, bay leaf, and wine. Stir and add salt.

4. Simmer, covered, over very low heat for half an hour. Use as directed in the recipes.

You may add any one of the following ingredients to the sauce after step 3: stew meat, meat balls, shrimp, squid, short ribs, etc.

Cook the meat until tender; shrimp and squid should be added to the sauce during the last 15 minutes of cooking time.

FAST TOMATO SAUCE, STYLE 2

4 chopped tomatoes, either fresh or canned
1 medium-size chopped onion
1 or 2 cloves chopped or sliced garlic
1 tbsp. fresh chopped parsley or 1/4 tsp. dried parsley
oil

1. Brown garlic in a small amount of oil. Remove from pan and set aside.

2. Add more oil if necessary and sauté the onion until tender.

3. Add the tomatoes, return the garlic to the pan, add parsley, salt, and a small amount of water if necessary. Simmer covered until the tomatoes are cooked, about 15 minutes.

TOMATO SAUCE AL COGNAC

Use this sauce the same way that you would use ketchup.

It's a ketchup replacement that was served to me in Spain.

> *1 tbsp. butter*
> *2 tbsp. ketchup*
> *1 tbsp. cognac*
> *1/2 cup tomato purée*
> *pinch pepper*
> *1 tbsp. water*

1. Melt butter.

2. Add the rest of the ingredients. Use more than 1 tbsp. water if necessary.

3. Simmer for 3 or 4 minutes and serve warm.

PINK SAUCE MAJORCA STYLE
(Salsa rosa Mallorquina)

This recipe, which is from Majorca, may be prepared the day before serving. Use it as you would use ketchup.

> *butter*
> *flour*
> *tomato paste*
> *brandy*

1. Melt butter in pan.

2. Add flour slowly and stir it until it is smooth.

3. Add tomato paste and blend it in.

4. Add brandy, stir, and serve the sauce hot.

MAYONNAISE

Señor Ferrándiz, who is now Profesor de Solfeo in the Royal Conservatory of Madrid, was at our house when he heard me say that I needed a mayonnaise recipe. "I'll show you the recipe my father taught me," he said. So we went into the kitchen, he took off his jacket, and made up a most delicious mayonnaise.

His father was born in the city of Mahon, the capital of the Island of Menorca in the Islands of the Baleares. According to some people, mayonnaise originated on that isle, and they say that the original spelling of the word was "mahonesa," named from that city.

There are several ways to prepare mayonnaise; the oldest form is to use a fork, and the fastest is to use the blender. Also, one beater of the mixer may be used.

Whichever way you prepare it, always do it on a day when you are not in a hurry and when you are in a good mood! Patience is one of the unlisted ingredients.

There are certain rules which must be followed when preparing mayonnaise. These are:

Always have all the ingredients and the bowl and fork at room temperature. Once you start stirring the mayonnaise, never stop. Always stir in the same direction.

Add the oil very, very slowly DROP BY DROP, when using the fork or mixer method. Add it in a thin, steady stream when using the blender. Always be sure that you are blending the oil in well before adding more.

When you separate the egg yolk from the white, no part of the yolk should be in the white.

If the mayonnaise doesn't take at first and curdles, there are several remedies:

Start again from step 1 by placing an egg yolk in a warm bowl and beat it until it is a light yellow. Add the curdled mayonnaise, a drop at a time, until it's blended in. Then continue with the rest of the recipe.

Another way to rectify the curdled mayonnaise is to beat the egg white to a stiff peak, then add one tablespoon of it to the curdled sauce and stir it rapidly until the mayonnaise becomes creamy.

Store the mayonnaise in the refrigerator as soon as it's made.

Blender method

1 egg (the yolk and white)
3/4 cup oil
   less than 1/2 tsp. salt
   1 tsp. lemon juice or 1 tsp. vinegar
1/2 clove mashed garlic (optional)

1. Place whole egg, vinegar, garlic, and salt in the blender. Start it at low speed, and blend the ingredients until smooth.

2. Slowly, in a steady, thin stream, add about 1/4 of the oil through the opening of the blender top.

3. When about 1/4 of the oil has been added, stop the blender. When the motor has stopped, push down the mayonnaise from the sides of the container with a rubber spatula.

4. Start the blender again at high speed and add the remaining oil in the same slow, steady, thin stream until all the oil is used.

Fork or beater method

1 egg yolk
3/4 cup oil (place it in a small pitcher for easy pouring)
 less than 1/2 tsp. salt
1 tsp. lemon juice or 1 tsp. vinegar

Use only one beater of the mixer. If you're using a fork, stir in one direction only.

1. Place the egg yolk in a warm china or glass bowl. (Put the beater at lowest speed) and beat the egg yolk until it is light yellow.

2. Drip the oil into the yolk, a drop at a time, and continue beating without stopping, until all the oil is blended in and the sauce is fairly thick.

3. Beat in the salt.

4. Slowly beat in the lemon juice.

If a thinner mayonnaise is desired, beat an egg white in a separate bowl until it forms peaks. Slowly fold some of it into the mayonnaise.

GARLIC AND OLIVE OIL SAUCE
(Alioli)

This is the story of Alioli, the forerunner of mayonnaise: In the war of 1705, the English encircled the Island of Menorca, of which Mahon is the capital. A blockade was formed and no food was allowed into the island. However, the people did have wheat, olives, and garlic; items which grew there. From these they made olive oil, prepared alioli, and baked bread to eat with it.

So powerful is this sauce that they were able to sustain themselves from it and survive!

This sauce, which has a very strong garlic flavor, may be used with cooked tongue, boiled meats, or plainly cooked vegetables.

Prepare it by the same method used to prepare mayonnaise.

> garlic
> olive oil
> 1/2 tsp. lemon juice (optional, it makes the sauce thinner)

Start with 5 cloves garlic and add about one cup oil to make sauce.

1. Mash garlic very well and place it in a bowl.

2. Add the oil, drop by drop, in very small amounts. Beat it in, moving in one direction only, without stopping, and form a thick paste.

3. After all the oil is blended and the sauce is thick, add salt. Then blend in lemon juice, drop by drop. Don't stop beating until all the sauce is done.

BECHAMEL SAUCE

Bechamel sauce is a white sauce which was named after the man who originated it, Louis, Marquis de Béchamel, who was a steward of Louis XIV of France.

Even though it originated in France, people in other lands find this creamy sauce a useful addition to many foods.

Very simple to prepare, it can be used with almost any dish to add flavor and eye appeal to it.

Sometimes the sauce is stirred into the food, as it is done with chopped spinach, and sometimes it's placed on top of the food, as the recipe directs in Royal Chicken. Also, the sauce itself can take on a shape, as it does in the Croquette recipe.

If it is prepared the day before using, place it in a bowl, put pats of butter on top, cover it, and store it in the refrigerator until needed. To reheat, place the sauce in a double-boiler and stir in the butter.

Make it in a heavy saucepan so that it will not burn.

After you make it twice, you won't need to read the recipe, it will be so easy!

Two cups sauce

6 tbsp. butter or oil
4 tbsp. flour
2 cups milk
  salt and white pepper
  a pinch nutmeg
1/2 sliced onion (optional) (chop onion for Croquette recipe)

One cup sauce

3 tbsp. butter or oil
2 tbsp. flour
1 cup milk
  salt and white pepper
  a pinch nutmeg (optional)

A half cup sauce

2 tbsp. butter or oil
1 tbsp. flour
1/2 cup milk
  salt and white pepper
  a pinch nutmeg

1. Heat milk to scalding (just before it boils) and set aside.

2. Melt the butter in a heavy pan and sauté the onions until tender. Remove onions if you don't want them in the recipe.

3. Blend the flour into the butter. Remove pan from heat.

4. Blend the milk into the flour very gradually, stirring it into a smooth sauce. Add salt, pepper, and nutmeg. Return to heat.

5. Stir constantly until a sauce is formed, about 10 minutes for the two-cup sauce, and less for the half-cup sauce.

Bechamel sauce may be mixed into cooked, drained vegetables, or poured on top of the vegetable, sprinkled with cheeese, and baked in the oven. Also tasty is to mix a beaten egg into the vegetable, then blend in the sauce, and bake. Just pouring the sauce on top of the vegetable or meat makes it tastier, too.

HOLLANDAISE SAUCE

This sauce may be made the day before serving. Store it in the refrigerator until needed.

Serve the sauce warm, NOT hot. If it gets hot, it will separate.

It's good on fish, poached eggs, cooked vegetables, and fried potatoes.

> *1/4 lb. butter*
> *1 tsp. water*
> *3 egg YOLKS*
> *1/4 tsp. salt*
> *1/8 tsp. ground white pepper*
> *1 tsp. lemon juice*

1. Melt butter in pan, skim the foam off the top of the butter and discard the foam. Keep the butter warm, but do NOT let it cook.

2. Place egg yolks and water in the top of a double-boiler (or in a pan on very low heat), and beat constantly with a wire whisk until the mixture is thick.

3. Pour the melted butter from a tablespoon, DROP BY DROP, into the thick egg mixture, and stir it while it is dripping in. (Do NOT use the last dregs of the butter.) Remove double-boiler from heat.

4. When the mixture is well blended, add salt, pepper, and lemon juice. Mix it in well.

How to re-heat the sauce

1. Place sauce in double-boiler and heat slowly. Do NOT let it get hot.

2. In another pan, heat 1 tsp. lemon juice and 1/2 tbsp. water.

3. When sauce is warm, slowly drip the mixed lemon juice and water into the sauce, in a steady stream, until it is all blended in.

MORNAY SAUCE

This sauce may be prepared the day before using. To save it for a later date, place a pat of butter on top of the sauce and store it in the refrigerator until you're ready to use it. Re-heat the sauce in the top of a double-boiler on low heat. Do NOT let the water in the bottom of the double-boiler come to a boil.

This sauce is good on fish, vegetables, hard-boiled eggs, or poached eggs. Either heat the sauce and pour it on the food, ready to eat, or pour the sauce on the food and brown it in the oven.

bechamel sauce, page 253
1 1/2 cups sweet cream
2 tbsp. grated cheese

1. Prepare bechamel sauce.

2. Stir the sweet cream into the bechamel sauce.

3. Stir the grated cheese into the bechamel sauce.

BERNAISE SAUCE

Use on steak or grilled fish.

> *hollandaise sauce, page 255*
> *1/2 tsp. tarragon*
> *1/2 tsp. chopped parsley*
> *pinch pepper*
> *1 tbsp. vinegar*

1. Prepare hollandaise sauce.

2. In a separate pan, bring vinegar and tarragon to a boil, and remove from heat immediately.

3. Add this, drop by drop, into the hollandaise sauce, and stir it until it is well mixed.

4. Add parsley and pepper, and mix it in.

TARTAR SAUCE

Serve with fish and seafood.

> *mayonnaise*
> *capers*
> *chopped sour pickle*
> *finely chopped onion*
> *finely chopped parsley*
> *chopped hard-boiled egg*
> *fish court boullion, page 15 6, or water*

Add the above ingredients to the mayonnaise. Use a very small amount of boullion, just enough to make the sauce creamy.

VINAGRETTE SAUCE
(Salsa Vinagrette)

This recipe, which makes about 2 1/2 cups sauce, can be stored in the refrigerator and used when needed for vegetables and fish.

> *1/2 cup oil*
> *1/2 cup vinegar*
> *1 1/2 cups water (use less water if vinegar is not strong)*

Mix the ingredients listed above in a jar, add 1/2 tsp. salt, and stir.

Chop the following ingredients very finely and add to the oil and vinegar mixture:

> *1 tbsp. fresh parsley*
> *1/2 hard-boiled egg*
> *1 tsp. capers*
> *1 tiny pickle*
> *1 tiny canned red pimiento*
> *a pinch black pepper*
> *1/4 cup chopped onion*

Cover the jar and shake the ingredients very well. Store in the refrigerator until ready to use.

GREEN SAUCE
(Salsa verde)

This sauce, which is enough for 6 large slices of fish, may be prepared the day before using.

> *1 tbsp. oil*
> *1/2 medium onion, very finely chopped*
> *1 clove garlic, very finely chopped*
> *1/2 cup flour*
> *1 tbsp. fresh, very finely chopped parsley*
> *1/2 cup asparagus liquid*
> *1 1/2 cups fish court boullion, page 156*

1. Heat oil in pan and sauté onion. Remove onion from pan and set aside.

2. In the same pan, sauté garlic, sprinkle in flour and parsley, and stir them in.

3. Return onion to pan and stir it in.

4. Add boullion slowly and stir it in well so that the flour doesn't lump. Add asparagus liquid. Simmer a few minutes, and use.

If the sauce is not green enough, do either of the following to make it greener:

1. Grind a little fresh parsley with a mortar and pestle, add a little sauce to it and return it to the pot. (Or put the parsley and a little sauce in the blender.)

2. Mash a few canned peas in a dish, add a little of the sauce to it and return it to the pot.

ORANGE JUICE SAUCE FOR ROAST CHICKEN, DUCK, OR PORK

1 1/2 tbsp. sugar
1 tbsp. vinegar
2 glasses water
1 tbsp. beef extract
1 tsp. potato starch
1 cup orange juice

1. Heat sugar in a saucepan until it browns. Blend in vinegar and remove pan from heat.

2. Blend in orange juice, the water, and beef extract. Cover pan and simmer on low heat for about 10 minutes.

3. Put the starch in a bowl and blend in 2 tbsp. water. Add it to the orange juice sauce and simmer another 2 minutes. Remove from heat.

To blend it into the pan gravy, first remove roast, then take off as much fat as possible from the roast gravy.

Add about 5 tablespoons hot water to the pan and scrape off the gravy that is stuck. Bring to a boil.

Blend in the orange juice sauce and simmer another minute or two.

ANCHOVY SAUCE

This sauce may be made days in advance and stored in the refrigerator. Use it on vegetables. It's especially good on boiled potatoes.

1 tbsp. prepared mustard
1 tbsp. vinegar
2 tbsp. butter
1 can anchovies, mashed
3 tbsp. oil or liquid from cooked vegetable on which you're going to use sauce

1. Melt butter.

2. Place mustard in a bowl, add vinegar, and stir until smooth.

3. Add butter and stir until smooth.

4. Add anchovies and blend them in.

5. Add oil in a slow, steady stream and blend it in while stirring constantly.

SAUCE FOR BOILED FISH

2 sliced potatoes
1 chopped tomato
1 chopped green pepper
1 cup water
1/4 tsp. ground cumin seed
1 whole clove
1 bay leaf

1. Fry the potatoes, tomato, and pepper in a small amount of oil. Add the cumin, bay leaf, clove, salt and water. Cook until the vegetables are tender.

2. Put it in the blender or through a strainer. Simmer it again and remove foam that may rise to the top.

Serve in a bowl next to the fish.

CHESTNUT PUREE

This is something like whipped potatoes, only it's made with chestnuts. Serve it with turkey.

Up to and including step 6 may be made the day before and then re-heated in the top of a double-boiler before continuing with the rest of the recipe.

Serves 4.

1/2 lb. chestnuts
1 tbsp. butter at room temperature
about 2 tbsp. sweet cream or milk (the sauce should be thick, so use less if necessary)
1/4 tsp. ground nutmeg
salt and pepper
1 onion
2-inch piece celery

1. Make a slit in each chestnut.

2. Put a very small amount of oil in a frying pan and shake the chestnuts for a few minutes in the hot pan, coating them with oil.

3. Bake them in a 350 degree oven for about 10 minutes (or less) just until they can be peeled. Peel while still warm and remove the brown skin as well.

4. Cook the peeled chestnuts in just enough water to cover them, with an onion, a stalk of celery, and salt and pepper to taste. When they are tender enough to mash with a fork, drain. Discard the onion and celery.

5. Purée the chestnuts in a blender, or put them through a ricer.

6. Add butter, and work into a paste. (If this is difficult to do, heat it in the top of a double-boiler, but do not let the water in the bottom pot come to a boil.)

7. Stir in cream, a little at a time, until you get a purée that resembles thick whipped potatoes. Use less cream than called for in the recipe if necessary. The purée has to hold a shape when served.

8. Stir in nutmeg, salt and pepper.

9. Serve a tablespoon or so of purée on each person's plate, or decorate the serving platter with mounds of it.

Desserts

> Hombre de buena pasta.

This expression, which says, " the man is made of good dough," means that the person has a peaceful nature. The blandness and texture of dough is used to allude to the character of people.

A TRUE STORY

This is a true story, but the names have been changed to protect those involved.

Mrs. Jones hired a new cook. (In those days cooks were still available at very reasonable salaries). Instead of giving her detailed instructions and showing her around the new job, Mrs. Jones, a very busy lady, assumed the cook would know exactly what to do.

She told her to prepare dinner and then bake a birthday cake because a few friends were coming in to celebrate her husband's birthday that evening. As Mrs. Jones left the house, she called out, "Put the birthday candles on the cake. They're in the drawer."

The dinner was delicious and Mrs. Jones was very pleased with the new help. Then the birthday cake was brought out. "But," the cook lamented, "the candles would not light."

No wonder. They were suppositories!

PLUMP IS BEAUTIFUL

My daughters and I had a hard time keeping our weight down. We were on Spanish hours and we seemed to be eating all day long! What added to our difficulty was that plumpness was considered healthy and beautiful, so our motivation to lose weight was not always present.

Just to show you how different values are from country to country, listen to this dialogue which took place between a Spanish friend and me when we met after not seeing each other for a month.

Friend: ¡Hola! ¿Qué tal? How's the family? I see you gained some weight. Now you must be feeling good. You look better.

Me: Ah, umm, well, actually...

Friend: I saw your oldest daughter Carol last week. She gained a lot of weight. ¡Qué gorda está! How fat she is, how beautiful.

Me: Ah, umm, well, actually...

Friend: (Turning to my seven-year-old standing next to me). But the one who is really beautiful is Nancy. (Pinches her cheek.) Is she ever fat! ¡Guapa!

There was no nastiness in that conversation; she really meant what she said. Now that we had fattened up we looked healthier and lovelier to her. A comment that I heard frequently was, "She's fat and beautiful."

This is the attitude we need to have before we eat dessert! But also, the calories should be worth eating.

There are some desserts in this section which are not high in calories, also, there are some variations which can easily be made by omitting sugars and liquers.

CARAMEL-COVERED ALMONDS

1/2 cup almonds, shelled and skins removed
8 1/2 cups sugar

1. Blanch almonds by rinsing quickly with boiling water and remove skins.

2. Heat sugar in saucepan until it becomes a caramel brown color.

3. Add the almonds, stir them so that they get covered with the syrup, and immediately remove to a wet board.

The syrup hardens very quickly. Serve when dry.

CREAM PUFF SHELLS

I had always thought it was so difficult to make Cream Puffs and Eclairs until I tried this recipe. Now I know that it is one of the easiest things to prepare, and well worth the few minutes it takes to make.

After the dough is baked, the inside is hollow, so there is plenty of room to fill it with anything you like. For dessert you may fill it with Pastry Cream, page 281, or whipped cream. It can be filled with tuna fish salad or chicken salad for lunch. Also, smaller shells can be made for appetizers.

This dough, which is usually baked, may also be fried when cold.

The important thing to remember when preparing the dough (which is made in a pot) is to ADD THE FLOUR ALL AT ONCE.

Heat oven to 400 degrees.

> *1 cup water*
> *1/2 cup butter*
> *1/4 tsp. salt*
> *1 cup flour*
> *4 eggs*

1. Put the water, butter, and salt in a saucepan and bring it to a boil. When the butter is melted, remove the pan from the heat.

2. Add all the flour immediately and stir it in vigorously with a wooden spoon until all the flour is blended into the liquid and a ball of dough is formed. (The dough sort of wraps itself around the spoon.) Cool the dough slightly.

3. Add the eggs one at a time. Each time you add an egg, beat it in well until it's mixed in with the dough and the dough is shiny.

4. To make the Puff Shells, drop the dough from a tablespoon onto a greased baking sheet. (If you want Eclairs, squeeze the dough out of a pastry tube or form it with two spoons into the shape of a finger.) Make sure there is plenty of room between shells because they expand very much.

5. Bake in a 400 degree oven for about 15 minutes, or until the shells are firm and done.

6. When cool, cut the top off carefully, fill, and replace top.

ORANGE CREAM GELATIN

This is a very light dessert, especially if egg whites are used instead of cream.

The molds may be filled with the gelatin alone, or lined with sponge cake (page 275) of Lady Fingers.

Four large portions.

> 1 1/4 cups orange juice
> 2 tbsp. sugar
> 1/4 cup cold water
> 1 tbsp. unflavored gelatin
> 1/4 cup hot water
> 3 egg whites or 2 cups whipped cream

1. Soften gelatin in the cold water.

2. Add the hot water to dissolve gelatin.

3. Blend in sugar.

4. Add orange juice.

5. Let it set until it begins to thicken.

6. Beat egg whites until they form stiff peaks, or whip the cream.

7. Fold in to gelatin with as few strokes as possible.

8. Pour into molds and let set until firm.

APPLESAUCE SOUFLEE

This is such an easy, beautiful souflée; however, it should be eaten immediately after taking it out of the oven because it falls in the cooler room temperature.

It takes about a half hour to bake, so time the dessert course accordingly.

The cream of tartar and sugar may be omitted. The cream of tartar makes a firmer meringue, but it is somewhat bitter and needs the extra sugar.

Step 1 may be done in advance.

Heat the oven to 350 degrees.

> *1 cup applesauce*
> *1/4 cup sugar*
> *1/4 cup rum or cognac*
> *3 egg yolks*
> *4 egg whites*
> *about 1/8 tsp. cream of tartar*

1. Beat egg yolks and sugar. Blend into applesauce. Add rum.

2. Beat egg whites in a separate bowl until they foam, then add cream of tartar. Continue beating until they form stiff peaks.

3. With a rubber spatula, fold the egg whites into the applesauce with as few strokes as possible.

4. Pour into a buttered souflée dish or a 6- or 7-inch ceramic or glass baking dish. Place in a pan of water, and bake for about 30 to 35 minutes, or until a knife when inserted near the center comes out clean.

FRIED LITTLE CREAM PIES

Very easy, fast and most delicious.

Let the filling get very cold so that it will be easier to handle.

May be prepared in advance and fried before serving.

Makes 14 pies.

> *Pastry Cream recipe, page 281*
> *Pie Dough recipe 2, page 279*

1. Prepare the Pastry Cream filling and let it cool while the pie dough is being prepared.

2. Cut the dough into circles with a water glass. Place a teaspoonful of Pastry Cream on one circle and cover it with the other circle. Press the edges together with the tines of a fork.

3. Fry in hot oil until brown, place on a serving dish and sprinkle with powdered sugar and cinnamon.

CHURROS
(Spanish Doughnuts)

It's a Spanish custom to buy churros from street vendors on New Year's Eve, after midnight, and to eat them with hot chocolate. (At the stroke of midnight on New Year's Eve you're supposed to eat 12 grapes before the clock strikes its last gong.)

Churros taste something like light doughnuts, although they have a different form; the churro is in the shape of a loop.

These doughnut-like cakes fried in deep fat look pretty and are delicious, and once you get the knack of pushing the pastry out of the tube, they're easy to prepare.

Churros may be served warm or cold. Also, they may be made earlier and re-heated in the oven before serving.

There is one very important rule to remember about making churros, and that is to prepare the batter only when you are ready to fry the churros. Churro batter CANNOT be prepared in advance. As soon as you mix the batter, you must finish the recipe. Prepare all the utensils and ingredients before you start mixing the batter, including the hot oil in the pan for frying the churros.

There are several slightly different types of batter you can make. For example, one type of batter, type 3, uses no eggs and very little oil.

To form the churros, use a pastry tube with a ragged tip. If you don't have a pastry tube, two paper cups will work very well if used in the following manner:

1. Make a pencil hole in the bottom of one cup.

2. Fill with batter, half-way full. (The batter is thick and will not run out of the hole.)

3. Place bottom of second cup into batter, and push batter through hole into frying pan.

Batter for churros

Type 1

2 eggs
1 cup water
1/4 tsp. salt
3 tbsp. oil
3/4 cup unsifted flour

Type 2

Prepare exactly like type 1, but omit eggs.

Type 3

Prepare exactly like type 1, but use 1 tbsp. oil instead of 3 tbsp. oil. Omit eggs.

Type 4

Prepare exactly like type 1, but use 2 tbsp. oil and 1 egg

Also needed will be oil for deep frying and confectioner's sugar to sprinkle on churros when they are done.

1. Heat oil for deep frying.

2. Beat eggs and set aside.

3. Place water, salt, and oil in a saucepan and bring to a boil.

4. When it boils, remove from heat and add flour, A LITTLE AT A TIME.

5. Add eggs, A LITTLE AT A TIME, and mix it all in well until a smooth batter is reached. DO NOT LET BATTER GET COLD. If the batter gets cold, the churros will not form into a shape, but will disintegrate in the oil.

6. Place batter into a pastry tube immediately.

7. Squeeze out about three inches of batter directly into the hot oil in the frying pan to form the churro. Let it brown on one side, then turn it over to brown on the other side. Remove from pan when done and drain on paper toweling. (Always test the oil to see if it's hot enough with one churro first before making the entire batch.)

8. When the churros are done, sprinkle them with confectioner's sugar, and serve.

ICE CREAM CAKE

1/2 gallon ice-cream
   Sponge Cake recipe, page 275,or store-bought sponge cake or
   Lady Fingers (the equivalent of four 8-inch layers)

1. Cut cake into narrow rectangular slices, about 2 inches long.

2. Place 1/3 of the cut cake on cookie sheet in the shape (length and width) of the ice-cream.

3. Place the ice-cream on top.

4. Place the rest of the slices of cake on top of and around sides of ice-cream, covering ice-cream completely with cake.

5. Whip cream and cover the whole cake with it. (Sides, too.)

Cake may be served now, or placed into freezer for later use.

A half hour before serving, remove cake to refrigerator so that it will be soft enough to cut.

BAKED ALASKA

Up to and including step 7 may be made well in advance and frozen.

This recipe serves 8 people.

> *1/2 gallon vanilla ice-cream, in the shape of a brick*
> *sponge cake, page 275, or lady fingers (the equivalent of 4*
> *8-inch layers)*
> *8 egg white Meringue, page 276*
> *1/2 cup rum*

1. Cut cake into narrow rectangular slices, about 2 inches long.

2. Make meringue and set aside.

3. Place 1/3 of cut cake on cookie sheet, in the shape (length and width) of the ice-cream.

4. Place the ice-cream on top of the cut cake that is on the cookie sheet.

5. Place the rest of the slices of cake on top of and around sides of ice-cream, covering ice-cream completely with cake.

6. Beat meringue once more, slightly, and cover cake completely with meringue, putting it on like icing. It's important that the meringue seals the cake to the pan. (Bring meringue to seam where the cake meets the pan. Cover the cake liberally with meringue, bringing the meringue on to the pan. This will seal in the ice-cream).

7. Sprinkle with a small amount of confectioner's sugar, preferably from a shaker.

8. Bake in 425 degree oven for 10 minutes. When the top starts getting brown, remove from oven.

9. To warm rum: place in saucepan and slowly bring to a warm temperature. WARM SLOWLY. It is very important that you do NOT let it get hot or boil. If it gets too hot, the alcohol evaporates, and the liquer will not light up. Just get it warm.

10. Pour warm rum over cake (at the table) and immediately light it with a match. Eat immediately.

MERINGUE COOKIES
OR WHAT TO DO WITH LEFTOVER EGG WHITES

2 egg whites
2 1/4 tbsp. sugar
pinch cream of tartar

3 egg whites
3 1/4 tbsp. sugar
pinch cream of tartar

1. Beat egg whites until they begin to foam. Sprinkle in sugar. Continue beating. Sprinkle in cream of tartar. Continue beating until they form stiff peaks.

2. Melt an equal amount of jam and water in a pan over low heat.

3. Fold the jam syrup into the egg whites little by little.

4. Wet a cookie sheet and sprinkle it with sugar. Drop the meringue by the tablespoonful onto the sugar and bake in a very slow oven (about 200 degrees) for one hour, or until a toothpick when inserted into the meringue comes out clean.

When done, remove pan from oven and let set awhile. Remove cookies with a spatula.

Place the flat side of one cookie onto the flat side of another to make one cookie out of the two.

SPONGE CAKE
(Bizcochón)

This cake is very easy to make, and it may be prepared the day before using. It serves 5 people.

4 eggs
3 tbsp. sugar
3 tbsp. flour
1/4 tsp. grated lemon rind

1. Separate egg whites from yolks. Be very careful not to let A DROP of yolk enter the whites, or the whites won't beat well.

2. Beat YOLKS well, and add sugar, one tablespoon at a time. Beat between additions.

3. Add lemon rind to the yolks.

4. Add flour, one tablespoon at a time, beating between additions. Beat well.

5. Beat egg whites until they stand in peaks.

6. Add beaten egg whites to batter, and fold in QUICKLY with rubber spatula, until all the whites are thoroughly blended with the batter. (This should take only 25 seconds. Don't mix too much, or the fluffiness of the cake will be ruined.)

7. Grease jelly roll pan or 12'' x 6'' cake pan and pour batter in. Spread batter evenly and bake for about 10 minutes, or until toothpick comes out clean. Bake in a 350 degree oven.

8. Let cool 5 minutes. Loosen edges with spatula, and turn pan upside down on wax paper, thereby turning out cake.

9. Fill with desired filling, and roll up jelly roll fashion WHILE STILL WARM. (Or use as directed in the recipe.)

Fillings

Spread cooled cake with either one of the following fillings:

A. A thin layer of jam and ice-cream.

B. Jam and sour cream.

C. Jam and yoghurt.

D. Whipped cream and sliced strawberries.

E. Pastry cream filling.

1. Roll cake gently, so as not to squeeze out filling.

2. Place cake with seam side down on plate.

3. Pour a jigger of sweet wine over rolled cake.

MERINGUE

Meringue is very easy to prepare; however, the following hints are very important:

Beat egg whites in a copper bowl if possible; they whip up better. When separating egg whites from yolks, be sure that not a drop of yolk falls into the white, or the white will not beat up well. To prevent "weeping," the item that the meringue will be placed on should always be cooled first.

To prevent shrinkage, the meringue should always touch the edge of the crust. Also, cool the baked meringue slowly, not in a refrigerator.

8 egg whites
9 tbsp. sugar

1. Separate the egg whites from the yolks.

2. Beat egg whites very stiff, until they hold a peak.

3. Slowly beat in the sugar, a tablespoon at a time. Beat until the meringue is stiff and shiny.

Use as directed in the recipe, or bake in a 425 degree oven until lightly browned.

MERINGUE SHELLS

These shells are empty in the center so that they may be filled with ice-cream, for example, or any other suitable item.

Meringue recipe
1/4 tsp. cream of tartar

Add the cream of tartar to the egg whites when they begin to foam. Use a pastry tube to form rings of the meringue, placing one layer upon another, for about four or five rings high, on a baking sheet that has been lined with brown paper.

Bake in a 250 degree oven for about one hour and 15 minutes.

Let it set for a few minutes before removing from pan with a spatula.

GYPSY'S ARM
(Brazo de Gitano)

This recipe serves about 6 people.

make sponge cake recipe, page 275
make half amount of pastry cream filling recipe, page 281
1 pint whipping cream
1 tbsp. brandy

1. Fill baked, unrolled Sponge Cake with Pastry Cream Filling. Let it set half an hour before rolling it. Then roll it up gently so that the filling is not squeezed out.

2. Whip the cream, fold the brandy into the whipped cream, and frost the roll all over with the whipped cream.

Place into refrigerator until ready to serve.

SPANISH APPLE PIE

This pie may be made the day before using, but it must be stored in the refrigerator, and it cannot be kept for more than two days because the pastry cream filling is perishable. Bake it in a 450 degree oven. Use a 9-inch pie pan or spring form.

> prepare Dough for Pies, recipe style 1, page 279
> prepare Pastry Cream Filling, page 281
> 2 large apples
> sugar
> butter
> 1/4 cup apricot marmelade
> 1 marachino cherry
> confectioner's sugar

1. Roll out the dough and place it in an UNgreased pan. Prick all over with a fork. Trim off excess overlapping dough.

2. Make pastry cream. Pour it onto UNbaked dough.

3. Peel and core the apples. Slice them so that they are as thick as a nickel.

4. Place the apples on top of the pastry cream filling, in a circle, slices slightly overlapping, until all the pastry cream is covered with apples. Make a circle of the sliced apples in the center of the pie to look like a flower.

5. Sprinkle apples with 1 tsp. sugar and bits of butter.

6. Coat rim of dough with beaten egg yolk.

7. Bake for about 15 minutes, until the apples are soft and the dough is done.

8. When the pie is cold, heat the marmelade with 1 tbsp. sugar and stir till it's well mixed. Put it through a sieve.

9. Spread this mixture over the apples on the cold pie.

10. Sprinkle confectioner's sugar around rim of pie, on the dough only. Place Marachino cherry in center.

DOUGH FOR PIES, STYLE 1

This dough takes five minutes to prepare, it's that easy to do. Once prepared, the dough has to "rest" for 20 minutes before it's rolled out and baked, so allow enough time for that. Also, the butter should be removed from the refrigerator a half hour before so that it becomes soft enough to use.

This recipe makes enough dough for a one-crust nine-inch pie.

To use this crust for meat or fish pies, omit the sugar and add 1/4 teaspoon grated cheese.

> *1 cup unsifted flour*
> *1/4 tsp. baking powder*
> *1/4 cup sugar*
> *1/4 tsp. salt*
> *1 whole egg*
> *1 egg yolk ·*
> *1/4 stick butter (two tablespoons) at room temperature*

1. Mix the sugar, salt, and baking powder with the flour.

2. Beat whole egg and egg yolk slightly. Make an indentation in the center of the flour, and place the eggs and butter in it. Quickly mix it with a fork, then, using the fingers, continue blending it in. Do not knead the dough. Form a ball, cover it, and let it "rest" for 20 minutes.

3. Roll out dough, place into pie plate, and prick all over with a fork. Trim off excess dough. Bake in a 450 degree oven.

VERY EASY PIE DOUGH, STYLE 2

This is an easy dough to make; just stir everything together and roll it out!

If the recipe calls for tart shells and you don't have them, fit the dough over the bottom of muffin tins, prick all over with a fork, and bake them upside down.

An easy method of rolling out dough is to dampen the table top, place a sheet of wax paper on top, put the ball of dough on it, and cover with another sheet of wax paper. Then roll it out, moving the rolling pin on the wax paper.

To place the dough into the pie pan, remove the top layer of wax paper. Lift the bottom layer of paper with the dough and fit the dough side into the pie pan. Then gently remove the remaining wax paper.

If you're having trouble with the texture of pie dough, the following information might help: too little liquid makes the dough crumble; too much makes it tough.

For this recipe, bake an empty pie shell or tarts in a 475 degree oven for about 8 to 10 minutes.

one-crust 9-inch pie or 6 tart shells

2 2/3 cups SIFTED flour
1 tsp. salt
2/3 cup oil
1/2 cup milk

Two-crust 9-inch pie or 12 tart shells

5 1/3 cups SIFTED flour
2 tsp. salt
1 1/3 cups oil
1 cup milk

1. SIFT flour and salt together.

2. Put oil and milk together in a separate bowl. Don't blend.

3. Pour the oil and milk all at once into the flour and stir it until it's blended and forms a dough.

4. With your hands, shape the dough into a ball then gently roll it out, starting from the center, to form a circle or whaterver shape is needed.

PASTRY CREAM FILLING

This recipe makes enough filling for one 9-inch pie.

Pastry cream is a creamy filling which is used for pies, cakes, pastry shells, etc.

> *2 cups milk*
> *1 piece lemon peel or 1/8 tsp. lemon extract or 1/8 tsp. vanilla*
> * extract (peel the lemon so that the white rind is not included)*
> *1 tbsp. butter*
> *1 whole egg*
> *2 egg yolks*
> *1/4 cup flour*
> *1/2 cup sugar*

In order to get everything ready at the right time, you are going to start the milk boiling while preparing the first part of the sauce.

1. Place the lemon peel in the milk, and bring the milk to a boil. If you're using extract instead of lemon peel, add it in step 6, not now.

2. Bring water in the bottom part of a double-boiler to a boil.

3. Place the TOP part of the double-boiler on the COUNTER (not yet in the bottom part of the boiler), and mix sugar, flour, and eggs in it, while it is off the heat. After it is mixed, immediately place the pot into the bottom part of the double-boiler, over the boiling water. STIR CONSTANTLY.

4. When the milk in the saucepan comes to a boil, remove the top part of the double-boiler from the bottom part, add the milk all at once to the sauce, and stir it in well.

5. Return the pot to the bottom part of the double-boiler, and continue stirring until the sauce thickens, about 5 minutes.

6. Add butter, and stir for 2 minutes.

If the sauce is lumpy, put it through a sieve.

VERY EASY PEAR PIE

> *pie dough recipe 1, page 279*
> *1 can pear halves*
> *sugar to make a caramel*
> *slivered or chopped almonds for decoration*

1. Prepare the dough, line an ungreased pie plate, prick all over with a fork and trim off excess dough. Bake in a 450 degree oven for about 8 to 10 minutes or until done. Cool.

2. Arrange the drained pear halves on the baked pastry crust.

3. Heat about 3 tablespoons sugar with one teaspoon water and when it begins to brown, pour it over the pears.

4. Sprinkle with almonds.

PEACH PUDDING PIE

Fast and simple to prepare, and very delicious.

Heat oven to 350 degrees.

> *3 eggs*
> *canned or raw sliced peaches*
> *1/3 cup sugar*
> *1 cup milk*
> *1 ounce rum or cognac*
> *sponge cake (see recipe, page 275*

1. Butter a deep pie plate and line the bottom and sides with sponge cake.

2. Place canned peaches in a bowl, add the rum, and let set for a half hour. If you're using raw peaches, place the peeled, halved peaches into a small amount of water, rum, and sugar, and simmer, until tender but not very soft.

3. Drain the peaches and place them in a circle on the cake. (Slice the raw peaches.)

4. Separate the egg yolks and whites.

5. Stir sugar into the beaten egg yolks, then combine with milk.

6. In a separate bowl, beat the whites until they form stiff peaks, then fold them into the egg yolks. Pour over peaches.

7. Put the pie plate in a pan of water and bake in a 350 degree oven for about a half hour, or until a knife when inserted near the center comes out clean. Serve cold.

SPANISH CUSTARD
(Flan)

A very popular dessert in Spain, this recipe serves six people and is very easy to prepare.

Pre-heat oven to 350 degrees.

> *9 eggs*
> *9 tbsp. sugar*
> *4 cups milk*
> *1/4 tsp. vanilla*
> *extra sugar for caramel topping*

1. If you're using a metal custard mold, cover bottom of it with sugar and a little water and cook on medium heat until sugar melts and becomes a light caramel color. Tilt mold and swirl caramel around bottom of mold so that it gets covered with the caramel. Set aside to cool.

If you're using a glass or ceramic baking dish, heat about three tablespoons sugar with one teaspoon water in a saucepan on medium heat until it reaches a light caramel color. Then pour it into the baking dish and tilt it so that the caramel covers the bottom of the dish. Set aside to cool.

2. Bring milk to a boil and remove from heat.

3. Put eggs in a bowl and beat well. Beat in 9 tablespoons sugar.

4. Mix in the hot milk very slowly. Add vanilla and mix well.

5. Pour into baking dish on top of caramel. Place baking dish in a pan of water and bake in a 350 degree oven for about 35 to 40 minutes, until a knife inserted near the center comes out clean. Cool before placing into refrigerator.

Let custard cool. Shake mold a little and slide a knife around sides. Place a plate over mold, turn upside down, and tap bottom. Custard will unmold easily.

Serve with caramel side up.

AN ECONOMICAL COFFEE CUSTARD
(Flan Económico)

A very delicious custard, using less eggs than the original recipe.

It may also be made plain, without the coffee. Add a few drops lemon juice and a drop or two of vanilla, instead.

> *1 cup milk*
> *2 tbsp. strong coffee liquid*
> *3 slices white bread (crusts removed) made into soft bread crumbs*
> *1/4 cup sugar*
> *3 eggs*
> *4 tbsp. sugar for making the caramel*

Preheat oven to 350 degrees.

1. Prepare the caramel by heating on medium heat the four table-spoons sugar and one teaspoon water in a saucepan (or metal custard mold) until sugar becomes brown. Coat custard cups with it by pouring it in and very quickly swirling it around.

2. Combine the coffee liquid with the milk, then add the sugar. When the sugar dissolves, add the bread. Bring to a boil, then remove from heat.

3. Beat together three egg yolks and two egg whites. Blend into milk, a little at a time.

4. Pour into custard cups and set into a pan of water. Bake in a 350 degree oven for about a half hour or more. (When a toothpick inserted into the center comes out clean.)

Let custard cool. Shake mold a little, and slide a knife around sides. Place a plate over mold, turn upside down, and tap bottom.

Custard will just slide out.

Serve with caramel side up.

FRUIT AND BREAD CUSTARD

Easy, delicious, and nutritious.

Serves 2.

1 cup unseasoned bread stuffing or soft bread crumbs
1 cup milk, or a half-cup cream and a half-cup milk
1 tbsp. sugar
1 egg
a few slices drained canned peaches or any other fruit

1. Soak bread in a half cup milk (or the cream) until soft.

2. Beat egg, add a pinch salt, and combine with the half cup milk, sugar, and the soaked bread. (Do NOT press out milk from bread.)

3. Butter a small baking dish and pour it in. Put in the sliced peaches.

Bake in a 350 degree oven for 40 to 50 minutes, or until a toothpick inserted into the center comes out clean.

FRIED CUSTARD
(Leche Frita)

The man who gave me this recipe had lived in an orphanage as a child, and "Leche Frita" was a treat he had always looked forward to.

He remembered how much he enjoyed this when the monks who took care of him made it, and now he cooks it up for his children.

At first Fried Custard didn't sound very appealing to me, (it translates into Fried Milk!), but he insisted that I try it because he loved it so much, so I did, and I found it quite delicious.

This is a soft, custard-like marshmallow with a crisp fried exterior.

2 cups milk
3 egg yolks
6 tbsp. sugar
1/4 cup cornstarch
1-inch piece lemon peel (remove white part from peel)
a few drops vanilla
1 or 2 eggs and bread crumbs for coating

1. Bring milk with lemon peel to a boil.

2. Blend egg yolks, sugar, vanilla, and cornstarch in a bowl.

3. Slowly add the milk, little by little, to the cornstarch mixture, stirring it in well.

4. Put it in the saucepan and cook over low heat stirring constantly until it becomes very thick.

5. When the sauce is thick, remove pan from heat and cool.

6. Coat a large platter with butter and pour the sauce onto it. Let set until firm and cold.

7. Prepare a dish of beaten egg and a dish of bread crumbs. Heat the oil for frying. Cut the firm sauce into very small (about 3/4 inch squares.)

8. Dip each square into the beaten egg, then into the bread crumbs, and fry on medium heat until brown on both sides. When done, sprinkle with powdered sugar.

FRUIT COCKTAIL PUDDING

1. Butter an 8-inch round casserole or soufflée dish. Drain canned fruit cocktail (mixed fruit) and place into dish.

2. Line the sides with Lady Finger biscuits or sponge cake squares.

3. Prepare Pastry Cream filling, page *281*

4. Pour it into the fruit and let it set for about a half hour.

5. Heat oven to 350 degrees and bake for a half hour. Serve cold.

APPLESAUCE PUDDING

applesauce
4 to 6 slices bread, crusts removed
butter
2 beaten eggs
4 tbsp. milk
3 tbsp. sugar
1/4 tsp. vanilla

1. Butter bread (use melted butter) and line bottom of baking dish.

2. Cover with applesauce, and top with another layer of buttered bread.

3. Blend sugar, milk, vanilla, and beaten eggs. Pour on bread and let set for about a half hour so that the liquid is absorbed.

4. Place into a 375 degree oven until pudding is firm inside and browned on top. (Insert a knife near center to test for firmness.) Remove from oven and let cool. Slide a knife around the edges to remove pudding.

RICE WITH MILK DESSERT

1 cup rice
1 1/2 cups water
1 cup milk
1-inch piece cinnamon or a pinch ground cinnamon
a piece lemon peel, white removed
2 tbsp. sugar

1. Cook rice in the 1 1/2 cups water with the lemon peel, cinnamon and a pinch salt until all the water is absorbed.

2. Dissolve the sugar in the milk in another pot and add it to the rice. Continue cooking until all the milk is absorbed and the rice is done.

3. Remove the lemon peel and cinnamon stick, place the rice into a serving bowl, and sprinkle sugar and cinnamon on top.

RICE SOUFLEE DESSERT

Do the last four steps about 15 minutes before serving.

Preheat oven to 350 degrees.

1 cup rice
3/4 cup milk
4 eggs
sugar
Cointreau (optional)
cinnamon

1. Cook rice for 20 minutes with two and a half cups water, sugar to taste, and a pinch of salt.

2. Bring the milk to a boil in a pan large enough to hold rice later on. Remove from heat.

3. When the rice is done, drain it and add to milk. Add more sugar if necessary. Cook for another five minutes. Remove from heat. Let cool.

4. Beat egg yolks with the Cointreau, and blend into cooled rice, a little at a time.

5. Beat the egg whites until they form stiff peaks and fold into the rice with as few strokes as possible.

6. Pour into a deep casserole dish and place into a 350 degree oven for 10 to 15 minutes, until the rice is browned on top and a knife inserted near center comes out clean. When done, sprinkle with cinnamon. Eat immediately.

COOKIE BALLS

Makes about 48 cookies.

> *1 cup butter*
> *1/2 cup firmly packed brown sugar*
> *1 tsp. vanilla*
> *2 1/4 cups SIFTED cake flour*

1. Cream butter with the sugar until it is light and fluffy.

2. Blend in vanilla, then gradually add the flour. Mix it until smooth. Chill in refrigerator.

3. Shape dough into balls the size of a walnut, then dip into granulated sugar. Bake on a buttered cookie sheet in a 350 degree oven for about 12 to 15 minutes, until they become a light brown.

ANNISETTES
(Roscos)

These are hard, puffed-up cookies that may be stored for a long time.

This recipe makes 20.

> *3 eggs*
> *3 cups flour*
> *1/4 cup oil*
> *1/2 tsp. ground anise*
> *1/4 cup sugar*

1. Blend the eggs and the sugar.

2. Blend the oil and the anise with the eggs.

3. Put the flour into a separate bowl, make an indentation in the center and add the egg mixture. Blend it in, stirring for about five minutes or more. The dough should be bubbly.

4. Sprinkle flour on top of dough and form small balls the size of a golf ball.

5. Place on a greased baking sheet, and let it rest for about fifteen minutes.

6. After this time, paint tops with beaten egg and bake in a 400 degree oven for 10 to 15 minutes, until brown.

COOKIES

Makes about 35 large cookies.

The butter should be soft, at room temperature.

> *1/2 cup butter*
> *2 1/2 cups flour*
> *3/4 cup sugar (or 1/2 cup sugar for a less sweet cookie)*

1/8 cup Sherry
1 tbsp. orange juice

1. Beat the butter until it's light and fluffy. Beat the egg yolks and blend into the butter. Beat.

2. Blend in the Sherry, orange juice, and sugar. Gradually blend in the flour until a dough is formed. Let rest for a half hour.

3. Roll it out and cut circles with the rim of a water glass. (Or a smaller glass if smaller cookies are desired.)

Bake on a greased cookie sheet in a 350 degree oven until done, about 10 or 15 minutes.

POLVORONES COOKIES

Makes about 36 walnut-size cookies.

1 cup butter (2 4-oz. sticks) at room temperature
2 cups unsifted flour
1/2 cup sugar
3 tbsp. ground almonds
1 egg at room temperature
1/8 tsp. salt
1/4 tsp. powdered cinnamon
confectioner's sugar (optional)

1. Toast the flour on a flat pan on medium high heat until it becomes a golden tan color. Toss it constantly so that it doesn't burn.

2. Remove from pan when done and cool. Place in a bowl and mix in salt, cinnamon, and almonds.

3. In another bowl, blend the butter with the sugar.

4. Make an indentation in the center of the flour and in it place the butter and sugar mixture and the egg. Blend well to form a dough.

291

5. Make small balls the size of a walnut, and place them on an ungreased cookie sheet. Bake in a 350 degree oven for about 25 minutes.

When cool, sprinkle with confectioner's sugar.

VERY DELICIOUS NUT COOKIES

Makes four dozen cookies.

> *1 cup soft butter*
> *1/2 cup sifted confectioner's sugar*
> *1 tsp. vanilla*
> *2 1/4 cups all-purpose flour*
> *1/4 tsp. salt*
> *3/4 cup finely chopped nuts*

1. Blend butter, sugar, and vanilla thoroughly.

2. Blend flour and salt, and stir it in.

3. Blend in nuts. Chill.

4. After this time, roll into one-inch balls. Place on ungreased cookie sheet and bake 10 to 12 minutes in a 400 degree oven.

While still warm, roll in confectioner's sugar and cool. Later roll in confectioner's sugar again.

JANE BAXTER'S NUT CAKE

> *1 1/2 cups sugar*
> *1/3 cup lard*
> *2 eggs, beaten*
> *2 egg whites*
> *2 1/4 cups SIFTED flour*
> *1 tsp. soda*
> *1 tsp. cinnamon*
> *1/2 tsp. cloves, all spice, and nutmeg*

1/2 tsp. salt
1 cup currant jelly
1/2 cup pineapple juice
1 tsp. vanilla
1/2 tsp. dried lemon rind
3 1/3 lbs. shelled walnuts
1 lb. toasted shelled almonds
1/8 cup brandy

1. Chop nuts into coarse pieces and dredge in one-quarter cup of the flour.

2. Sift dry ingredients three times.

3. Combine juices, vanilla, and jelly.

4. Cream sugar and lard. Add two whole beaten eggs.

5. Add dry ingredients alternately with the juices and jelly, beating after each addition.

6. Add nuts, a little at a time. Add brandy.

7. Fold in stiffly beaten egg whites with as few strokes as possible. Pour into bread pans which are greased and lined with wax paper.

Bake in a 250 degree oven for two and a half hours.

When done, remove paper and cool. Age for about two weeks in a covered container. Place a rag soaked in brandy over cake during the aging.

CHOCOLATE SOUFLEE

4 oz. unsweetened cornstarch
1 tbsp. rum
1 cup sugar
1/3 cup cornstarch
2 cups milk

4 egg yolks
6 egg whites
a pinch salt
1/4 tsp. cream of tartar
whipped cream for the topping (optional)

The first three steps can be prepared earlier.

1. Melt the chocolate with four tablespoons water in the top part of a double-boiler. When it's melted, blend in the sugar. Remove from heat.

2. Put the cornstarch in a pan and slowly blend in the cold milk. Place on heat, stir constantly, bring to a boil, and remove.

3. Add the chocolate mixture to the cornstarch mixture. Add the rum, cover and set aside.

4. Heat oven to 375 degrees now so that it will be hot when the souflée is ready to be baked.

5. Beat egg yolks well and add to chocolate sauce.

6. Beat egg whites until they begin to foam, add cream of tartar and salt, and continue beating. Before they get very stiff, add two tablespoons sugar, then continue beating until they form stiff peaks.

7. With a rubber spatula, first fold a small amount of egg white into the chocolate sauce, then fold in the rest of the sauce to the whites with as few strokes as possible.

8. Butter a two-quart round ceramic or glass casserole or souflée dish, sprinkle it with granulated sugar, and pour in souflée. Bake for about 30 to 40 minutes, or until a knife inserted near the center comes out clean.

Serve immediately. If desired, top with whipped cream.

FRITTERS
(Buñuelos)

These may be prepared with or without a filling.

Some of the fillings used are mashed tuna fish, thinly-sliced pieces of apple, finely chopped fried onions, small pieces of shrimp or chicken. After preparing this recipe a few times, you'll have your own ideas.

If you're not using a filling (and they're very good without one), sprinkle with powdered sugar when done.

Batter should be as thick as pancake batter.

1 cup flour
1/4 tsp. salt or more (taste batter)
1/4 tsp. baking powder
1 egg yolk
1 egg white
1 tbsp. rum (optional)
oil for deep frying
about 1/4 cup water

1. Blend flour, salt, and baking powder in a bowl. Make an indentation in the center and drop in the egg yolk and rum. Slowly drip in water, a little at a time, and blend it with the egg yolk and rum. Slowly blend in the flour until a batter is formed.

Set aside for a half hour.

2. Now is the time to prepare the filling.

3. After the dough rests for a half hour, heat the oil.

4. Blend the filling into the dough.

5. Beat the egg white until it forms stiff peaks and fold in with as few strokes as possible.

6. (Drop a cube of bread into the oil to test for readiness.) Slowly pour the batter off a tablespoon into the oil. Brown on one side, then on the other. Remove with a slotted spoon and drain on absorbant paper.

De Lux Apple Fritters

Slice an apple into thin, small pieces.

Blend two tablespoons sugar with four tablespoons cognac, and stir it into the apples. Let it set for one hour.

Dip the apples into flour, then into the batter, and fry.

CRESCENTS

This is a recipe for making a crescent-shaped edible craker which can decorate a serving plate by standing the craker on its side.

Dough for pies recipe, style 1, page 279, For this recipe, omit the sugar in the Dough for Pies recipe, add 1/4 cup grated cheese, and increase the salt slightly.

1. After the dough is rolled out, cut it with the rim of a glass into a quarter moon shape.

2. Coat the dough with egg YOLK.

3. Bake it in a 400 degree oven on an UNgreased cookie sheet until done, about 10 minutes.

After the crescent is baked, cut off a small piece of each tip. Dip the tips into a paste of flour and water, and place each crescent on its tips around the edge of the serving platter, thus making a border around the food on the plate.

OMELETTE IN FLAMES
(Tortilla Quemada)

Isabel, the lady who occasionally cleaned for us, said she loved this dessert and that I had to include it in the book.

>*1 egg for each omelette*
>*butter*
>*sugar*
>*2 tbsp. cognac*

1. Make a Plain omelette, page 85

2. Place omelette on a plate and sprinkle powdered sugar on top. Score omelette with a red-hot skewer, burning lines across the top.

3. At serving time, place cognac in a saucepan and slowly bring it to a warm temperature. Do NOT let it boil or get very hot or the cognac will not light up.

4. Pour the warm cognac on the omelette at the table. Light it with a match.

ORANGES IN KIRSCH
(Naranjas al Kirsch)

This recipe is for 6 people.

>*6 oranges, one orange per person*
>*1/2 cup sugar*
>*1/2 cup Kirsch liquer*
>*strawberries or marachino cherries*

1. Peel oranges, slice into rounds, remove seeds, and place on a flat serving dish. (This may be done hours earlier.)

2. A half hour before serving time, sprinkle oranges with sugar, and then with Kirsch. Place in the refrigerator.

3. Decorate with strawberries or cherries at serving time.

PRUNES IN COGNAC

Rinse prunes and dry. Place into a jar and cover with cognac. Let set for two weeks before using.

Serve with other fruit, or decorate a turkey or chicken platter.

FRUIT CUP IN ORANGE SHELLS

1/2 orange per person
Sherry or cognac
sliced strawberries or cherries
sliced bananas
chopped almonds
powdered sugar

Cut the oranges in half and scoop out the center carefully. (Don't cut shell.) Combine strawberries, bananas, the scooped-out oranges, Sherry, and a small amount of powdered sugar. Chill in refrigerator.

Before serving, fill the orange shells and top with chopped almonds.

Serve cold.

BAKED APPLES WITH PASTRY CREAM FILLING

Prepare the Pastry Cream in advance and place a pat of butter on top.

1 apple per person
Pastry Cream recipe, page 281, (enough for 6 to 8 apples)

1. Scoop out center core and some of the apple to make a space for the filling. Be careful not to break the skin. Coat lightly with oil to prevent wrinkling.

2. Make four slits, one on each side of the apple opening, to prevent splitting while baking and to make stretch room for the filling.

3. Place the apples on a baking dish and bake in a 375 degree oven for about 35 minutes, until the apple is soft.

4. Prepare Pastry Cream filling.

5. Remove apples from oven and fill. Serve hot or cold.

PASTRY-WRAPPED BAKED APPLES

Pie dough recipe style 2 for a two-crust pie
> *1 apple per person*
> *1 tsp. butter per apple*
> *1 tsp. sugar per apple*
> *a drop vanilla per apple*
> *a few seedless raisins per apple*

1. Prepare dough and roll it out. Cut it into squares large enough to cover the entire apple.

2. Peel and core the apples.

3. Mix together sugar, butter, raisins, and vanilla.

4. Fill each apple and place on square of dough. Bring the sides of dough together forming a point at the top, and pinch them to seal.

5. Place on an ungreased baking pan and bake in a 400 degree oven for 20 minutes on the center shelf until the dough browns. Then remove pan to lower shelf, cover lightly with tin foil, and bake for another 15 minutes.

BAKED APPLES WITH HONEY

> *1 baking apple per person*
> *honey*
> *cinnamon*

1. Wash apple and scoop out the center core.

2. Coat outside of apple with oil to prevent wrinkling.

3. Place 1/2 tsp. honey in the center of each apple and sprinkle cinnamon on the honey.

4. Bake in a 400 degree oven for 20 minutes, or until the apple is soft.

Serve with sweet cream or eat it as it is.

BAKED APPLES WITH COGNAC

1 apple per person
1 tsp. sugar per apple
1 tsp. cognac per apple

1. Wash apples and scoop out center core. Lightly coat skin with oil to prevent wrinkling.

2. Fill center of each apple with the sugar and cognac.

3. Bake in a 375 degree oven for 35 minutes or until apples are soft.

4. Sprinkle with confectioner's sugar. Serve warm.

BAKED APPLES IN WINE SAUCE
(Manzanas al Vino Blanco)

If you like baked apples, this fruit baked with wine is extra special. Serve one apple per person. This recipe may be made the day before serving. Heat the oven to 375 degrees.

6 baking apples
1/4 stick butter
6 tbsp. sugar

1/2 cup water
1/4 cup dry white wine
  6 marachino cherries (optional)

1. Wash apples and scoop out center core. Be careful not to break through the bottom of the apple when removing the core. Coat skin lightly with oil to prevent wrinkling.

2. Make some slits inside the apple in the pulp. Be careful not to cut through to the outside skin. The slits will let the sauce penetrate the pulp. Also make 4 cuts on the top opening of the apple to prevent the apple from splitting while baking. The cuts should be one on each side of the apple.

3. Place apples on baking dish and pour mixture of water and wine into the hole of each apple and over the apples.

4. Divide butter into 6 pieces and place into each hole.

5. Place one tablespoon sugar into each hole and around top of each apple.

6. Bake for 35 minutes.

7. Remove apples to serving dish, pour sauce from pan over apples, and BEFORE SERVING place a cherry into each apple and sprinkle each apple with confectioner's sugar. Serve warm.

BAKED APPLE FLAMBE

For a nice effect, light the apples at the table in a dimly lit room.

One apple per person.

1. Remove the core of the apples, coat the outside of each apple with oil so that the skin won't wrinkle, and bake them in a 375 degree oven for about 35 minutes, or until tender.

2. When done, place them close together on a plate. Heat 4 tablespoons sugar (or enough sugar to make a syrup for each apple),

the apple syrup from the baking pan, and a small amount of water (about one teaspoon) in a pan until it becomes a syrup.

3. At serving time, warm the syrup and pour over apples

4. Warm two ounces of cognac or rum in a pan. Do NOT let it boil or it won't light up. Pour on apples and immediately light them with a match and serve.

BANANAS FLAMBE

This recipe serves 4 people, and is the easiest thing to make.

> *cut 2 bananas in half lengthwise (1 banana for 2 people)*
> *3 tbsp. rum*
> *3 tbsp. cognac*
> *sugar*
> *butter*
> *lemon juice*

1. Place peeled, cut bananas on a buttered baking dish.

2. Sprinkle bananas with sugar, bits of butter, and lemon juice.

3. Place them into a 350 degree oven and bake until the bananas are tender.

4. Remove from oven and set aside.

5. Place rum and cognac in a saucepan and slowly bring it to a warm temperature. Do NOT let it boil or get very hot because if it does it will not light up.

6. Pour rum and cognac over bananas at the table, and immediately light them with a match. Shake pan, and serve immediately.

FRUIT SALAD IN BANANA SHELLS

This recipe serves 4 people.

> *2 bananas*
> *1 apple*
> *6 strawberries, fresh or frozen*
> *cognac, 1 cup*
> *lemon juice*

1. Wash banana, cut in half lengthwise, and remove banana from skin carefully with the back of a teaspoon. Keep banana skin from tearing.

2. Dice banana, slice strawberries, and peel, core, and dice apple. Sprinkle banana and apple with lemon juice inmediately after dicing.

3. Place all the fruit in a bowl, add cognac, and carefully mix together.

4. Place banana skins on lettuce leaves, fill with fruit and serve cold.

ICE-CREAM WITH BANANA

Prepare the following amount for each person:

> *strawberry ice-cream, 1 scoop*
> *2 lady fingers*
> *1/2 banana*
> *1/4 cup Kirsch liquor*

1. Slice banana (after peeling) and soak in Kirsch for a half hour.

2. Half fill champagne glass with ice-cream, and top with banana.

3. Pour a little more Kirsch over banana and ice-cream.

4. Place lady finger cakes on dish that glass rests on.

ICE-CREAM WITH PEACHES

Prepare the following amount for each person:

> *1 scoop vanilla ice-cream*
> *1/2 peach, canned or home cooked*
> *1 tsp. cherry preserves*
> *whipped cream*
> *1 marachino cherry*

1. Place ice-cream in champagne glass.

2. Place peach half on top of ice-cream.

3. Spread preserves on peach.

4. Cover with whipped cream and marachino cherry.

ICE-CREAM CUP WITH CHAMPAGNE

Prepare the following amount for each person:

> *1 scoop vanilla ice-cream*
> *2 tbsp. canned fruit cocktail or fresh fruit that is in season*
> *1/4 cup cold champagne*

1. Place ice-cream in a champagne glass.

2. Place fruit on top of ice-cream. If raw fruit is used instead of canned, sprinkle confectioner's sugar over the raw fruit.

3. Pour champagne over the fruit and ice-cream at serving time.

CREPES
(Tortillas Rellenas)

Makes 10 6-inch crépes.

> *6 tbsp. flour*
> *1/2 cup milk*

2 beaten eggs
1/8 tsp. salt

1. Put the flour in a bowl. In a separate bowl, beat the eggs until fluffy, then pour them into the flour and beat until blended.

2. Add the milk and salt, and beat until well-blended. (This will be a loose smooth batter.)

3. Heat a 4- or 6-inch pan (to medium heat) and brush with butter.

4. Pour in about one tablespoon of batter (only enough to coat pan thinly), and immediately tilt the pan so that the bottom of it is completely and evenly covered. Pour out excess batter. (Use one hand to pour in the batter, and another for tilting the pan.)

Fry until edges of batter get dry. Lift around edges with a spatula and roll crépe out onto plate. Unroll flat and stack until all are done.

Put filling in center of crépe, fold over, and fry in butter, seam side down first. Then turn over and fry on the other side until golden brown.

Filling suggestions for crépes:

Pastry cream filling, page 281
ice-cream (fry 2 crepes separately, then sandwich in a slice ice cream, on plate)
sliced, peeled apple soaked in rum or cognac for 2 hours, then sprinkled with sugar and cooked slightly
cooked shrimp cut into tiny pieces, mixed in bechamel sauce, page 253
meat mixture from Ground Meat Pie recipe, page 195, and crépe covered with a tomato sauce

Beverages

El español fino con todo bebe vino.
The Spaniard who is fine eats everything with wine.

WINES

One cannot write a Spanish cookbook without mentioning wine, a beverage which is served with every meal except breakfast.

Spain produces a large amount of wine; it's probably ranked third in production behind France and Italy.

Usually people drink the local dry red or white Spanish wine with their meals, wines which are not sweet. (The word "dry" means not sweet. In Spanish it is called "vino seco.")

If you order "vino de la casa" (wine of the house) in a restaurant, you will probably get a very good dry red wine.

In a private home you might be served two wines, a white one with the first course, and a red one with the meat; it all depends on the hosts.

Sangría is served in the summer months because it is lighter and more refreshing in hot weather than straight wine, and it can be diluted to suit one's taste.

I found the following advice for serving wine in a Spanish cookbook called *The Art of Preparing and Serving the Table*. (1). It seems to be an ideal list for serving wines and liqueurs during and after a meal. However, all that is really needed to take care of guests are a dry red and white wine, and a liquer or two.

(1) G. Bernard de Ferrer. Editorial Molino, 1962, *Arte de Preparar y Servir la Mesa*, page 8.

With the soup, serve dry Madera, Jerez (Sherry), and the like.

With the meat or fowl, the red wine of Burdeos (Bordeaux) or a superior Rioja is good.

With game or cheese, bring the red wine of Borgoña to the table.

With light desserts such as flan or fruit, serve either a sweet or dry champagne.

With cake serve Oporto (Port), Alicante, Málaga, etc.

With coffee serve liquers such as Chartreuse, Cognac, Anis, Cointreau, Curacao, Benedictine, Kummel, and others such as these.

Many wines suggested on this list are not Spanish; however, Spanish wines are good and most people in Spain use them.

WINE PUNCH
(Sangría)

Sangría, a wine punch, is served in the summertime in Spain. It's a lighter drink than straight wine, and pleasanter to have on a hot day. Because it can be so refreshing, it's easy to drink a lot before realizing that it has quite a sock.

Sangría is very easy to prepare, and much of it can be done in advance, even the day before. However, the soda should be added just at serving time so that it doesn't go flat, and so should the ice-cubes and fruit slices.

There are many variations of Sangría because each person can add his own ideas to it. These recipes were given to me by Dr. Dionisio Ollero, profesor of Linguistics in the University of Madrid. He got them for me from a friend who owns a bar in Madrid when I prepared Sangría for a party.

The following will make enough Sangría for six eight-ounce servings, or twelve four-ounce servings. One recipe is for a Sangría made with red wine, and the other is for a Sangría made with white wine.

In addition to the sliced lemon, any or all of the following fruit may be added:

1. Sliced oranges, seeds removed.

2. Sliced apples, seeds removed.

3. Peeled, sliced bananas.

4. Sliced strawberries.

RED WINE SANGRIA

1 quart dry red wine
2 tbsp. lemon juice
1 tbsp. orange juice
2 tbsp. cognac
1 sliced lemon
1 tray ice-cubes
2 cups plain carbonated water (club soda)

1. Pour the first four ingredients into a pitcher. If the Sangría will not be served immediately, store these four ingredients, in the pitcher, in the refrigerator until serving time.

2. At serving time, add the lemon slices, carbonated water, and ice-cubes. Place a wooden spoon into the pitcher to stir the drink and to hold back the fruit and ice-cubes when pouring. Put some of the fruit into the glasses.

WHITE WINE SANGRIA

1 quart white wine
1 tbsp. cognac (optional)
1 sliced lemon
1 cup carbonated, lemon-flavored drink
1 cup plain carbonated water (club soda)
1 tray ice-cubes

Pour all the ingredients into a pitcher at serving time. Add fruit if desired, place a wooden spoon into the pitcher to hold the fruit back when pouring. Put some of the fruit into the glasses.

EGGNOG
(Ponche de Navidad)

Serves 10:

1 dozen eggs
2 cups heavy cream
2 cups milk
1 pint brandy, rum, or bourbon
4 tbsp. powdered sugar

Serves 2:

1 egg
1/3 cup milk
1/3 cup heavy cream
1 1/3 ounces rum, brandy, or bourbon
1/3 tsp. powdered sugar

1. Beat yolks until they become thick, then add liquor.

2. Beat milk into egg yolks.

3. Beat egg whites until they foam, add sugar, and continue beating until they form stiff peaks. Fold into egg yolks.

4. Beat cream until thick and add to yolks.

HOT MILK AND EGG PUNCH

Serves 2:

2 eggs
3 1/2 tsp. rum
3 1/2 tsp. brandy
1 cup milk
cinnamon (optional)
2 tsp. sugar

Serves 6:

6 eggs
1/4 cup rum
1/4 cup brandy
3 cups milk
cinnamon (optional)
2 tbsp. sugar

1. Beat egg yolks with sugar.

2. Bring milk to a boil.

3. Beat egg whites until they form peaks.

4. Add rum and brandy to egg yolks, and a pinch cinnamon.

5. Fold in egg whites.

6. Blend in the milk, little by little.

Serve immediately in mugs.

VODKA FRUIT DRINK

Serves 2.

1 jigger Vodka
2 jiggers orange juice
2 jiggers pineapple juice
2/3 of a jigger lemon juice (preferably from fresh lemon)
1/2 of a jigger Grenadine

Put everything into a tumbler with crushed ice and shake vigorously.

HOT CHOCOLATE, SPANISH STYLE

This recipe, which is for 6 people, makes a thick, rich hot chocolate drink the way it's served in Spain.

1. Place grated chocolate in a pot (off the heat) with the flour and sugar, and stir in a small amount of the milk. Then slowly stir in all the milk, and place the pan on low heat.

2. Simmer it slowly, and stir it constantly. Let it come to a boil. Remove it immediately. Let it come to a boil a second time, and remove it immediately again.

3. Beat it quickly with a whisk so that it is foamy, and serve hot.

A STORY WITH A MORAL

Don Juan Manuel, a Spanish writer of the fourteenth century, wrote short stories that had a moral.

It seems that children in that century also were unhappy with parents' decisions, and so to teach a moral, Don Juan tells a story about a son who asks his father to listen to the advice of others more often.

The father knows that he cannot teach his son by lecturing, but by experience; therefore, he arranges a journey to the market in town for the two of them and their donkey.

They start out leading the donkey behind them.

No sooner do they get on the road when they meet several people who laugh at them for walking when they have a donkey on which one of them could ride. The son turns to the father and says, "Of course, that makes sense." "All-right," the father says, "get on the donkey."

They continue down the road, and soon they hear some people say, "What a shame! The son rides while the father walks." Embarrassed, the son gets off so that the father can get on.

On the way they run into another group of people clucking their tongues. "It's wrong," they say, "for the son to walk. An older

person can suffer better because he's more accustomed to it."
"Get on behind me; we'll both ride," the father tells the son.

On they go towards the market when they again meet concerned individuals who inform them that two people on a donkey is much too heavy a load for the poor animal.

At that point the father turns to the son and says, "Look at all the advice we have gotten. No matter what we did, we couldn't satisfy everyone."

"Para mí, es cierto que si uno quiere hacer bien, le conviene hacer todas las cosas a lo mejor de su habilidad. Uno no puede seguir el consejo de todo el mundo, aunque le gusta a todo el mundo dar consejos," says the father.

Wich translates, "In my judgment, in order to do things well, one has to do things to the best of his ability. One cannot follow everyone's advice although everyone likes to give it."

To take the liberty to apply this to cooking, select those recipes which you feel are suitable, read the directions thoroughly, and prepare them carefully. Then you will be cooking to the best of your ability.

THE DIFFERENCE BETWEEN "HORSE" AND GENTLEMAN"

I couldn't speak Spanish very well when I arrived in Spain, and this sometimes caused me a lot of embarrassment.

One of those times was when I went to the Club Real de Madrid to find out about horseback riding for my eldest daughter.

In halting Spanish I asked questions about the club, and I felt that I was doing very well for a foreigner. However, when it came time to ask about horseback riding, I wasn't sure about the choice of words.

"Horse" and "gentleman" are very similar: "caballo" and "caballero," and the term I knew in Spanish for horseback riding was "to mount horses." Unfortunately, I couldn't remember which of the two words I needed to put into the spot after "mount"!

I stalled for time while my daughter Carol tugged on my sleeve. "Ask," she kept saying, "ask." I took a deep breath and said in all earnestness. "¿Aquí se puede montar caballeros?"

The minute I said it I knew I had made a wrong choice. Carol left; the secretary sucked in her breath; and the manager, looking at me in disbelief, turned beet red.

Somehow we each composed ourselves, and I left, never to return.

Because of such experiences, I prepared the following list of useful Spanish words and sentences.

"This painting will be worth a fortune back home"

Useful Spanish words and sentences for market and restaurant:

coffee	café
tea	té
milk	leche
water	agua
eggs	huevos
fried	fritos
scrambled	revueltos
boiled	cocido
medium boiled	cocido blando
hard boiled	cocido duro
bread	pan
butter	mantequilla
jam	mermeladas
meat	carne
steak	bistec
veal	ternera
lamb	cordero
chicken	pollo (pronounced pole - yo)
pork	cerdo
chops	chuletas
hamburger	hamburguesa
sausages	salchichas
ham	jamón (pronounced ha-mon)
Spanish ham	jamón serrano
cold cuts	fiambres
meatballs	albóndigas
roastbeef	rosbif
egg and potato omelette	tortilla (pronounced tor - tea - ya)
fish	pescado
shrimp	gambas
squid	calamares
soup	sopa
vegetables	verduras
salad	ensalada
beer	cerveza
wine	vino
cognac	coñac
whisky drinks have the same name in Spanish	
cheese	queso
fruit	frutas

In a restaurant:

Waiter: ¿Qué quería usted?   What would like?

Customer: Pollo asado con patatas y ensalada.   Roast chicken with potatoes and salad.

Customer: Tráigame agua, por favor.   Bring me water, please.

Waiter: En seguida, señor.   Right away, sir.

Customer: Tráigame la cuenta, por favor.   Bring me the bill, please.

Waiter: Aquí está.   Here it is.

Customer: How much is it?   ¿Cuánto es?

INDEX

A

Abbreviated terms, 36
A few notes about the food in the reci-
pes, 33-34
Albóndigas, 196-197
Aleta, 191-193
Alioli, 252-253
Anchovy,
– sauce, 260
  cauliflower, tomato, and anchovy,
    salad, 150-151
  potato and anchovy salad, 150
Anecdotes,
  A story with a moral, 314-315
  A true story, 264
  ¡Ay señora!, 19-20
  Even a plate of beans can be prepared
    beautifully, 23-25
  If you don't show who you are in
    the beginning, 41
  Isabel's kitchen, 153
  Plump is beautiful, 264-265
  "Sign your flourish," 103
  The bus ride and the shoe, 29-30
  The difference between "horse" and
    "gentleman," 315-316
  "What kind of meals do they serve?"
    83
  Why there are no snail recipes in this
    book, 185-187
Angulas, 57-58
Annisettes, 290
Appetizers, 41-58

baby eels, 57-58
bean "nuts", 43
chopped green peppers and tomatoes,
  44-45
eggplant dip or salad, style 1, 45
– – –, style 2, 46
french-fried squid, 49-50
garlic shrimp, 54
marinated cauliflower a la Isabel, 46-
  47
– octopus, 56-57
mixed-fry croquettes, 51-52
Moorish kabobs, 54-56
pickled smelts, 47-48
shrimp in pajamas, 52-53
soufleé canape, 42
Spanish croquettes, 50-51
tuna or meat-filled pastries, 48-49
Apples, baked, 298-302
– – flambé, 301-302
– – Fritters, 295-296
– – in wine sauce, 300-301
– – with pastry wrapped, 299
– – with cognac, 300
– – with honey, 299-300
– – with pastry cream filling, 298-299
Applesauce,
– pudding, 287-288
– soufleé, 268-269
Artichoke
– fresh, 119-120
– hearts, 118-119

– potato and artichoke heart salad, 150
A Spanish day, 26-28
Asparagus omelette, 91
Aspic,
– fish, 181
  stuffed fish Bella Vista, 180
A story with a moral, 314-315
A true story, 264
A typical menu from a restaurant in Spain, 21-22
Avocado, orange and tomato salad, 145
!Ay señora!, 19-20

B

Baby eels, 57-58
Bacalao a la Riojana, 161-162
Bacalao al pil-pil, 160-161
Baked,
– Alaska, 273-274
– apples, 298-302
– – flambé, 301-302
– – in wine sauce, 300-301
– – with cognac, 300
– – with honey, 299-300
– – with pastry cream filling, 298-299
– eggs, 91-92, 94
– – on spinach, style 1, 91-92
– – – – style 2, 92
– – with ham and grated cheese, 94
– fish and potato chips, 178-179
– trout, 159-160
  puffed baked eggs, 92-93
Bar-b-qued lamb ribs, 210-211
Batter, 156-157
  deep-fry for fish, 157
  – – for seafood, 157
  – – for vegetables, 157
Beef or veal stew with potatoes, 202-203
Beans, 135-141
– "nuts", 43
– soup from Gallego, 81
  bean and vegetable soup Majorcan style, 75-76
  cocido gallego, 218
  how to prepare beans, 136
  lima bean salad, 152

omelette with cooked beans, 90
pote gallego, 216-217
Bechamel sauce, 253-255
Beef,
– boullion, 61
– or veal stew with potatoes, 202-203
  diced meat and tomatoes, 194
  ground meat pie, 195-196
  Madrid-style stew, 199-202
  meat and potatoes, Extremeño, 190-191
  – and vegetable stew, Extremeño, 198-199
  – balls, 196-197
  – in onion sauce, 193-194
  – loaf, 197-198
  short ribs of beef, 195
  – – with rice, 211
  stuffed meat roast, 191-193
Beets,
– and hard-boiled egg salad, 150
– and potato salad, 150
Bernaise sauce, 256-257
Beverages, 307-314
Blended tomato, potato, and onion soup, 78-79
Blond sauce, 246-247
Boiled potatoes with parsley, 128
Boquerones, 159
Boullion,
– fish court, 156
Bread-balls for soup, 60
Breaded veal chops or cutlets, 204-205
Bulería, 31
Buñuelos, 295-296

C

Cabbage, cooked, 108
Cake, nut, 292-293
Calamares,
– en su tinta, 184-185
– in tomato sauce, 185
– fritos, 49
– stuffed, 183-184
Caldo gallego, 81
Calves feet with chick peas, 223

Caramel-covered almonds, 266
Carrots,
− a la Santanderina, 105-106
− pureé soup, 78
− with spinach in vinegar sauce, 104-105
Cartoons,
   Showing off your Spanish, 317
   "That`s not a bug. . .", 167
   "This painting will be worth a for-
      tune. . .",
Cauliflower,
− cooked, 108
− creamed, with egg, 107-108
− − with grated cheese, 107
− marinated a la Isabel, 46-47
− salad, 151
− soufleé, 99
− with tomato and anchovy in salad,
   150-151
Centigrade, 37-38
Cheese,
− omelette soufleé, 87
− soufleé, 87, 98-99
   baked eggs with ham and grated
      cheese, 94
   gruyere cheese omelette, 91
Chestnut pureé, 261-262
Chicken, 93, 230-240
− broiled, 230
− country-style, 239-240
− custard, 93
− in garlic and wine sauce, 238
− in rum, 233-234
− in tomato sauce, 239
− medley, 235-236
− roast, 230-231
− − and stuffed with apples, 231-232
− − − − with applesauce, 232-233
− soufleé, 99
− soup, 68
− stewed with tomatoes, peppers, and
   potatoes, 238-239
   fried chicken breasts supreme, 237-
      238
   royal chicken, 234-235
Chicken, duck, rabbit, partridge, 229-243
Chick peas,
− − how to prepare, 136

− − stew, 218
−. − with calves feet, 223
   spinach soup with chick peas, 76
Chopped egg and onion salad, 149
− green peppers and tomatoes, 147-148
Chocolate, hot, Spanish style, 314
− soufleé, 293-294
Chops or cutlets, breaded, 204-205
Churros, 270-272
Clams,
− and rice, 163-164
− mussels, and oysters (tips), 33, 65,
   156, 163-164, 168-171, 173
− soup, 65
Cocido Gallego, 218
− Madrileño, 199-202
Coddled eggs, 84
− − Villaroy, 100
Cod, dried, salt,
− − − in its own sauce (al pil-pil), 160-
   161
− − − with peppers and tomatoes (a la
   riojana), 161-162
Cold jellied consomé, 74
− Spanish vegetables soup (gazpacho),
   67
Consomé
− cold jellied, 74
− with Sherry, 74
Converting Fahrenheit and Centigrade,
   37-38
− weight, 38
Cooked
− beets with hard-boiled egg salad, 150
− cabbage, 108
Cookies, 290-291
− balls, 289
− (polvorones), 291-292
   very delicious nut cookies, 292
Cooking utensils mentioned, 37
Cream puff shells, 266-267
Creamed,
− cauliflower with egg, 107-108
− − with grated cheese, 107
− spinach, 114-115
− vegetable soup, 62-63
Crépes, 304-305
Crescents, 296

Croquettes,
— mixed-fry, 51-52
— Spanish, 50-51
  hard-boiled egg croquettes, 94-95
  stuffed-egg croquette, 96
Cutlets, breaded, 204-205
Custard,
— garnish for clear soup, 61
— ham or chicken, 93
— potato, 129
— Spanish, 283-284
— spinach, 116-117
  economical coffee custard, 284-285
  fried custard, 286-287
  fruit and bread custard, 285

D

Decorations, 40, 155
  crescents, 296
  custard for clear soup, 61
  potato garnish, 128
  to place around fish serving platter,
    155
Deep-fry batter, 157
Definitions of terms used, 34-35
Desserts, 263-305
  also see table of contents under Des-
    serts
Diced meat and tomatoes, 194
Dip,
— eggplant, style 1, 45
— — style 2, 46
Don Juan Manuel stories, 41, 314-315
Dough for pies,
— — — style 1, 279
— — — style 2, 279-280
Doughnuts, Spanish, 270-272
Dried cod, 160-163
— — in its own sauce (al pil-pil), 160-
    161
— — soup, 69-70
— — spicy, in tomato sauce, 162-163
— — with peppers and tomatoes (a la
    riojana), 161-162
Duchess potatoes, 132
Duck in orange sauce, 240-242

Dumplings, 190

E

Ears, pigs a la León, 228
Easy food decorations, 40
Economical coffee custard, 284-285
Eggnog, 312-313
Eggplant dip or salad, 45-46
— — — — style 1, 45
— — — — style 2, 46
— — — — supreme, 109-110
  pisto with zucchinni squash or egg-
    plant, 104
Eggs, 83-101
— salads,
  potato and egg salad, 150
  chopped egg and onion salad, 149
  cooked beets with hard-boiled egg
    salad, 150
  also see table of contents under Eggs
Empanada,
— de lomo, 209
— gallega de mariscos, 173-174
Empanadillas, 48-49
Equivalents and measures, 36
Even a plate of beans can be prepared
  beautifully, 23-25

F

Fabada Asturiana, 138
Fahrenheit, 37
Fifteen-minute soup, 63-64
Fish and seafood, 153-185
  soup, 66-67
  also see table of contents under Fish
  baby eels (angulas), 57-58
  clam soup, 65
  court boullion, 156
  dried salt cod soup, 69-70
  french-fried squid, 49-50
  garlic shrimp, 54 (al ajillo)

grilled shrimp (gambas a la plancha), 43-44

marinated octopus, 56-57

mixed-fry croquettes, 51-52

pickled smelts, 47-48

pisto, 164

sardine or perch salad, 151-152

shrimp in pajamas, 52-53

shrimp-shell soup, 71-72

tuna-filled pastries (empanadillas), 48-49

Flamblé, 301-302
- baked apple, 301-302
- bananas, 302

Flamenco, 31, 32
    a Bulería, 32
    a Milongas, 31

Flan, 283-285
    an economical coffee custard, 284-285
    Spanish custard, 283

French-fried squid, 49-50

Fresh artichokes, 119-120

Fried,
- custard, 286-287
- eggs with lentils, 94
- fish, 158
- little cream pies, 269-270
- potatoes in sauce, 130-131
- smelts, 159
- trout, 159

Frite Extremeño, 190-191

Fritters, 295-296

Fruit,
- cocktail pudding, 287
- salad in banana shells, 303
    baked apples, 298-302
    - - flambé, 301-302
    - - in wine sauce, 300-301
    - - with cognac, 300
    - - with honey, 299-300
    - - with pastry cream filling, 298-299
    ice-cream, 303-304
    - - cup with champagne, 304
    - - with banana, 303
    - - with peaches, 304

pastry-wrapped baked apples, 299

Frying, notes, 156-157

G

Galician,
- fish and seafood pie, 173-174
- stew with navy beans, 216-217

Gallego, bean soup from, 81

Gambas,
- al ajillo, 54
- a la plancha, 43-44
- con pijama, 52-53

Garlic,
- and olive oil sauce (alioli), 252-253
- shrimp (gambas al ajillo), 54
- soup (sopa de ajo), 73-74

Garnish crescents, 296

Garnish, potato, 128

Gazpacho, 67-68

Green,
- pea soup with spinach, 77-78
- peas with sausage, ham, and onions, 120-121
- pepper, tomato, salad, 147-148
- peppers with raisins, 107
- sauce, 258-259

Grilled,
- fresh sardines or perch, 172
- shrimp, 43-44

Ground meat pie, 195-196

Gruyere cheese omelette, 91

Gyspy,
- arm, 277
- salad, 146
- stew, 226-227

H

Ham,
- and egg custard, 93
- and potato omelette, 89-90
- omelctte, 88
    baked eggs with ham and grated cheese, 94

Hard-boiled eggs, 84
– – –, croquettes, 94-95
Hollandaise sauce, 255-256
How to calculate how much meat to buy,
How to grind saffron, 34
How to hard-boil eggs, 84
How to prepare,
– – – dried beans, 136
– – – fish, 154-156
– – – freesh tripe, 223-224
How to work up a recipe, 33

I

Ice cream,
– – cake, 272
– – with banana, 303
– – with champagne, 304
– – with peaches, 304
If you don't show who you are in the
     beginning, 41
Isabel's kitchen, 153

J

Jane Baxter's nut cake, 292-293
Jellied consommé, cold, 74

K

Kidney, 222
– bean stew, 138

L

Lamb, 210-216
– and potato stew, 212
– ribs with rice, 211
     bar b-qued lamb ribs, 210-211
     roast leg of lamb, 213
     – stuffed leg of lamb with tomato
          sauce, 214-215
     – whole baby lamb, 216
     stewed lamb shanks, 215

     stuffed leg of lamb, 213-214
Leche frita, 286-287
Leg of lamb,
– – – – roast, 213
– – – – – stuffed, in tomate sauce,
          214-215
– – – stuffed, 213-214
– – – shanks, stewed, 215
Lentils,
– how to prepare, 136
– stew, 139
– with fried eggs, 94
– with tomato sauce, 137-138
Lettuce,
– salad, 146
     shrimp in a lettuce blanket, 151
Lima bean,
– – salad, 152
– – stew, 140
Liver, 319

M

Macaroni,
– in bechamel sauce, 133
– in sauce with baked eggs, 134
– with tomato sauce, plain or baked,
     133-134
Madrid-style stew, 199-202
Majorcan style bean and vegetable soup,
     75-76
Marinated,
– cauliflower a la Isabel, 46-47
– octopus, 56-57
Mayonnaise, 250-252
Measures and equivalents, 36
Meat, 189-228
– filled pastries, 48-49
     also see table of contents under Meat
     beat soup from gallego, 81
     beef boullion, 61
     Moorish kabobs, 54-56
Meringue, 276
– cookies, 274
– shells, 276-277
Merluza a la Vasca, 174-175

Metric system, 38
Milongas, 32
Mixed-fry croquettes, 51-52
Moorish kabobs, 54-56
Mornay sauce, 256
Mushrooms,
– omelette, 90
– plain, sautéed, 121
– with bread crumbs and parsley, 121
Mussels, clams, and oysters, notes, 33, 156, 163-164. 168-171, 173

O

Omelette,
– asparagus, 91
– gruyere cheese, 91
– ham, 88
– in flames, 297
– plain, 85
– shrimp, 88
– Spanish (tortilla), 85
– spinach, 91-92
– spring, 89
– with cooked beans, 90
   cheese omelette soufleé, 87
Octopus, marinated, 56-57
Oil for frying, notes, 34
Onion soup, 72-73
   blended tomato, potato and onion soup, 78-79
Orange,
– avocado and tomato salad, 145
– cream gelatin, 267-268
– juice sauce, 259
Oranges in Kirsch, 297
Oven temperatures, 39
Oysters, mussels, and clams notes, 33, 65, 156, 163-164, 168-171, 173

P

Paella,
– style 1, 168-170
– style 2, 170-171

Panaché de verduras, 111-113
Partridge in chocolate sauce, 243-244
Pastry cream filling, 281
– wrapped baked apples, 299
Peach pudding pie, 282-283
Peas, green, with sausage, ham, and onions, 120-121
– with onions and mint, 120
Peppers,
– stuffed with rice, 124-125
– – with veal and chicken, 207-208
Picadillo de carne, 194
Pickled smelts, 47-48
Pies,
   fried little cream pies, 269-270
   Galician fish and seafood pie, 173-174
   ground meat pie, 195-196
   peach pudding pie, 282-283
   pork pie, 209
   salmon pie, 182-183
   Spanish apple pie, 278
   very easy pear pie, 282
Pig's ears a la León, 228
Pinchos Morunos, 54-56
Pink sauce Majorca style, 249-250
Pisto,
– fish, 164
– with zucchini squash or eggplant, 104
Plain,
– omelette, 85
– sautéed mushrooms, 121
Plump is beautiful, 264-265
Polvorones cookies, 291-292
Pork,
– pie from Galicia (empanada de lomo), 209
   Galician stew with chick peas (cocido gallego), 218
   – – with navy beans (pote gallego), 216-217
   rice with pork, 127
   roast whole baby pig, 210
   smoked chops with cabbage and potatoes, 208
Potatoes
– and anchovy salad, 150
– and artichoke heart salad, 150

— and egg salad, 150
— and ham omelette, 89-90
— blended with tomato and onion soup, 78-79
— omelette (tortilla), 85-86
— salad, 148-149
— soup pureé, 79-80
    also see table of contents under Potatoes
    beet and potato salad, 150
    shrimp and potato salad supreme, 144-145
    stringbean, tomato, and potato salad, 146-147
Pote gallego, 216-217
Preparation of fresh tripe, 223-224
Proverbs,
    Barriga llena corazón contento
    A full stomach makes a happy heart, 135
    Bueno es el vino cuando el vino es bueno
    When the wine is good it's really good, 189
    El español fino con todo bebe vino
    The Spaniard who is fine eats everything with wine, 307
    En boca cerrada no entran moscas
    Flies don't enter a shut mouth, 143
    Entre col y col, lechuga
    Between something ordinary, something good, 26
    Has bien y no mires a quién
    Do good deeds; it doesn't matter who the recipient is, 229
    Hombre de buena pasta
    A person with a paceful nature, 263
    La mejor salsa es el hambre y buenas ganas
    Hunger and desire are the best sauce, 245
    Las sopas y los amores, los primeros son los mejores
    Of soup and love, the first is the best, 59
    Para trabajar, mañana; para comer, ganas

Work can be put off till tomorrow, but not the desire for food, 23
Todo el monte no es orégano
All that glitters is not gold, 123
Prunes in cognac, 298
Pudding, 165-166
— applesauce, 287-288
— fish, 164- 165
— fruit cocktail, 287
Puffed baked eggs, 92-93
Punch, hot milk and egg, 312-313
Pureé potato, 79-80
— Blended tomato, potato, and onion soup, 78
— carrot soup, 78

R

Rabbit, hunter`s style, 242-243
Rice, 124-127
— boiled, 125-126
— paella, style 1 and 2, 168-171
— soufleé dessert, 288-289
— with milk as a dessert, 288
— with tomato and peppers, 124-125
— — — sauce, sausage and peppers, 126
— with veal or pork, 127
    clams and rice, 163-164
    peppers stuffed with rice, 124-125
Roast,
— stuffed leg of lamb with tomato sauce, 214-215
— — meat, 191-193
— whole baby lamb, 216
— — — pig, 210

S

Saffron, how to grind, 34
Salads, 143-152
— dressing, 246
    also see table of contents under Salads
    eggplant dip or salad,
— — — — — style 1, 45
— — — — — style 2, 46
    shrimp and potato salad supreme, 144-145

Salt cod, 160-162
   dried salt cod soup, 69-70
   see table of contents under Fish
Salsa rubia, 246-247
Salmon pie or tarts, 182-183
Sangría, 310-311
Sauces, 245-261
  – for boiled fish, 260
    also see table of contents under
    Sauces
Seafood, see Fish
Short ribs of beef, 195
Shrimp,
  – and potato salad supreme, 144-145
  – garlic, 54
  – grilled, 43-44
  – in a lettuce blanket, 151
  – in pajamas, 52-53
  – mixed-fry croquettes, 51-52
  – omelette, 88
  – shell soup, 71-72
  – soufleé, 99
  – soup with mayonnaise, 70-71
Smelts,
  – fried, 159
  – pickled, 47-48
Smoked pork chops with cabbage and
  potatoes, 208
Songs,
    children's cod fish song, 160
    flamenco, 31-32
    Santurce sardine song, 172
Sopa de ajo, 73-74
Soups, 59-81
    also see table of contents under Soup
Soufleé, 87-88
  – applesauce, 268-269
  – basic, 98-99
  – canape, 42
  – cauliflower, 99
  – cheese omelette, 87
  – chocolate, 293-294
  – rice, dessert, 288-289
  – shrimp, 99
  – spinach, 117-118
Spanish,
  – apple pie, 278
  – croquettes, 50-52

– custard, 283-284
– doughnuts, 270-272
– omelette, 85-86
– tomate sauce,
– – – style 1, 247-248
– – – style 2, 248-249
Spinach,
– and green pea soup, 77-78
– and onions, seasoned with cinnamon,
  114
– baked, 116-117
– creamed, 114-115
– omelette, 91
– pie, 113-114
– soufleé, 117-118
– soup with chick peas, 76-77
– style 1, 115-116
– style 2, 116
  baked eggs on spinach
  – – – – style 1, 91-92
  – – – – style 2, 92
  carrots and spinach in vinegar sauce,
  104-105
Sponge cake,
  plain, 275-276
  gypsy's arm, 277
Spring omelette, 89
Squid,
– french-fried, 49-50
– in black sauce, 184-185
– in tomato sauce, 185
– stuffed, 183-184
Stew, see Meat
Stewed lamb shanks, 215
Stories,
  A Spanish day, 26-28
  A story with a moral, 314-315
  A true story, 264
  "¡Ay señora!", 19-20
  Even a plate of beans can be prepared
    beautifully, 23-25
  Isabel's kitchen, 153
  Plump is beautiful, 264-265
  "Sign your flourish," 103
  The bus ride and the shoe, 29-30
  The difference between "horse" and
    "gentleman," 315-316

"What kind of meals do they serve?",
83
Why there are no snail recipes in this
book, 185-187
Stringbeans,
− tomato, and potato salad, 146-147
− with tomato, 109
Stuffed,
− egg croquette, 96
− fish, 179-180
− − Bella vista, 180-181
− green peppers with weal and chicken,
207-208
− leg of lamb, 213-214
− meat roast, 191-193
− peppers with tomatoes and anchovies,
106
Substitutes, 34

anchovies, 106
Tongue,
− beef, 220-221
− lamb, 219-220
Tortilla española, 85-86
Trout,
− baked, 159-160
− fried, 159
Tuna- or meat-filled pastries (empanadillas), 48-49
Two-bean soup, 80-81

U

Useful Spanish words and sentences for
market and restaurant, 317-318
U. S. system of measurement, 38

T

Tapioca soup, 81
Tartar sauce, 257
Tarts, salmon, 182-183
Temperatures,
Fahrenheit and Centigrade, 37
oven, 39
Tips on preparing fish, 154-155
Tomato,
− and green pepper salad, 147-148
− salad, 148
− sauce,
− − al cognac, 249
− − style 1, 247-248
− − style 2, 248-249
− with stringbeans, 109
avocado, orange, and tomato salad,
145
blended tomato, potato, and onion
soup, 78-79
cauliflower, tomato, and anchovy salad, 150-151
chopped green peppers and tomatoes,
44
stringbean, tomato, and potato salad,
146-147
stuffed peppers with tomatoes and

V

Veal,
− cordon bleu, 205- 206
− roast with vegetables, 203-204
− stew with potatoes, 202-203
− Villaroy, 206-207
breaded veal chops or cutlets, 204-205
Galician stew with navy beans, 216-
217
rice with veal or pork, 127
stuffed green peppers with veal and
chicken, 207-208
Vegetables, 103-121
− soup, 62-63
also see table of contents under Vegetables
bean and vegetable soup Majorcan
style, 75-76
mixed-fry croquettes, 51-52
Very easy pear pie, 282
Villaroy,
− fried chicken breasts supreme (pollo
Villaroy), 237-238
− coddled eggs, 100
− veal, 206-207
Vinagrette sauce, 257-258
Vodka fruit drink, 313

W

White mountain eggs, 101-102
Wines,
   notes on wine, 308-309
   punch (sangria), 310-311

Z

Zucchini, pisto with squash or eggplant,
   104

Otros títulos de la Sección de Cocina-Repostería

de Editorial

ENCICLOPEDIA DEL WHISKY

Por Bento Luiz de Almeida Prado
220 págs.— Ilustraciones a todo color.— 20 x 27 cm.— Rústica.
ISBN: 84-283-0938-8

Resumen interesante y ameno del mundo del Whisky con abundantes datos sobre esta bebida y su entorno.Excelente obra por su cuidada presentación y calidad de sus láminas a todo color. Terminología. Historia. Cocktails. Disposiciones legales. Consejos. Bibliografía. Todo lo que el aficionado al whisky debe conocer sobre esta bebida.

300 RECETAS CULINARIAS PARA ADELGAZAR

Por Béhotéguy de Teramond
312 págs.— 4 desplegables dobles sobre la composición química de los alimentos.— Numerosos dibujos.— 13,5 x 19,5 cm.— 2ª edición.— Rústica.
ISBN: 84-283-0280-2

El libro que ha hecho adelgazar a medio millón de franceses por el método de "Bajas calorías". Cómo seguir una dieta agradable a la vista y al paladar y con gran variación en el número de platos sin los inconvenientes del cansancio que produce un régimen alimenticio falto de calorías. Incluye en 4 desplegables dobles, unas Tablas con la composición química de los alimentos.

LA INDUSTRIA DEL CHOCOLATE, BOMBONES, CARAMELOS Y CONFITERIA

Por Carlos Gianola
280 págs.— Con ilustraciones.— 15,5 x 21,5 cm.— Rústica.
ISBN: 84-283-0874-8

Obra que vulgariza el empleo de las nuevas materias primas y los nuevos procedimientos de fabricación poniendo los conocimientos necesarios para ello al alcance de pequeños artesanos y de pequeña y gran industria de golosinas. Fórmulas para la fabricación de caramelos, bombones, turrones, etc. Materias más utilizadas en la industria de la confitería. Gomas, grasas, sustancias aromáticas y frutos secos. Indice alfabético.

LA INDUSTRIA DE LA FRUTA SECA EN ALMIBAR Y CONFITADA

Por Carlos Gianola
184 págs.– 15,5 x 21,5 cm.– 2ª edición.– Rústica.
ISBN: 84-283-0553-6

Obra de interés para los profesionales de la industria de la conservación de la fruta: a los jefes de empresa para saber dirigirla. A los técnicos para poder ampliar y perfeccionar los conocimientos adquiridos. A los que se incorporan a la profesión para adquirir los conocimientos esenciales en base a la práctica. Nociones sobre la maquinaria más moderna y los procedimientos y productos actuales.

LA INDUSTRIA MODERNA DE GALLETAS Y PASTELERIA

Por Carlos Gianola
272 págs.– 16 págs. más con fotografías.– 15,5 x 21,5 cm.– 2ª edición.-
Rústica.
ISBN: 84-283-0533-1

Cerca de 500 recetas para fabricar galletas, bizcochos, pastas para té, plum-cakes, tostadas, etc. Parte de un estudio detallado de las materias primas en que basa sus recetas, explica detalladamente cada receta e incluye un estudio, no menos detallado, de las máquinas necesarias en esta industria.

LA COCINA SABROSA Y PRACTICA

Por J. Jamar
304 págs.– 13,5 x 19,5 cm.- 19ª edición.– Rústica.
ISBN: 84-283-0353-3

1.100 recetas dedicadas a las amas de casa, especialmente a las que disponen de poco tiempo que dedicar a la cocina. Recetas muy sencillas, fáciles de preparar y de excelente resultado aún para los paladares más exigentes. Cocina casera, condimentada con el mayor esmero y guisos especialmente sabrosos y algunos platos más complicados, de más lujo o regionales, especialmente de cocina vasca.

MENUS FAMILIARES Y DE INVITADOS

Por J. Jamar
316 págs.– 14 x 19 cm. –2ª edición aumentada.– Rústica.
ISBN: 84-283-0070-4

Numerosos menús para fiestas, reuniones, invitados, fiestas infantiles, etc. Todos ellos económicos, fáciles de preparar y capaces de contentar a los más exigentes. Se completa con un interesante capítulo que contiene las normas generales para la recepción de invitados.

COCINA PARA PROFESIONALES
Hoteles. Restaurantes. Residencias

Por E. Loewer
394 págs.— Con ilustraciones.— 15,5 x 21 cm.— 2ª edición.— Rústica.
ISBN: 84-283-0283-0

Instalación. Productos. Técnica culinaria. Platos. Estudio de minutas. Rendimientos económicos. Ciencias alimentarias. Vocabulario en cinco idiomas. Conocimientos generales para usos de los profesionales de la cocina. Dedica el último capítulo al estudio de algunos alimentos del código alimentario español e incluye índice de materias e índice alfabético.

EL MEJOR CONSEJERO DEL DIABETICO

Por el Prof. Dr. K. Schöffling, Dr. K. Petzoldt y A. Fröhlich-Krauel
248 págs.— 17 x 24 cm.— Rústica.
ISBN: 84-283-0679-6

Obra de divulgación sobre el diagnóstico y tratamiento de la diabetes. Régimen del diabético. Numerosos consejos médicos y recetas de cocina que permiten una sola dieta alimenticia para toda la familia. Dedica un capítulo a la terapia de la diabetes destacando la importancia de que el propio paciente se convierta en un verdadero colaborador y ayudante de su médico durante el tratamiento. Las recetas que incluye permiten al diabético el comer a la mesa con su familia y alimentarse, como ella, de forma sana, sabrosa y variada.